VAUGHAN PUBLIC LIBRARIES

3 3288 10052415 8   OCT 2020

A Bite of the Apple

D1636082

**WITHDRAWN**

WITHDRAWN

# A Bite of the Apple

## A Life with Books, Writers and Virago

### LENNIE GOODINGS

BIBLIOASIS
Windsor, Ontario

Copyright © Lennie Goodings 2020

First published in Canada by
Biblioasis
Windsor, Ontario

First published in Great Britain and the United States by
Oxford University Press
Oxford and New York

All rights reserved. No part of this publication may be reproduced or transmitted in any
form or by any means, electronic or mechanical, including photocopying, recording, or
any information storage and retrieval system, without permission in writing from the
publisher or a license from The Canadian Copyright Licensing Agency
(Access Copyright). For an Access Copyright license visit www.accesscopyright.ca
or call toll free to 1-800-893-5777.

FIRST EDITION

Library and Archives Canada Cataloguing in Publication
Title: A bite of the apple : a life with books, writers and Virago / Lennie Goodings.
Names: Goodings, Lennie, author.
Description: Includes index.
Identifiers: Canadiana (print) 20200205919 | Canadiana (ebook) 20200205943 |
ISBN 9781771963602
(softcover) | ISBN 9781771963619 (ebook)
Subjects: LCSH: Goodings, Lennie. | LCSH: Virago Press—Employees—
Biography. | LCSH: Virago Press—
History. | LCSH: Women publishers—Great Britain—Biography. | LCSH:
Women editors—Great Britain—
Biography. | LCSH: Book editors—Great Britain—Biography. | LCSH:
Feminist literature—Publishing—
Great Britain—History. | LCSH: Publishers and publishing—Great Britain—
History. | LCGFT:
Autobiographies.
Classification: LCC Z325.G66 G66 2020 | DDC 070.5092—dc23

Readied for the press by Daniel Wells

  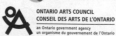

Published with the generous assistance of the Canada Council for the Arts, which last year
invested $153 million to bring the arts to Canadians throughout the country, and the
financial support of the Government of Canada. Biblioasis also acknowledges the support
of the Ontario Arts Council (OAC), an agency of the Government of Ontario, which last
year funded 1,709 individual artists and 1,078 organizations in 204 communities across
Ontario, for a total of $52.1 million, and the contribution of the Government of Ontario
through the Ontario Book Publishing Tax Credit and Ontario Creates

PRINTED AND BOUND IN CANADA

*To John, Amy, and Zak,*
*and to all Virago women and men*

# Contents

*Preface*                                                                        ix

PART ONE

## A New Kind of Being

1. First Bites: The Early Years                                                   3
2. Setting the World on Fire                                                     23
3. The Acceptable Face of Feminism? Why Not!                                     47

PART TWO

## The Books

4. The Virago Modern Classics                                                    69
5. 'Fuck the Patriarchy!': Non-fiction                                           91
6. What Stories Can Do: Fiction                                                 105

PART THREE

## The Politics: Office and Otherwise

7. The Dramas                                                                   121
8. Disrupting the Old Stories                                                   133
9. Beyond Borders                                                              159
10. Up, Down, and Up Again                                                     173

PART FOUR

## The Power to Publish is a Wonderful Thing

11. The Intimacy of Editing                                                     199

12.    Does Any Other Successful Publisher Get Asked
       Constantly If They Are Still Necessary?                    221

13.    Why Can't a Man Read Like a Woman?                         235

14.    Giving and Taking Courage                                  249

       Notes                                                      263
       Index                                                      283
       Acknowledgements                                           301

# Preface

Soho, London, early evening, late 1970s, and the sounds of Friday-night revelries rise up to our window on the fourth floor in Wardour Street where I'm still working my way through piles of paperwork in the Virago office. I am not alone. We do everything ourselves in this company—including the dusting and vacuuming of our one largish room and small kitchen/bathroom—and it is Carmen Callil's turn to clean. If it's your week you can come in on Saturday or stay late after work on Friday. Carmen is vigorously polishing one of our three telephones. I am just twenty-five, Canadian, new to Britain, and in awe of this formidable woman, but as there are only two of us in the office I feel emboldened to ask: 'Why did you start Virago?' She looks up and, without missing a beat, replies, 'To change the world, darling. That's why.'

I know I am in the right place.

I am a fervent believer that books can affect, even change, lives. It was a memoir about bookselling that partly drew me to Britain to begin with. *84 Charing Cross Road* by Helene Hanff—funny, sharp correspondence between a girl from the new world and older gentlemen in a London bookshop—had been one of my favourites as a young woman. (Satisfyingly, now a Virago Modern Classic.) Before I arrived in London in 1977, I felt I already knew the redoubtable Foyles and the famous street of second-hand bookshops which threaded its way from Oxford Street to Trafalgar Square. I longed for a relationship with London and its booksellers and publishers.

Clutching a temporary working visa, shrugging off the new-to-me idea that I was a slightly inferior character from the colonies who, as the immigration paperwork had it, 'understandably wants to visit the mother country', I packed my bags. I was not long out of university, had travelled to the west coast of Canada, where I had worked in a bookshop, and back to my home near Niagara Falls. Now, at last, I would go to London. I bought a round-trip air ticket and told myself and my family that I would stay for one year to try anything and everything and then head home, probably to Toronto, to get a proper job.

Over four decades later, still in London, married to an extraordinary man who has lived the Virago story with me, and now with two grown children, I write this book about Virago, the feminist press.

*A Bite of the Apple* is part memoir, part history of Virago, and part thoughts on more than forty years of feminist publishing. I consider myself so very lucky and privileged to be part of Virago. I have tried to be straight and not shy from awkward and painful times, as well as to tell of the truly great ones. At times the conflicting demands of the press have nearly capsized our ship but, to stretch that metaphor just a bit further, the Viragos—by whom I mean authors, founders, staff, and our readers—were always going to rock the boat. We always meant to disrupt, to make a difference.

This is not an aggrandizing hagiography, though I remain deeply indebted to and impressed by the authors and staff who have made Virago what it is. There are some pretty fabulous women who deserve to have their praises sung.

What I love about publishing is that no matter how sophisticated, how technological, how digital our industry becomes, one fact remains: publishing still comes down to one person telling another, you must read this book. Publishing is driven by that passion, conviction, and excitement.

You also need courage to publish and, certainly, to write. To write this book means taking risks, which makes me feel a deep empathy with my authors. I am highly aware of laying claim to a story that so many have witnessed and participated in. Even as I try to be honest and represent myself and others, I am, of course, editing, deleting, and leading readers to believe that what I saw, what I thought, and what I think is the truth. That both humbles and scares me.

One of my favourite kinds of book is one that doesn't quite fit neatly into categories and it turns out that's what I have written too. I have followed the chronology of the press and try to represent the enormous breadth of the Virago titles published over these years, set against the background of the march of feminism, but I also segue into thoughts on editing, on post-feminism, on reading, on breaking boundaries, and at times I fast-forward or think back. The chronology might lose you at times but that's okay, even understandable: we've had ten different offices and seven different forms of ownership. I have had four different jobs: Publicity Manager/Director, Marketing Director, Publisher, and now Chair. Over these years probably close to one hundred women have worked at Virago and we've published nigh on 4,000 titles and just over 1,000 authors. That's a lot of history. But I am not trying to capture every detail; what I want to portray is how it *felt* to be there. So it's a hybrid book.

I have come to see that the connecting thread of this book is tension. Tension, though uncomfortable at times, is not necessarily bad: it makes creative sparks and even maddening constraints can be productive. Virago lives within the tension between idealism and pragmatism; between sisterhood and celebrity; between art and commerce; between independence and being owned; between behaving independently but for over twenty-five years being part of a conglomerate; between watching feminism wax and wane and then become popular again, while at the same time knowing so many of the battles are still to be won; between being modest and yet aware of one's power; between trying to do good in the world and some-times failing. Tension does seem to be an integral part of change.

There is no doubt that I too have my own tensions: I have made foes as well as friends, mistakes as well as good choices, and I have taken unpopular decisions. I also have power—at some times more than at others in this career of mine—and it is not without challenge to try to handle that intelligently and generously. But it's important that women have power. Women's former lack of the power to decide what was published is at the very heart of Virago, our *raison d'être*.

I also find, somewhat to my surprise, that on the other side of this daring to record these times and thoughts is the deep pleasure of shaping a story, giving an experience a narrative. I have learned that I love to tell the stories. Marilynne Robinson says, 'writing takes you inward, seeing what your mind contains', and I discover that she's right.

*A Bite of the Apple* is my memories of these decades. Virago has been a life-changer for me.

But certainly not only for me.

### PART ONE

# A New Kind of Being

'The sense of limitless freedom that I, as a woman,
sometimes feel is that of a new kind of being'

Angela Carter

# CHAPTER ONE

# First Bites
## The Early Years

When I got a part-time position at Virago in 1978, I wouldn't have had the brazen hope then that I would become the Publisher, but I did know that I had found my home — once, that is, I caught my breath after toiling up the five steep flights to the one-roomed Virago office.

It was a heady time for feminism at the end of the 1970s, though not in ordinary offices and businesses, and certainly not in the boardrooms. Virago set sail in those winds.

My first publishing job had been in another tiny office, on Maiden Lane in Covent Garden where three of us—male owner and two women—worked. It was an independent publicity company set up in the wake of the relatively new idea that books could be actively promoted beyond the review pages and, particularly, the stories of authors' lives and personalities could be told to sell their books. When I first arrived in London I had a floor to sleep on in a Canadian friend's bedsit in Swiss Cottage for a few weeks before she went back home, and one contact in London: another Canadian, a woman I hadn't met before, who is the sister of a man I knew at university and was a publicist at William Collins publishers. She showed me an ad she had just prepared, noting, with laughter from us both, that only recently had she been allowed to include the cover price in the advert; before that it had been thought vulgar to mention that books cost money. Publishing was a gentleman's profession in so many ways. And it was so...imperial. I was often asked, slightly sneeringly, or at least with some disbelief, about Canadian culture. Margaret Atwood picked up the same feeling in the 1970s: 'In England, then, being Canadian was sort of like being cross-eyed, only less interesting; most people would gamely pretend not to notice, or throw you a look of pity and then swiftly escape to talk to someone else.' Atwood's rise to fame was a mercy to us Canadians abroad.

In my job at the publicity company, the boss sat in the front room overlooking the street and I and the other woman pounded electric typewriters in the back room. Or rather, my colleague, Fiona Spencer-Thomas, did; I, having seriously exaggerated my typing skills, tried to do most work on the telephone. My first book tour around Britain was with the Australian Colleen McCullough for her bestselling novel, *The Thorn Birds*—ironically, now a classic on the Virago list. Soon after, I worked on the paperback of Robert Lacey's *Majesty*, his biography of the Queen. My boss believed (correctly) that in order to nab the media's attention we needed something eye-catching, so for nearly two weeks Robert and I travelled the length and breadth of the UK, to radio and television interviews in a chauffeur-driven Phantom IV Rolls-Royce—just like the Queen's, apparently—discussing, at my initiative, left-wing politics while sipping whisky from crystal tumblers.

The boss was only about three years older than Fiona and me but it was not uncommon for him to interrupt us and bellow out from his front room, 'Coffee please!' When I once suggested that if he didn't have a guest and he wanted coffee he might come out and make it for himself and even offer us some, he paled; alarmed, he asked, 'Are you communist? They always want to share everything.' When I saw him after Margaret Thatcher became Prime Minister, he rubbed his hands in glee and greeted me with, 'Ah, the socialist ...'

I was a young woman with a head full of literature, waking up to feminism and thrilling to the change in the air. It felt like the time to look for another position.

22 May 1978

Dear Ms Callil,

After ten months with one of the most successful publisher's publicity companies I am convinced by the power of the media in the task of exposing books to the public and the booksellers ... your co-operative too uses free media time effectively. Even though your group adopts an alternative approach to publishing, it must sell its goods in the traditional market place; if your message through your books is to reach people other than the converted and already aware sector of the population—sales, advertising, and media must be employed ... I wish to employ this learning towards a better end.

It is for this reason that I am writing to you to see if there is any outlet for my energy, interest and experience. Although full-time involvement would be ideal, I am just as interested in working with you on a part-time basis. It is important for me to feel honestly enthusiastic about the books that I am promoting and the environment in which they are produced.

These requirements I see reflected in your co-operative and book list . . .

What I would appreciate is the chance to meet with you and discuss some of the ideas I have about free publicity for your books and the same meeting would give me the welcome chance to learn more about the Virago Co-operative.

Yours sincerely,

Lennie Goodings

This stiff, earnest little letter was answered with one that put me quickly right, but also gave me a small opening at which I jumped.

9 June 1978

Dear Ms Goodings,

I was interested to read your letter, though I think you are under a bit of a misapprehension about our company. We are not a co-operative but a limited company and we operate in a normal business way.

However, I would be interested in talking to you about your promotional experience, and in fact we do from time to time need freelance help with publicity and promotion. Perhaps we could meet for half an hour within the next month to talk about what you do and what you could possibly do for us?

Yours sincerely,

Carmen Callil

Virago's small rooms in Wardour Street, on the edge of Soho, were near the then seedy Leicester Square. Number 5, a tall, narrow Victorian building, had a pinball arcade on the ground floor, a 'gentlemen's club' on the first, other closed doors on the third and Virago perched at the very top. A small corridor for storage and a photocopier led into one largish working room facing the street, with a nook that held a fridge and counter space. At the back there was a tiny room with a sink and a loo, and a window out of which we could climb to sit on an asphalted roof and, after making me a sandwich, having learned I hadn't yet eaten, that's where Carmen interviewed me. Quick and intense, she discovered that I didn't know quite as much about publicity as I had claimed, but what I did have was new-world confidence (or naivety). I suspect she, being from Australia, recognized a fellow colonial not bowed by British traditions. She declared I had 'clout' and on 1 August 1978 offered me a freelance job: 'For the sum of £200, you will work on the promotion of *Make it Happy* [*What Sex is all About*] by Jane Cousins as follows. First of all, you'll prepare a promotion outline including Jane Cousins's proposed tour of the UK; you'll also work on the possibility of her talking at teachers' centres and teaching colleges sometime around or after publication.' I was also to spend two weeks full time, 'tying up Jane's tour . . . and if possible, and there's time available, during those two weeks you'll also work on Patti Smith's *Babel* and anything else that comes to hand'.

I learned that Virago *really* was not a collective, nor egalitarian in the way business decisions were taken—certainly not. It was run with a firm, hierarchical grip on finances, schedules, staff, and detail by Carmen Callil, Managing Director, in conjunction with Ursula Owen, Editorial Director, and Harriet Spicer, Production Director, but it did have a most generous attitude towards sharing things like tea- and coffee-making—and cleaning the office. Important, for me, was that its books were real and exciting: about the ideas and the passions that were coming up from the streets, in collective houses, in consciousness-raising groups, in feminist history workshops, in political rallies, *Spare Rib*, and other feminist magazines and newsletters. Virago books were part of the movement that would utterly alter women's place in the world.

Virago was founded in 1973, a dramatic time of political change, with the Western world on the cusp of power shifts: Britain entered the European Economic Community (EEC); the trade unions held the country to account, with strikes and a three-day working week; the Watergate investigation was about to bring down President Nixon and forever challenge the idea of the integrity of political office; the American Psychiatric Association removed homosexuality from the *DSM* (the *Diagnostic and Statistical Manual of Mental Disorders*); it was three years since the Equal Pay Act of 1970 and just two years away from the Sex Discrimination Act of 1975; and in a tennis match billed as the 'Battle of the Sexes', Billie Jean King accepted a challenge from Bobby Riggs. The female sex won.

By the time I arrived at Virago it had published around thirty books, launched the Virago Modern Classics list, and was becoming a recognizable force.

The girl who'd been a passionate reader, studied English literature and worked in a bookshop, had been raised, the oldest of five, by a bookish mother with feminist instincts and a liberal father, had landed where she felt she belonged. I'd left my country alone, to try my hand in Britain, and through a sort of blind instinctual feeling that it was right to pursue a job that felt like it might make a difference, had found it.

Creating a list that has a political and philosophical mission gives a publishing house tremendous energy. Victor Gollancz's Left Book Club, active from 1936 to 1948, is a significant example of a radical publishing house responding to a particular political time. The club's aim was to 'help in the struggle for World Peace and a better social and economic order and against Fascism'; its members were avid readers who were looking for a solution to the moral issues of the day and were provided with a monthly book club choice, a newsletter—even an annual rally. And its books wore a very distinctive livery of yellow and red.

Virago's list began with that same sense of purpose, urgency, and a deep awareness of its audience—and a view that there were many others out there who wanted to understand and be part of this world-changing 'club'.

Virago and the other feminist houses which preceded and soon followed in Britain and across the world published instinctively, knowing that there was a readership hungry for their books. Carmen Callil, Ursula Owen, and Harriet Spicer knew who they were publishing for; they shared their readers' concerns, quests, and passions. Beginning on the crest of the Women's Liberation Movement, Virago, unlike most publishing enterprises that work from nothing to build an audience, was almost immediately recognized as a living and breathing realization of many readers' wants and desires. Women wanted a voice, women wanted to understand their history, women wanted to see themselves on the page, women wanted a champion, and women wanted their share.

The feminist politics of the 1970s were complex and, like any social and political revolution, had many splinters. It also included those who didn't want to speak out or get involved but who were deeply stirred and found themselves cheering silently from their own lives. The one thing all these groups had in common was a desire to be heard. The female voice had something to say. Women felt they had been left out, not asked and not represented, even in socialist politics—or perhaps especially in socialist politics. It was to this eager audience that Virago and the other feminist organizations of the time launched themselves.

Carmen Callil said about Virago's beginnings, 'I was inspired by the explosive energy of the underground press . . . but frustrated by its lack of engagement with women's ideas, their work, their opinions, their history.'

'Their opinions' sounds almost tame compared to the other noble pursuits—ideas, work, history—in her list, but it was key to the sense of the time. Women were just not listened to— particularly not in public debate and certainly not in the media, where if women voices were heard it was as adjuncts to men's. It was not until 1975 that women were heard on the news regularly; before that, public-opinion surveys said women's voices were not acceptable. The broadcaster Joan Bakewell remembers that 'in the '70s, I asked the head of BBC News, "Might a woman one day read the news?" and was told, "Absolutely not."' #MeToo and other feminist campaigns of many decades focus on the power of breaking the silence with the female voice: one that is even now still muted in some places, some industries, and some countries.

But probably the most dramatic changes are the way women view *themselves* today compared to the 1970s, and the way that we, in the West, are seen and heard. In the introduction to *I Call Myself a Feminist*, which Virago published in 2015, the young women who edited the collection write, perhaps over-optimistically, but certainly reflecting their world: 'It seems cool, vibrant, sexy to be feminist. We have access to ideas and resources and thoughts and articles that feminists in the seventies could only dream about...We have allies the world over and feminism is no longer seen as only a "women's" issue'.

Of course, we still have problems of male domination in all parts of life, but we cannot deny that the institutional changes—around taxes, banks, mortgages, marriage, divorce, domestic violence, childcare, work, MPs, civil partnerships—since then have been profound. And it's thanks to women speaking out. Demanding that women be heard fuelled the feminist presses, newsletters, and magazines.

When I ask Carmen to remember all these years later why she hired me, she says, 'Well, I liked you. And you had opinions! I liked that.'

Opinions. Part of the women's movement was discovering that women even *had* opinions.

Born out of this cacophony of voices, appealing to the various ways that feminism was being interpreted by the Women's Liberation Movement, the late 70s and early 1980s in the UK saw the emergence of a staggering number of publications including: *Shrew*, *Red Rag*, *The Feminist Review*, *Everywoman*, *Trouble & Strife*, *WIRES*, *Outwrite*, *Wasafiri*, *Revolutionary and Radical Feminist Newsletter*, *Cambridge Women's Liberation Newsletter*. America gave us many, among them *Sinister Wisdom*, *Quest*, and *The Women's Review of Books*, which later became a British publication too; Canada introduced *Amazones d'Hier, Lesbiennes d'Aujourd'hui*, and *Herizons*.

The most influential and wide-ranging feminist magazines were born in the same year: the American *Ms.*—founded by Gloria Steinem and Dorothy Pitman Hughes—and the British *Spare Rib*, founded by Marsha Rowe and Rosie Boycott, hit the streets in 1972; *Ms.* in January and *Spare Rib* in July. Crucially, what these two magazines wanted to do was to reach every woman and 'to put women's liberation on the news stands'. *Ms.* claimed to be the first mainstream publication of its kind to speak honestly and directly about real women's issues. These magazines were not just reaching out to women who already identified as feminists: they were out to compete with the glossy women's magazines. The *Spare Rib* founders believed: 'There is the most urgent need for a magazine that will reach ALL women—that is, women who are frustrated by the limitations of existing magazines.'

Virago began with the same mainstream mission. Carmen Callil Publicity Ltd ('Anything outrageous suitably publicized'), set up in 1972 when Carmen was aged thirty-four, helped to launch *Spare Rib* and it gave Carmen the inspiration to turn to the industry she was most familiar with—she had worked at André Deutsch, Granada, and Quartet—to start a publishing house championing women's writing. Carmen had been the publicist for Germaine Greer's *The Female Eunuch*; she knew that books could be an agent of change.

She remembers that 'one day, when having a drink in a pub in Goodge Street, the idea for my publishing company came to me like the switching on of a light bulb'. That drink was with John Boothe, Joint Managing Director and Editorial Director of Quartet. Asked if he would support it, he immediately said yes.

Initially she registered her idea as Spare Rib Books, to be published in association with Quartet. The name was changed to Virago in March 1973, just before the first official board meeting on 21 June with Marsha Rowe and Rosie Boycott of the recently formed *Spare Rib*.

Carmen remembers: 'Rosie and I sat on the floor of my flat and went through books on ancient gods etc and Rosie found the name.' Virago: provocative, a heroic war-like female, and 'a strong, courageous, outspoken woman, a battler. Irreverence and heroism, that's what we wanted.'

Virago wanted to address all women and all of women's experiences. It challenged the idea of niche publishing from the start: 'There is a specialist publishing imprint for almost everything, except for 52% of the population—women. An exciting new imprint for both sexes in a changing world,' announced Virago's first catalogue. The refusal to be seen as marginal; the desire to inspire and educate and entertain *all* women, and men too; to bring women's issues and stories into the mainstream; to demonstrate a female literary tradition: these passions and beliefs were the bedrock of Virago. 'It was not enough to publish for ourselves,' said Carmen.

That attitude remains ours today.

Not all of the feminist houses gave themselves this mission, this reach, these intentions.

Women's words were beginning to rock the status quo. Books reporting from the front line of womanhood were published by some of the male hierarchical establishments that these books criticized. Important and life-changing memoirs and polemics firing up the Women's Liberation Movement from academics, journalists, poets, and novelists could not be kept down.

*The Feminine Mystique* by Betty Friedan (1963) and Germaine Greer's *The Female Eunuch* (1970) took on the patriarchy; *Against our Will* by Susan Brownmiller (1975) took on rape culture; *Hidden from History* by Sheila Rowbotham (1973) told us why our stories had not been told; Angela Davis's *If They Come in the Morning* (1971) brought news of the Civil Rights Movement; and *Fat is a Feminist Issue* by Susie Orbach (1978) heralded the conversations around the female body. Then there were books that would later become Viragos: *Sexual Politics* by Kate Millett (1970) on literature; *Patriarchal Attitudes* by Eva Figes (1970) on history (with the strapline 'My Case for Women to Revolt'); *Of Woman Born* by Adrienne Rich (1976) on mother-hood; and the memoir *I Know Why the Caged Bird Sings* by Maya Angelou (1969).

Arguably the mother of all of this generation of feminist books, which proclaimed that 'one is not born, but rather becomes a woman', was *The Second Sex* by Simone de Beauvoir, published in 1949 and translated into English in 1953.

Novels too were picking up on the restless mood of the times: Margaret Atwood's *The Edible Woman*; Margaret Drabble's *The Millstone*; *The Golden Notebook* by Doris Lessing; *The Women's Room* by Marilyn French; *The Bluest Eye* by Toni Morrison; and, a few years later, Alice Walker's *The Color Purple* were among the many.

This rewriting, new telling, and, crucially, these new per-spectives were for many, to use a phrase of the time, mind-blowing. The crime writer Val McDermid remembers reading Kate Millett's book: 'It was as if an explosion had gone off in my head. My politics had always been of the left, but I'd never really encountered a feminist perspective before. *Sexual Politics* allowed me—it forced me—to look at the world in a different way. I was on fire with what I had read.'

Rosie Boycott remembers *The Female Eunuch* with similar amazement: 'She bowled me over. I was stunned by her extraordinary beauty and her daring, her openness about sex, her obvious pleasure in taking on men, her extreme cleverness which combined with her wicked sense of humour . . . I remember her writing that women should "consider the idea of tasting your own menstrual blood", something I doubt too many actually did, but ideas like this pushed back the boundaries of being female, making our claustrophobic female world suddenly much, much bigger . . . for me, her vibrancy and sheer zest for life played a key part in changing mine.'

The ideas grew, handed woman to woman. *The Women's Room*, remembered the writer Nuala O'Faolain, was 'slipped to me like Samizdat to pass on as quickly as possible'.

The books, bought in shops, borrowed from libraries, shared urgently among friends, taken home to read in bed, stuffed in bags to read on buses, in backpacks to read on trips—these words of women—were privately and eagerly consumed.

There were marches and conferences, and the beginning of consciousness-raising groups, but nothing compares to the intimacy of reading; the private seduction of being alone with words that are speaking just to you, the reader, cannot be over-estimated. The writer A. L. Kennedy understands: she says that when you read, you hear the words 'in your most intimate organ—the brain'.

In the year before I came to London, while living in a bedsit in Victoria, at the southern tip of Vancouver Island, I read a novel that transformed the way I thought about myself. Aged twenty-three, I had moved nearly 3,000 miles from my friends, family, and boyfriends at home in Ontario to the west coast of Canada to try my luck at making my own way. I worked in a spaghetti restaurant at night and Borogrove Bookshop (a name inspired by Lewis Carroll's 'Jabberwocky') in Centennial Square by day, and though I did make some friends I was lonely and turned often to books. *The Diviners* by the Scots-Canadian writer Margaret Laurence told the story of Morag Gunn. Morag had a great appetite for life, for ideas, for sex (memorably, on the kitchen floor) and was torn between two men: one an appealing intellectual, the other an earthy man of few words with strong feelings—which, as it happened, somewhat reflected my life at the time. Morag thought that whichever one she went with would define who she would become, and though I had already forged my own adventure and proved I could make a living and live alone, I too had the sense of myself as waiting to be defined by a man. I thought my life would be a reflection of whoever my husband might be. In a sudden epiphany, Morag saw there was another answer: she dropped them both and took herself off to London to live her own life. And, reader, so did I.

'Reading is a way of becoming the person you are interested in being,' says A. L. Kennedy. These words, these 'womenwords' that we were reading, were whispering recognition, revolution, and insurrection. It's no wonder to me that women wanted more. Women wanted their own magazines, their own papers, and their own publishing houses. ·

It's hard today to capture that feeling of optimism, the sense of possibility fearlessly pitched against entrenched patriarchy— all with the profound belief that we would win the battle, that we would change the world. Did we think it was going to be that simple? Possibly we did.

What I have come to see is that out of this sort of popular force, this massive wave of demand for change, singular characters will emerge. They are those who only see the goal, who are aware of the hurdles but believe they are right and invincible in their pursuit. Often these people have only a little experience of what they are about to throw themselves into, but by sheer belief in themselves and their mission they win through.

Carmen was such a person. Of course she could not have built Virago alone. First she had Marsha and Rosie with whom to dream and scheme, before they left to focus on *Spare Rib* and then resigned from the Virago Board in 1974 and 1975 respectively.

Then Ursula, beginning in 1973, becoming Editorial Director in 1974, was absolutely crucial and a brilliant, fiery complement to her. Carmen couldn't have done it without Harriet Spicer's vital, intelligent, steadying help right from the beginning of Carmen Callil Publicity Ltd. Alexandra Pringle and I, joining part time in 1978, and then the others including Kate Griffin (1979), Lynn Knight (1980), Ruthie Petrie (1982) of those early days, were also important, but Carmen, seizing the moment, seeing the possibility—she was the ignition.

It was rage against injustice that fuelled Carmen, made her blind to some of the obstacles, and gave her the courage and almost monomaniacal chutzpah to overcome them. In her case, the power of an absolute sense of being right was combined with a deep knowledge and love of literature, and the skill of obsessive, meticulous planning. It was a dynamite combination. I choose the word dynamite because that sort of raging passion and disregard is often combustible and can leave a burned path in its wake. Over the years, though many were cherished and inspired, many too got scorched. I think of the number of people I used to meet who would complain, 'Carmen isn't speaking to me.' I sit now in an open-plan office and think back to Carmen's style of management...It wouldn't wash now. (Though however one handles it, power brings complications; once I became Publisher I too found I have a few people who won't speak to me.) But it was her intense drive which inspired the rest of us and kept it going. Said Carmen, 'We must survive. It is our duty not to go bust. Virago must be here for future generations, ensuring that women writers are not forgotten again.'

I have known Carmen now for decades, and I know from what she has said that her sense of injustice started in part with the Catholic Church. It has always been a source of great pleasure to know that Carmen and Germaine Greer were educated at the same convent school, remembered by Carmen as 'rules, censorship and silence, and above all a sense of disapproval waiting to pounce on those rare times when you felt most entirely yourself. And an obsession with sin.'

Carmen came to London in 1960 and fell in with the Australians of the underground press at *Ink* newspaper, then worked in publishing before founding her own publicity company. But even though the times were liberal and changing, the patronizing attitudes of men, both those on the left and the old-fashioned ones ('beige men', Carmen used to call them) of the British publishing world, stoked the old feelings of injustice. Being unfairly treated, feeling powerless against a larger structure—first Catholicism, then patriarchy and the British establishment—made Carmen frustrated, and determined to take control and have her own power.

Every woman who becomes a feminist has woken up to an understanding of injustice, to the corroding effect of patri- archy. I grew up with petty and belittling remarks and expect- ations; I witnessed and was angered by unfairness for girls and women; and when I was at university I began to understand how we women have learned to be our own censors, voyeurs of ourselves, checking and modifying ourselves for correct looks, behaviour, and even dreams and ambitions. I believe the world is still far from equal but I wouldn't say I have that constant, burning howl of rage against injustice that seems to inhabit Carmen. (Even now she refers to herself as a 'seething pot'.) But it's a hot flame I was very drawn to. Drawn to that and the idea that books, particularly when collected under the Virago umbrella, could make a difference.

Carmen was famously outstanding at publicity and much of the Virago look and style and indeed 'branding' was down to her. Her intelligent and encouraging editorial skills became evident as Virago progressed.

Ursula was the Editorial Director and I warm to this descrip- tion of her from a *Guardian* profile in July 2001: 'The editor and publisher Ursula Owen has always considered herself an out- sider. A very English German, a very Jewish Christian, a rad- ical in a conservative world, a conservative in a radical world. Owen has often wanted to belong, to be quietly accepted. At the same time, part of her has always laughed, or scowled, in the face of convention.'

Ursula had come from a career in editorial—from Frank Cass publishers—and was highly experienced in commissioning and editing. Born in England to German-Jewish parents, she was an intriguing mix of an impassioned, rather explosive temperament combined with an English bluestocking education; her background and education gave her Oxbridge confidence and connections. She was part of one of the most famous women's groups, the Arsenal Women's Group (Arsenal due to location, not the football team) and so combined grass roots feminism with the analysis that was emerging from feminist academics. Articulate and clever, she had a nose for good books and was a very intuitive editor. Divorced, she had a child, Kate, who we all came to know and like very much.

Harriet, who has a sense of fairness through to her core, was Carmen's right-hand woman. Blessed with a literary and artistic eye, no doubt influenced by her mother's bohemian life (she moved in circles that included the sculptor Elisabeth Frink and the painter Duncan Grant) Harriet also cites her mother, a spirited woman who made her own way post-divorce in the 1950s, as inspiration for independent thinking.

Harriet, also Oxford educated and well read, is younger than both Ursula and Carmen by ten to twelve years and so was more attuned to Alexandra and me, who are three years younger again. She was well attuned to Carmen's ways. She is also a beacon of justice and was not against making her views known when she felt things were not right.

The Virago author Sarah Waters, looking back at the mid to late 1980s, observes that it was an extraordinary, exhilarating time, one of 'dismantling the grand narratives'. And that is right; there were fierce arguments and differences among feminists about how we should change the world and what it should be changed to, but what is unarguably true is that stories, histories, memoirs, rants, poems, articles, essays, explorations were like fireworks, rockets lighting up possibilities, blowing up old, entrenched ideas; words were going to tear down and rebuild the world. Words were incendiary and liberating. Words were heralding a new dawn.

Angela Carter wrote, 'The sense of limitless freedom that I, as a woman, sometimes feel is that of a new kind of being. Because I simply could not have existed, as I am, in any other preceding time or place.'

A new kind of being . . . Sitting in a tiny kitchen at the top of a collective house in Tufnell Park in north London, I turned the pages of my first *Spare Rib* magazine—shocked by the honesty of some of the articles, amused and gladdened by others—and felt the thrill of possibility.

## CHAPTER TWO

# Setting the World on Fire

'The one thing that's really memorable about those early days at Virago is the pace at which you worked...' Harriet remembers, and that 'it was all learning and doing things for the first time and thinking yippee!' Carmen concurs, 'Harriet was always very elegant. She...kept her cool and did her work... I just left things (re the publicity company) in her hands.'

Virago's first books, in association with Quartet, were published from Carmen's flat in Cheyne Place in Chelsea and were partially financed by Carmen Callil Publicity Ltd. An arrangement was made with Quartet: they would finance, produce, distribute, and own the books which Virago commissioned for them for a fee of £75 for each title and a royalty of 2.5 per cent on all sales.

The character and tone of the press was almost immediately established: *Fenwomen* by Mary Chamberlain was Virago's launch title in September 1975. A vivid social and oral history of an isolated village in the Cambridgeshire Fens, it provided a portrait spanning 100 years through the voices of the women who lived there. It signalled a crucial aim of Virago: to publish the stories of women's everyday lives, stories previously not thought worth telling and recording. Nancy Friday's *My Secret Garden: Women's Sexual Fantasies* followed in October and it was—and is—an eye-opening book that showed Virago was not afraid to publish provocatively.

In December 1976, having published ten books from Carmen's flat, where in a nod to the three cats who also lived there the address for cables and telegrams was caterwaul, Carmen, Ursula, and Harriet decided to leave the support of Quartet and go out on their own.

Sonny Mehta, then publisher at Pan, where he started the Picador imprint, and now Editor-in-Chief at Knopf in America, gave Carmen an article from the American *Publishers Weekly*— 'Mr Hopeful Starts a Publishing Company'—and taught her about profit and loss. Says Ursula, 'In our year with Quartet we had learned two things: how vital it is to have total financial control . . . and how any requirement to refer to others on editorial decisions . . . is a constraint . . . Armed with a cash flow sheet and a publishing proposal for the first three years, we set off.'

With a loan of £10,000 from the Rowntree Trust, money from Ursula's uncle Ernst Grunfeld, a good bit of Carmen's money, and £1,500 capital, Virago was relaunched as a fully independent company.

In the 2017 television documentary about Virago, *Changing the World One Page at a Time*, made by Claire Walley, Carmen remembers their small bank overdraft 'needed to be guaranteed by two men' and, laughingly savouring the irony, says she should have said, 'Would you mind guaranteeing my overdraft so that I can bring down the world?'

The two men loyal to Carmen were Bob Gavron of St Ives printers and the publisher Paul Hamlyn. So many men and women have helped Virago along the way and this period was no exception.

In July 1977 they moved to the fourth floor of 5 Wardour Street in Soho, which is where I found them a year later, and by then they had raised another £25,000 by selling some of the shares, with the majority held by the three women, which now included Harriet.

Having not really experienced mainstream publishing, I was under the impression that Virago was exactly what all publishers were like: a vigorous, driven, idealistic bunch of people. It accorded with the little I knew of Canadian publishing, where the small presses of 1960s Toronto—Anansi, Coach House— had the same sort of missionary zeal; in their case to publish, invent even, the dawning of what was called CanLit, or in the case of Canada's Women Press, feminist publishing. It didn't seem odd to me that one would throw one's entire life and spirit into the enterprise. Of course you did. But as I got further into publishing, I began to realize that no, this little enterprise was quite unlike the monoliths of British publishing and these passionate women were not at all the standard women in publishing, who at the time were clever types who mainly worked for the powerful men who defined the houses and took the publishing decisions. The Virago women were also clever but *they* took the decisions; they were the powerful ones. That delight in power and that passion for the project all contained in one small room was exhilarating but, to be frank, also often fraught and sometimes scary. It took me a few adrenalin-pumping years to find out it was not your average British publishing house.

The 'new kind of being' that Angela Carter identified was women hungry for their history. Thanks to Ursula's knowledge of the *History Workshop Journal* people, feminist academics, and socialist feminist groups, and inspired by Sheila Rowbotham's revolutionary *Hidden from History* (1973), Virago knew that there was so much women's history to be discovered.

One of the early initiatives was the Virago Reprint Library. Remembers Ursula, 'We were determined to reclaim a history, a feminism and a literature which had been lost or neglected. In this we were not only in tune with feminist historians...but were influenced by new writing in social and cultural history which was among the most important work being done in the 1960s and 1970s, most significantly E. P. Thompson's *The Making of the English Working Class* and Raymond Williams's *Culture and Society.*'

The first book of the newly independent Virago was *Life as We Have Known It*, edited by Margaret Llewelyn Davies, a collection of writings by working-class women first published in association with the Co-operative Women's Guild in 1931. It was reprinted with a new introduction alongside the original one by Virginia Woolf: 'These voices are beginning only now to emerge from silence...These lives are still half hidden in profound obscurity.' The history of women repeats itself and Virago was determined to get these histories in print and to keep them in print too—the commitment to backlist publishing was there from the start to avoid later generations, as Carmen said, 'searching through libraries and coming, with astonishment, upon the accounts of women who had the same hopes, problems and experiences'.

There followed, among others, *Maternity: Letters from Working-Class Women* edited by Margaret Llewelyn Davies; *Working-Class Wives* by Margery Spring Rice; the astonishing *Round About a Pound a Week* by Maud Pember Reeves; Florence Bell's *At the*

*Works*; *Women and Trade Unions* by Barbara Drake; the famous *Women and Labour* by the great South African writer Olive Schreiner; and the suffragist and suffragette histories *The Cause* by Ray Strachey and *My Own Story* by Emmeline Pankhurst.

Some of these books had originally been published by the Co-operative Women's Guild or the Fabian Women's Group, whose first aim was 'to study the economic position of women and press their claim to equality with men . . . to be secured by socialism'—and had long been out of print. Some were reissued with new introductions by feminist historians such as Sally Alexander and Anna Davin, and some with their original introductions.

This was an extraordinary period of study for women—both in and out of the universities and further education colleges.

The most successful of the early Virago non-fiction reprints was *Testament of Youth* by Vera Brittain, first published in 1933 and out of print for decades. It was given to Carmen by the academic Rosalind Delmar; Carmen read it through tears on a beach in Australia and returned to the office determined to put it back in print. And not only in print: she sent a copy to BBC TV and suggested they make a television series, which they did in 1979, with a marvellous series starring Cheryl Campbell. Virago was small at the time, with limited distribution, and wouldn't be able to enjoy the sales that would result from the programme, so a limited-licence paperback sale was made to Fontana, who produced a mass-market film tie-in paperback edition, to be sold alongside the Virago edition. When their licence elapsed, the Virago edition was once again the only one in the market. *Testament of Youth* remains in print today, a stalwart of the Virago backlist, still speaking to generations of readers and students, and most interestingly, as Brittain's biographer Mark Bostridge says in his introduction to the Virago centenary edition, from obscurity it has become a lasting testimony, 'more famous than the books by men that inspired it'.

The format known as trade paperback—originated first by Sonny Mehta at Paladin and Picador—was Virago's size of choice. It could take a slightly higher paperback price—£1.99—and its larger size allowed for an elegant cover. Because it was essential to have Virago books reviewed and there was then (and still is now) an old-fashioned idea that books were not worthy of attention unless they were in hardback, Virago also frequently published simultaneously a small hardback print run of around 500 copies, for the reviewers and the libraries. Carmen, queen of publicity, has said: 'Virago was founded with two main aims. One was ideological, the other a marketing belief . . . to get every inch of publicity we could for each book we published.' And we did.

Harriet turned eagerly to learning production: 'It was in my blood and I loved the tangible object.' Her father was a paper-maker, running Spicers Paper, and she embraced working with printers, typesetters, and indeed paper merchants. It was thrill-ing to learn.

Carmen also claims merchant blood in her veins. She recalls with huge fondness her Lebanese uncle's factory in Australia, which she often visited as a young girl. 'I loved the atmos-phere . . . I wasn't afraid of business, of the making of things. I absolutely knew that my business was possible.'

While in general feminists agreed with Simone de Beauvoir that women want to 'dethrone the myth of [inherent] femi-ninity', feminism also raised the question: what *is* femaleness?

What is the *essential nature* of women? And is our difference from men irrelevant to our equality with men? Are we different but equal? And do we want to be equal to men anyway? Why are men the standard?

(I still love the jokey slogan of that time, interestingly coined by a man, Timothy Leary: 'Women who seek to be equal with men lack ambition.')

Or, as Carmen said, 'There are the people who think women should become like men, but there are quite enough men around. We had something better in mind!'

Virago was often pressed to define feminism and that definition was something Virago has always refused to be hard-line about. The same is true today. Our books look at the world through women's eyes but we've never taken a stand on what is the 'right' kind of feminism. We have always thought that people should be their own judge of that. What we wanted to do was put women centre stage and highlight women's achievements and history.

Transgender rights and identity conversations have re-awoken those early discussions around what *is* woman. There is no doubt that women are still discriminated against but I think there is, at last, a general agreement that society *should* be trying to ensure that women, and now transgender and non-binary people, have the same rights, freedoms, and opportunities as men. But that was far from true back then, and the laws safeguarding equality were very new. Only a few years had passed since the Sex Discrimination Act had become UK law in 1975. In Canada the 1977 Human Rights Act was put in place around the time of the Equal Rights Amendment in the USA. Feminists were constantly put in a position of explaining, defending, and arguing their case.

As well as applying to Virago, I had sent my CV to another radical publishing house, Writers and Readers Publishing Co-operative. Virago's offer of one day a week coincided with them offering me a job too. We agreed that I would work for them four days a week; I handed in my notice at the publicity company and embarked on a year of contrasts.

Writers and Readers was a free-wheeling, high-minded co-operative 'run' by two married couples: Glenn Thompson (who had founded Centerprise Bookshop in Hackney, London) and Sian Williams, who handled the finance and sales, alongside the editors who were the then married couple Lisa and Richard Appignanesi (fellow Canadians, I discovered to my pleasure). To say they were idealistic publishers was an understatement: it was a company that seemed to be entirely fuelled by passion, ideas, and international feminist and socialist politics. The leaflet they gave me entitled 'A British Publishing Co-operative: Who We Are and What We Do' states they were formed in the autumn of 1974, 'with a minimum of theory, high hopes and no capital'. But this was prefaced by 'What theory do we espouse? Latter-day Phalansterian; Owenite socialism; Proudhonian mutalism?' And they were members of the Industrial Common Ownership Movement.

I was out of my depth in terms of their theory but I knew they published some outstanding, important titles and I liked their policy of encouraging writers to assume greater control over the production of their own books. Notable were the Beginners' Guides, one of the original, influential graphic series. This list of deeply intelligent and accessible books on political and cultural theory with texts written by experts and illustrated by impressive cartoonists was launched with *Marx for*

*Beginners.* They went on to publish *Trotsky*, *Mao*, *Freud*, *Einstein*, and *Feminism for Beginners*, among many others. Writers and Readers also published the left-wing playwright Arnold Wesker and the great novelist and cultural commentator John Berger, author of the ground-breaking *Ways of Seeing*. These authors were part of the co-operative; I have a treasured copy of John Berger's novel *Pig Earth*, which he has signed 'Thanks for keeping the faith'. In so many ways Writers and Readers were ahead of their time: publishing non-sexist children's books, novels in translation, books about education and literacy: writers including Paulo Freire, Frantz Fanon, Alejo Carpentier, Victor Serge. The emphatic aim was also to be international. One of their first titles was *Little Girls* by Elena Belotti, a brilliant book about the way girls, through home and school education, are turned into little women, translated from the Italian by Lisa. We also published the Irish writer Neil Jordan's first collection of stories, *Night in Tunisia*.

Glenn, an extraordinary, charismatic, self-educated man from Harlem who came to Britain in 1968, gave the job of production to me. I eagerly agreed and depended on printers and typesetters to learn how to make a book. Despite the fact that Writers and Readers often struggled to pay their bills on time, the printers (all mainstream) were kind and giving, with lovely reps who really wanted to help. Our typesetters were not at all mainstream: they did cheap book typesetting for radical presses such as ours on the side. Their main work was producing the International Marxist Group newspaper from a basement in Islington, which I would often visit. One of the other young people working at Writers and Readers at the time was the late Gary Pulsifer, who went on to found his own publishing house,

Arcadia. Many years later at Virago I had the pleasure of publishing Lisa Appignanesi.

When I came home to my shared house in Tufnell Park with tales of my days, one of my flatmates wisely gave me a copy of 'The Tyranny of Structurelessness' by Jo Freeman, a 1971 article which looked at the way in which feminist groups were creating groups without leaders and making structures flat and equal. She very clearly showed that structurelessness is 'a way of masking power'. In any group, informal and therefore unaccountable, she wrote, leaders will emerge. Interestingly, she argued that only when structure is formalized—even if it is flatter than the typical hierarchies—only then can it be subject to democratic scrutiny.

Yes, I thought. Yes. That is certainly what I experienced at Writers and Readers. So many great books and terrific goodwill from its authors but the lack of structure was incredibly time-consuming and ultimately, I think, part of its undoing.

Curiously, the offices were only a step away from Virago, at 9–19 Rupert Street, also in Soho. The Writers and Readers office was on a large, sprawling warehouse-like floor where we also kept our stock, at the top of a rundown building with no heat and rumours of rats in the basement where the toilets were. I remember running over to the pub across the way to pee.

I thought it was Dickensian, eccentric, and fascinating, and wore sweaters and long skirts, donning fingerless gloves in order to type, huddling over Calor gas canisters for heat.

The chaos, the ideas, the people, and the politics were intense, confusing, exhausting—but often fun and always fascinating. Their manifesto quoted Balzac, 'Debt is what our creditors do not have the imagination to understand', and said, 'As romantic socialists we thought it feasible to replace capital by being labour intensive . . . working at first for no wages, and now for very low ones; keeping overheads down; writers like John Berger and Chris Searle, waiving all advances and royalties as their temporary contribution for the co-op's take-off.'

I did get paid and I did get deeply involved with important ideals and ambitious projects, and I learned so much about making books.

For one year that was four days of my life: Monday, Wednesday, Thursday, and Friday.

On Tuesdays I went to the contrasting, highly ordered Virago in Wardour Street.

The main room was all tables: a large square surface had been created in the middle by pushing four tables together. Carmen had her own little table facing one of the walls below a pinboard with photos and cards and schedules –including a quote from the Russian revolutionary Alexandra Kollontai about a women's right to love and work—and along the front, under the windows, ran a long black table which had come from Carmen's dining room. Harriet, wonderful with order and process, sat at the end of it.

Three large, noisy electric typewriters and three black telephones completed the equipment; on the walls were suffragette photos, loaned to Virago by Jill Craigie, the documentary film maker (and married to the Labour politician Michael Foot). The office was a little ship: a place for everything and everything in its place. It was supremely organized by Carmen who was, and remains, a person who can impressively quell and order vast reams of paper, plans, finances, detail, and ideas. There was nothing anarchic or chaotic about this office. We worked rigorously to schedules, publication and otherwise. The day began at 9.30 sharp, officially ended around 5.30 or 6 p.m. and we ate lunch at our desks. Because the pay was low (my yearly salary when I was hired full time in 1979 was £3,750) food was provided by Virago; we took turns shopping. On my first day, at 1 p.m. I made myself a sandwich, opened a copy of the listings magazine *City Limits* to read while eating, and heard, 'Haven't you got anything to do, darling?' Ah, I thought—so we work at lunch too.

I was given a corner on the main table space, shared with Ursula Owen and with Alexandra Pringle, who was the assistant to all things. Alexandra, who had arrived at Virago a few months before me, was also working part time. Her other job was with *Art Monthly*, the editor of which was a neighbour of Ursula's, who had learned Virago was looking for an assistant. Alexandra remembers being interviewed by Carmen: 'She hired me and I started as her slave . . . otherwise known as the shit-worker.' It's true, that was the language used. But Alexandra has also said that we felt these two towering characters, Ursula and Carmen, were like our mothers. Carmen says we 'were family'. Of course that implies the full gamut of emotions: on both sides! Alexandra, who is English, and I are the same age and also like me, she had not come to publishing via Oxbridge. Her father was an English literature teacher and she was widely read in novels; she soon graduated naturally to assisting Carmen with the Classics, eventually becoming Editorial Director in charge of them. However, to begin with she was the general help, the 'shit-worker', though more decorously listed in the catalogue as Office Manager.

Alexandra and I often raised eyebrows to each other, though we didn't dare talk unless we were alone, which was very rare.

Alexandra has a loud, infectious laugh, but it was a good few months before I knew that. Outside the office, when we dragged sacks of review copies down the five flights of stairs and over to the post box, we had a lot to say about it all. Though I had the title of Publicity Manager—manager of me—I too was really an assistant to Carmen and I soon realized I had much to learn. I remember her counselling me against telling reviewers what to think—not to send a book saying 'I *know* you will love this' but instead to explain why we thought it important or special; a subtle but effective and respectful difference, and a lesson in how to 'position' a writer and her work. She also stressed the benefits of working at least six months in advance of publication. There were plenty of magazine and newspaper literary pages then—from the mainstream to women's liberation newsletters, all of whom we had contact with—and 'if our books are there first that's what they'll feature'.

Carmen was exacting, brisk, cajoling. One of my first press releases was returned to me marked throughout with corrections and comments in red ink. To this day, I remember that 'upcoming' was scrawled through with 'ugly Americanism' and replaced with 'forthcoming'. The difference between these two words was mystifying to me, but I quickly learned that there was a correct, Carmen way to do things. Maybe the people who work for me say the same about me now!

Carmen sometimes sported funny jumpers with koala bears on them; Ursula often wore a green turtleneck over a long tartan kilt; Harriet wore jeans and stripy tops. Alexandra, meanwhile, was all exotic earrings and perilously high heels. I can't think I was very distinguished in those days, though I did like vintage clothes and I credit my penchant for heels and a little black dress to Alexandra, in whom I observed that you could be feminist *and* dress up in fabulous clothes. Kate Griffin, a Kiwi who joined as our very impressive Sales Manager, wore fabulous bright red and yellow, and Lynn Knight, an office assistant who eventually graduated to become a Virago Modern Classics Editorial Director, I remember, came for her interview in a perfect 1930s suit. We were not flashy women but neither were we feminists who wore dungarees; that was not our style.

As well as sharing cleaning, food rotas, and all the work—including packing the review copies and licking the stamps (a swift assembly line that had to be seen to be believed)—we also made tea for one another. Making tea for Carmen, I discovered, was an art. 'It's because you are Canadian that you don't know. Look, this is how you do it,' she teased me. I was taught to warm the pot then spoon in an exact amount of tea leaves— a smoky blend of Lapsang souchong and English breakfast tea that Carmen mixed at home and put in old Fortnum & Mason tins—then wait the required brewing time before pouring and distributing the cups. Carmen regularly washed all the tea towels and the hand towels from the little bathroom/butler sink area. We had one loo with a door that didn't reach the floor or ceiling. That's where we went to have a cry when it was all too much. And, frankly, it often was.

Of course, everything was done by phone or letter. I began my work arranging promotion for Jane Cousin's *Make it Happy: What Sex is All About*, a provocative handbook which Ursula had commissioned. It was a new look at sex education for girls and boys, and I sat at my corner of the table with a telephone and plan, and within the hearing of the others pitched the radical book: talking about masturbation, orgasms, sexually transmitted

diseases to everyone from *The Times* to BBC Radio Solent. I
don't remember it being embarrassing or revealing—it was a
good thing that I was young and new to the country. For Jane
I arranged a publicity tour on which she had to embark by herself, which was most unlike my previous experience of author
publicity. On Robert Lacey's Rolls-Royce book tour we had
been joined at times by not one but two women from his publisher's office. Virago obviously couldn't afford that so off went
Jane by herself to travel by train up and down the country for
several weeks, as in those days a tour was very thorough and
covered press and radio and bookshops in all major, and some
smaller, cities. I rang her at her hotel in the evenings to see how
she was faring Jane's objective was to answer the questions
bothering teenagers, so everything was explained: incest,
paedophilia, masturbation, bestiality—the lot, and with photos. Her critics claimed the book had 'no moral context' and
was 'putting ideas into children's heads'. One religious magazine said it was yet 'another example of twentieth-century
arrogance', and had only two references to marriage; and in the
House of Commons an MP asked whether its content should
rightly be considered obscene. But most applauded her honesty
and the book sold well, and won a *Times Educational Supplement*
book award. For me this was exciting—and real: ruffling fea-
thers, speaking out, making a difference.

At the end of my year of living in two contrasting worlds,
Virago offered me a full-time job. I weighed up the two options.
Should I leave Writers and Readers? I dithered terribly. It was a
question of such contrasts and I made a list of the pluses and
minuses of each. For Virago: 'good career step, good list, better
pay and workers I respect and like, high morale, though

sometimes alienating'. Against Virago: 'very hard drudgery work, the commitment and energy required leaves little time for anything else'—and most surprising to me to read now: 'politics hazy'. That must have been because Writers and Readers was all politics and I was much swept up by their radical co-operative intents. In their favour I listed: 'high level of responsibility, fairly agreeable, good list'. Against was the terrible chaos and uncertainty, but 'Should I stay for moral reasons?' Oh the politics of the left, fuelled by idealism but also, frankly, by guilt.

I left the co-operative—on good terms—and chose Virago.

In October 1979 I moved to a full-time job at a salary of £3,500 with a promise of it going to £3,750 in three months, after which 'salary to be reviewed from thence as and when we can, and as we mutually agree'. I wrote to my parents that I wouldn't get home for Christmas that year because 'though their contracts specify holidays, it is like pulling teeth to actually get them ... *they* never take holidays themselves.' (However, not much later on part of my salary was the cost of a flight home every other year: and I *was* encouraged to go, so I was absolutely wrong there.) I revealed nerves about full time at Virago: 'I had a long chat with one of the women [it would have been Harriet] who work there—I told her that I was slightly nervous about coming in and she said she wasn't surprised (great comfort!) and gave me some tips and supportive hints. I think it will be okay.'

I plunged in. It *was* okay but it was challenging.

Because I now have a fond relationship with Carmen, I find it difficult to remember just how despairing I felt at times but I can also see how she shaped me. I find an old letter that I wrote to my parents around this time: 'Carmen doesn't get to me like she used to. She's still alternatively wonderful, inspiring, funny AND horrid, bullying and bitchy. But I really don't care—I'm able to stand up to her now. One thing Virago has done for me is to make me a much tougher character—and although it has sometimes been hell getting here—I *am* glad for that.'

I enclosed an article about Virago from the *Guardian* of 26 January 1981 by Polly Toynbee, who wrote of Carmen, 'She is an ebullient energetic character, and, one suspects, a powerful dynamic force,' and I put a large exclamation point beside that paragraph.

It was a bit like being in a very strict school, with rules and systems that if not followed were rewarded by cold silence or reprimands. Throughout my life I have been a person who finds mornings and being on time difficult—I am a night owl and a time-defiant creature. These traits were not really acceptable: the Virago office worked on Carmen-time. She was an insomniac, so by the official opening time of 9.30 she'd already been up for hours, reading and then arriving at the office at the crack of dawn. Ursula would drop off her little girl at school so she, like me, sometimes got there after 9.30, by which time the 'good mornings' were over. Good morning was said to those who arrived on time; those who didn't got a mere nod. But then, disconcertingly, Carmen could also be very kind, complimentary, and let you know how very pleased she was with your work. She has a marvellous laugh and was—and is—wickedly witty. I wanted to work well, I wanted her 'blessing', and even though I often did not approve of her behaviour I admired and respected her work: it was the same for all of us. For Carmen, the devil was in the detail and from her I learned meticulousness, high standards, and the rewards of hard graft. Though it

was often tough going for me—literally nightmarish at times—
I was absolutely determined not to be beaten by it. And there
was just so much about it that I loved.

In 1980 we published Dora Russell's memoir *The Tamarisk
Tree: My School and the Years of War*. It described the fascinating
experiment in education at Beacon Hill School, which she ran
with her husband, the philosopher Bertrand Russell—alongside the heart-breaking account of the end of her marriage. She
came to London for publication.

I was already well disposed to her because both Carmen
and Ursula would approvingly quote Dora Russell's daughter,
Harriet Ward, on her mother: 'She really believed in the value
of women as women. She didn't want them to be mere com-
panions of men she wanted them to be in every way equal, in
every way influential ... for the very essence of what they represent to count in politics and in society.'

To save Virago money I offered Dora an overnight stay in the
Victorian house I now co-owned in north London, between
Archway and Tufnell Park. (The days when you could buy
cheaply, even on paltry wages.) It was a very Virago household
that night because my co-owner was Cathy Porter, author of our
biography of Alexandra Kollontai, the only woman in Lenin's
government. Cathy and I sat in my embarrassingly shabby spare
room and talked with Dora, who reached back to another
fascinating era, recalling for example the writer and publisher
Leonard Woolf who, she said, 'put up with a lot' in regard to his
wife. We sat nodding, until we remembered who his wife was:
Virginia! The school Dora and Bertrand Russell had run was an
experiment in different ways of educating children, different ways
of living; a school set up between the wars; it was an optimistic

period. We were in such different times now, but Dora's openness to the possibilities of living a life that shunned convention and took risks felt relevant. I remember too that she wanted to see Doris Lessing, and Carmen and Ursula arranged a publication lunch upstairs in the famous Soho publishing hangout, the Gay Hussar, so she could do so.

Mentioning only a few of the many publications from the first few years of independence demonstrates that Virago was covering the classics, history, sex, memoir, education, and biography. I remember when I joined Virago friends asked if I would feel restricted publishing only women!

Ursula used to tell the story of talking to the press about Virago's first list of books and a reporter asking if Virago would find enough to publish the following year. As if.

Beyond my phone calls to the press and calls to authors and agents—Ursula and Carmen made most of those—Harriet rang typesetters and printers, but otherwise the room was disturbed only by the loud typewriters (by now my skill in that department was not great but a bit more respectable).

Once a month we had a meeting for which Carmen would set the agenda and it would include print runs, deliveries, cost of stamps, reports on publicity, subsidiary rights, and sales. (After Quartet, Writers and Readers had been Virago's sales reps, but by this time Wildwood House who had five UK reps were employed; export sales were arranged from the office.) And then there was the shopping and cleaning rota. Once or twice we had meetings at Carmen's house. Carmen has always had animals—cats and latterly dogs—and at that point she had a tabby cat named Mary, after Mary Wollstonecraft, and two grey cats named after her friends William Miller and John

Boothe, the latter an adviser to Carmen from her days at Granada. One of the cats immediately jumped onto my shoulder and curled around my frightened neck. I protested, weakly, until it was removed by Carmen, who declared that not liking cats 'showed a defect in your personality'.

When the office was Carmen's house, Harriet enjoyed that 'there were cats galore, which became a feature of working life—you had to be able to type with a cat around your neck or you wouldn't get anywhere'. Thankfully I arrived when Virago was in offices—without cats.

It was a quiet, focused office, though Carmen, smoking rollups, emitted a sucking sound as she held the cigarette-holder in her teeth between smokes. Most surprisingly, and rather delightfully, she would often suddenly burst forth with a line from 'I Don't Want to Set the World on Fire', a song she loved from the 1930s. Carmen adores singing and I have often seen her and her friends crowded around a piano, laughing and bellowing out old songs. Ursula too is a music lover; she plays the piano, though her taste runs more to classical.

We were a highly effective outfit and we all took great pleasure in that despite our differing individual temperaments. However, the ideas we were trying to disseminate through bookshops, media, and the Women's Liberation Movement were in many ways disruptive: because of course the point of the movement was to upset what had been seen as the 'natural' order of things. I love the fact that Virago has always been an interesting paradox: a well-run business with its own status quo set up to change the status quo of the world.

The Virago Advisory Group beautifully illustrates one of the ways Virago went about feminism. Soon after they became independent from Quartet, Ursula and Carmen invited thirty-four women to be in this group. They ranged from agents and fellow publishers such as Jane Gregory and Liz Calder to academics such as Rosalind Delmar, Elaine Showalter, and Sally Alexander. The writers included Angela Carter and Germaine Greer, and there were journalists including the Spare Rib Collective and Beatrix Campbell. The idea was to gather experts and helpers, advisers, and women who might suggest books for the press to publish or to give advice on publishing practice. But after a few meetings it quickly became apparent that these advisers had a different idea about their role—that is, some of them thought they were being brought in to the fold rather like a co-operative, but no, that was not what was intended. Meetings were abandoned and by the time I arrived only a few years later, the Advisory Group had become advisory individuals who did indeed make themselves and their expertise available to us. Their names were printed inside every Virago title for many years and they truly were a fabulous group of women to whom we often turned for help.

Printed alongside the list was a clarion call chosen to reflect the belief that when women work together real change is possible. Quoting Sheila Rowbotham:

'Virago is a feminist publishing company: "It is only when women start to organize in large numbers that we become a political force, and begin to move toward the possibility of a truly democratic society in which every human being can be brave, responsible, thinking and diligent in the struggle to live at once freely and unselfishly."'

The advisory women did suggest books: as mentioned earlier, Rosalind Delmar gave Carmen a copy of *Testament of Youth*; Sally

Alexander and Anna Davin helped find titles for the original Virago Reprint Library. All were very important and much welcomed ideas as a publishing house drawing on the women's movement for ideas and knowledge needs such voices. But Virago—Carmen and Ursula—made the decisions on what would be published; this was not a collective.

Many of the original feminist and radical organizations took to their heart the idea of doing everything in a brave-new-world way as Writers and Readers did: collectives, co-operatives, no shareholders was how some set up shop. They wanted to do business in a different mode; they wanted their companies to reflect the times. That wasn't Virago's way.

And yet even with this more traditional business model Virago was powered by idealism and altruism; workers and authors gave their all to the company because we believed in the larger enterprise—changing the world with women's stories—even if it meant taking low wages and working long hours. Authors too were willing to throw in their lot with Virago for low advances. They were very much on our side from the start.

Cynicism or pure opportunism; those have never been Virago motivations, though because we are a business they easily could have been. But over the forty plus years that Virago editors have chosen the books to publish, their guiding principle has always been to ask, what does this do to champion women's talent or what truth does it tell about women's lives? I do know that sounds impossibly idealistic and certainly I don't mean to say that we have done this at the exclusion of an eye to profit, but cynicism has rarely, if ever, played a role in Virago's book choices.

But from the beginning Virago has wanted to prove that the business of publishing books by women is a profitable enterprise and that the very existence of Virago shows the world that a feminist business run by women would work. In 1993 Harriet wrote, 'As with all publishers, books are our lifeblood, but at Virago, what we see as being of equal importance is the existence of the press itself . . . the belief that women's writing and issues could be the foundation of an inspirational, financially viable list.' To be financially viable you have to make a profit: this has always been crucial, because profit is protection, and Virago has almost always made a profit. When profit has been at stake the Virago directors made tough choices: about being independent, about selling ourselves, about, horribly, having to make people redundant. And now, when Virago is part of a larger publishing conglomerate, profit is still our protection— against people interfering in our editorial choices. When a publishing list does not make profit, it comes under scrutiny to find out why not.

Of course, keeping an eye on profit can mean turning down either less obviously viable projects or costly ones, but that problem—or choice—is not confined to imprints within a conglomerate. Taking risks affects both small and large houses; the difference between acquiring books as an editor in an independent and as one in a conglomerate is not about risk per se, it's that in the latter a commissioning editor has to convince many more people in the publishing house of their belief in a book or author. In so many ways the very act of writing and publishing means taking risks.

Idealism and commerce feel like strange bedfellows, as has often been proved, and usually one of those bedfellows gets kicked out. Does capitalism always have to mean growth for an ever-increasing profit? Or can 'enough' profit to keep the fires burning be sufficient? Virago's business model, with its lofty ideals, has at the same time always been rather modest. It began small. We did not ask for secretaries, cleaners, assistants. We could all type. We have always watched our outgoings in relationship to our income. We have been awarded grants for translations but not had grants to keep us going. When we did our management buy-out with Rothschild Ventures in 1987 the investors said, 'Virago washes its own face.' An awful expression but nonetheless we knew what they meant and were proud of that.

Growth and profit are things that Virago has had to wrestle with from the beginning. All directors and shareholders agreed that Virago needed to protect itself by making profit. So long as we achieved that any disagreements could be managed. But when we looked as if profits would not deliver—that's when we hit trouble between us. However, even at those very low points, through our passionate rows and factions, even then, we kept to the idea that Virago must survive us. Is that not a commitment to idealism that flies in the face of cold capitalism?

Interestingly, the old Virago mix of paradoxes again: the fact that we had a hierarchy and shareholders made us take our fiscal responsibilities seriously, and indeed it also meant that whoever had the most shares could sway the choice. Undoubtedly at times it was our traditional business model that held us together, but our idealism gave us the strength to battle—even against each other—to make sure the values that propel Virago live on.

## CHAPTER THREE

# The Acceptable Face of Feminism? Why Not!

There are many ways of describing Virago in a fulsome, comprehensive way, but one could simplify it as; bringing feminist ideas to a mainstream audience and championing women's talent. From the beginning, Virago had the drive to bring to prominence voices from the margins, to right the imbalance, to show the world that we are all enriched by women's voices. It comes from the belief—that I hold dear—that feminism benefits all people, not just women. Virago wanted to connect readers to these ideas. Today, Virago actively aims to be intersectional in a way that we recognize we had not achieved or perhaps understood before. But the conviction that feminism is not just for women has always been our bedrock.

When in the early 1980s Virago was becoming a force to be reckoned with, and one of the bridges between feminism and the mainstream—described by Harriet as 'a market-driven company, but we are attempting to change the market'—people responded to us in very different ways. One group—many writers, eager readers, teachers, librarians, booksellers; mainly women, but men too, feminists, but also those who didn't want to call themselves feminists—were thrilled to find the books and authors from Virago, Women's Press, Onlywomen,

Pluto, Penguin, Pandora, Sheba *et al*. They wrote to us, asked us to speak, wanted posters, suggested what we should publish; to them we were good news. This was by far the majority of our readers.

Then there was the mainstream press: quixotic, changeable, and unpredictable, not unlike today. We were a news story, so they wanted to know about us and some wrote genuinely good pieces about our authors; others patronized and disparaged us. 'Paper Tigresses' was one headline. A literary editor told me he had told his office he was going to have lunch 'with a Virago', implying it was an excitingly dangerous activity. People, well, men—including Kingsley Amis—would say 'you don't look like a Virago'. Men, and women too, wanted to argue with us: women have always been published, so why a publishing house just for them? Do we even need feminism? We have the Equal Pay Act: many women work; women can take care of themselves, can't they? The view of writers such as Eva Figes that 'now and in the future patriarchal attitudes will benefit no one, least of all men' *was* gaining currency and today many men understand that power and patriarchy are the corrupters of private and public relationships between men and women, but back then such ideas were voiced almost solely by women and feminism was often caricatured as anti-men rather than pro-women. (For some, it still is.) Hovering over all feminists, ready to damn them, was that word only ever used to try to silence women: 'shrill', meaning unreasonable and out of control. Feminists—and their publishers—were all too aware of that. The blurb for the 1972 paperback edition of Eva Figes's *Patriarchal Attitudes*, published by an imprint of Granada, says, 'Social progress for all of us! This is the essential conclusion of

Miss Figes's intelligent, *unhysterical* [my italics] book.' A quote from *New Society* hails it as 'a rational text' and it's accompanied by a comment from Gore Vidal (that gives and takes with the same hand): he writes that women are responding to patriarchy 'with a series of books and position papers that range from shrill to literature. In the last category one must place Eva Figes who, of the lot, is the only one whose work can be set beside John Stuart Mill's celebrated review of the subject and not seem shoddy or self-serving.'

It was tiresome and sometimes outrageously sexist or patronizing but at the same time there were many journalists right across the political spectrum, real allies, who actively looked out for Virago titles to feature or review. We have never lacked media coverage.

Then there were the feminists who didn't agree with us. They were not a homogenous group, of course; there were—and are—many strands within feminism. From some feminists we received grateful recognition and from others downright criticism: to be a mainstream publishing house was not something 'good' feminists should aspire to. Remembers Carmen: 'Those early days of feminism were serious days, which in many ways took me back to the atmosphere of my convent. In the service of The Cause, we were monstrously hard on each other. All movements thrive on a sense of pouncing disapproval in the air.'

I believe there are so many ways to make society change and there is no one right way: a better, fairer world for everyone will come when a multitude of forces, from grassroots to established institutions, sweep in the changes. But loud voices protested that we weren't a collective; we made our books look too beautiful; we occasionally published men; we had male designers; we had shareholders; we 'marketed' feminism. In a letter dated 1980 written from Virago to describe (defend might be a better word) us to a group of feminist presses in Europe one can see the stubborn justification of our position in the face of these feminist criticisms:

> Feminism is still, in Britain, quite a 'dirty' word, still open to grotesque stereotyping, which discourages some women. We want our books to be read by these women as well as feminists. This sometimes leaves us open to the charge that we do not make our feminism explicit enough. Our policy is based on our belief that our books must 'start where people are at'. Much of our list is therefore for a general as well as a feminist audience...There are some people who disagree with our policies, but many give us immense support...It could be argued that this support was a sign that we 'water down' our feminism. We ask ourselves such questions repeatedly, but at present we remain convinced of the need to publish for a general audience primarily.

And then almost protesting too much, but I understand why!

> Side by side with this aim of 'infiltrating' feminist ideas into the book market is that of publishing books which are progressive, provocative, and reflect the consciousness of women, the wide variety of ways in which they view their lives...We also encourage the writing of collective books. In sisterhood, All at Virago.

'In sisterhood' should read as a reminder that we're all in this together, and often it did and was meant sincerely, but I also remember really harsh, critical notes and letters that would be signed off 'in sisterhood'. Maybe it was meant to galvanize one to better behaviour?

Harriet and I often received these accusations to our faces because we went together to radical bookshop events. I remember most distinctly a Saturday afternoon (without Harriet this time) at a large gymnasium in London packed to the roof with women for a Women and Media event. I was not speaking, was a mere member of the audience, when a woman took the mic and turned to me and said, 'What do you say to the accusation that Virago is the *acceptable* face of feminism?' I slowly looked around the hall, up and down the huge room. It felt to me that every single woman was turned to me, waiting for my answer. 'It's great!' is what I wanted to say. But I knew that wasn't the right thing to say that day, with that crowd. I was frightened, I must admit. I squeaked out something weaselly about it being 'good to have plurality' and slunk off after the coffee break, cross with myself—and them too.

I know now that probably many of the women in that room felt as I did, that Virago was a good thing and that there is more than one way to bring about change, but it was a lesson in the bullying tactics that go alongside radical politics; that a small group can have a punishing voice way beyond their size. Virago too has always punched above its weight, but I believe we are not advocating the idea that there is only one way to be a feminist. To my mind, a radical approach to pushing for change is good—we do need that—but it has no more intrinsic value than a moderate approach: we need them both. What I feel strongly about is the way that radicals—and this applies to women as much as men—feel they can shout down a moderate view rather than accommodate it alongside their stance. Has anything changed?

When I see, as I have, Virago described as slick, sold out, self-mythologizing—even if it is by a tiny minority—it makes me angry and frustrated. I recall when we published Maya Angelou and some people—again a minority—said the same about her. I wanted to say back to them: How many people have you reached? How many lives have you touched? Have you changed anyone's mind? Given anyone joy? Inspired change?

At a recent book festival, a woman, a self-proclaimed Virago fan who works in academic publishing, came up to me after the talk and said (rather accusingly, I thought) that it was very disappointing that Virago was no longer independent. I don't entirely disagree but I gave her some of the reasons—need for capital, a changed bookselling landscape, desire to grow, board disagreements—that were behind our decision to sell ourselves to Little, Brown in 1995 and pointed out that, as a result, we are here and thriving, publishing some great authors, whereas had we not done so, we would not have survived. She sniffed, not giving an inch: 'Still disappointing.'

I heard myself reply, tersely, 'You, who are a publisher and therefore know the economics of it all, are being romantic.'

I was a little shaken afterwards—angry with the woman, but also surprised by what was a slightly hardline response from me, not least as I do consider myself a romantic—an idealistic publisher, even!

The romantic notion of the feisty indie; the demands from radicals that a feminist company be scrupulously, politically correct; the dry, disapproving feminist academic analysis of business decisions—they are all there to haunt Virago and, to be honest, it's because they are feminists that their criticisms and observations cut deeper than the casual misogyny of the media. But I wonder ... are their observations helpful or productive? What do they contribute? And, hey, aren't we on the same side? Shouldn't we all be focusing on the bigger picture?

I understand that they feel Virago—unique in the world as a mainstream feminist imprint—has obligations to its supporters, and that is true. However deeply flattering it is that we matter that much, I guess I would wish for clearer-eyed support. We're not a lobbying group, a charity, or a public service; we are part of the feminist movement and we are a proud feminist business which makes a profit in order to publish; we have to get our hands dirty and sell our wares. In other words, we have to compromise.

But the fact that people care, that we have the power to make a difference, that we are worthy of study and are held in esteem, that we can still publish the less mainstream alongside bestselling authors, that readers look to us, that readers still say, you changed my life—that is what matters. Always, Virago has been more supported by feminists than criticized. We have grown up alongside so many who have fought and continue to fight for a better world for us all: consciousness-raising groups, grassroots activists, politicians who have changed the law, teachers who have challenged the curriculum, lawyers who have fought the status quo, journalists who have been real allies, those who have demanded change for the status of women, campaigners who have taken up feminist causes, and readers who have embraced us and our authors. We work beside and are indebted to them.

Making a change is never easy. Three of the authors we published in the 1970s and 80s, Adrienne Rich, Beatrix Campbell, and Grace Paley, radicals all, have shown me that compromise is not capitulation, that accommodation of others' views is a way to teach and learn the truth about women and politics.

In 1973 Adrienne Rich, American poet, essayist, lesbian, feminist, won the National Book Award for her collection *Diving into the Wreck*, which established her as a major poet and moved her into the avant-garde of feminist thinking. She accepted the award, radically, on behalf of herself and two of her fellow nominees, Audre Lorde and Alice Walker, and 'the silent women whose voices have been denied us, the articulate women who have given us strength to do our work'.

Adrienne Rich wrote and talked about feminism as a way of thinking that went beyond the struggle for mere legal equality, arguing for a dramatic new way of looking at women's experiences, an uncovering of a female tradition. She saw herself as part of 'the long process of making visible the experience of women . . . [who are] in ignorance of their place in any female tradition'.

Her trajectory as a writer prefigured the journey of the women's movement. She was always just ahead of her time: ushering in new thinking, pointing out truths of women's lives and injustices. She told us how an understanding of feminism could bolster us and give us courage: 'When a woman tells the truth she is creating the possibility for more truth around her.' Much of what she said we understand now, but so many of us didn't know and feel it then.

Margaret Atwood (in her *New York Times* review) remembered hearing Adrienne Rich read her poetry and wrote approvingly of its anger and art: it 'felt as though the top of my head was being attacked, sometimes with an ice pick,

sometimes with a blunter instrument: a hatchet or a hammer ...
One of those rare books that forces you to decide not just what
you think about it but what you think about yourself.'

Adrienne Rich first came to us as the author of the utterly
revolutionary *Of Woman Born: Motherhood as Experience and
Institution*, which Virago published in 1977; she wrote of the
elevation of motherhood as a patriarchal myth and pinpointed
the 'exquisite suffering of ambivalence' that is the state of being
a mother. When we published her essays, *On Lies, Secrets and
Silence* in 1980, she travelled to Britain for publication. London
feminists and poets were ecstatic to have this erudite, inspiring
woman in our midst and quickly I was able to arrange events
for her at the Poetry Society, Conway Hall, and the ICA in
London, and later in Brighton.

She was a small woman, aged sixty, and wise in the ways of the
world; though daunted by her genius, I quickly saw that she took
a generous measure of me and others. I accompanied her to her
hotel with her partner, the novelist, Michelle Cliff. (I didn't have
to put her up—Virago paid for that—but I did, proudly, have a
dinner for her at my house.) The receptionist looked at the room
information and then, blushing, said, 'Oh, so sorry, we've got a
*double* bed reserved for you! Oh dear ...' As I was rushing to
smooth things Adrienne, calmly, graciously, put out her hand for
the key and said, 'Yes, that's right.' She looked frankly into the
eyes of the young woman. 'Thank you.' Acknowledging being
lesbian in such a public way was still far from common.

Then in Brighton, at an all-women event, a very worried
young woman asked Adrienne, 'What about men? My boyfriend?'
Adrienne nodded and said, 'Take care of yourself.' She knew that
women had to understand and liberate themselves to begin with.

After that trip she sent me a Christmas card: 'We thought of you as we drove through Canada from Buffalo to Detroit in September. May the new year treat you well and your holidays be full of joy. With affection, Adrienne.' These are small things to remember against the towering intellect revealed in her writing, but I recall them because they were kind gestures and showed she understood that in order to learn and to change you need a teacher who does not condescend.

Her tiny, grey-haired presence on stage at the ICA was electric. In a precise, soft American accent she answered questions about motherhood, about feminism, about poetry and about the possibility of change, the importance of words. One answer she gave spoke to me deeply: she said the world pretends to universality, as if 'mankind' refers to us all, but no. This word is more than mere incorrect terminology; it is demonstrably telling us women that our experiences are invisible, of no count. When people use the word 'universal', she said, it doesn't mean humankind, 'it means male'. As she writes: 'Feminism begins but cannot end with the discovery by an individual of her self-consciousness as a woman . . . Feminism means finally that we renounce our obedience to the fathers and recognize that the world they have described is not the whole world. Masculine ideologies are the creation of masculine subjectivity; they are neither objective nor value-free, nor inclusively "human." Feminism implies . . . that we proceed to think, and act, out of that recognition.'

I sat in that audience feeling a visceral, physical response— as if a lens over my eyes had been lifted, as if I had been duped or blindfolded and only now could see clearly. It took my breath away.

That observation of Adrienne's, and my response, I know, now reads as almost commonplace but it wasn't then. I am not alone in marvelling at the difference in our understanding between those days and now. The poet and essayist Katha Pollitt wrote after Adrienne's death in 2012, 'Woman as Other is such a familiar trope now it's hard to imagine it was ever a hard-won intellectual discovery . . . She took on our gravest perplexities and injustices . . . and asked . . . Who would we be if we could change our world?'

I remember Adrienne with such fondness. Thinking of her makes me long for her wisdom to help negotiate the world today. She understood the obligation we have to one another, however imperfectly we manage it: 'We cannot wait to speak until we are perfectly clear and righteous. There is no purity and, in our lifetimes, no end to this process.'

The Jewish American writer Grace Paley, the doyenne of the short story, called herself a 'somewhat combative pacifist and co-operative anarchist'. She lived her politics: in the 1960s campaigning against Vietnam, going to jail, organizing marches and neighbourhood campaigns. But she showed through her writing that the female world of childcare, husbands, food, and care was just as important politically as the big gestures of the more male socialist and anti-war politics of the time. She was so busy living her politics and her life—teaching, and managing family and community—that the world had to be satisfied with her extraordinary but small body of work. 'Life is short and art is long,' she used to say.

Her collections of stories, *Later the Same Day*, *Little Disturbances of Man*, and *Enormous Changes at the Last Minute*, which were published as Virago Modern Classics, are dialogue-driven vignettes of noisy, boisterous, largely immigrant New York. 'When you write, you illuminate what's hidden, and that's a political act.' She said, 'I wanted to write about women and children, but I put it off...I thought people will think this is trivial, nothing. Then I thought, It's what I *have* to write. It's what I want to read. And I don't see it out there.'

I went to visit her in New York and met her in a noisy little café, where we sat in the nook of the window, around the corner from her Greenwich Village apartment. Her five-foot figure, topped with wild, white hair, was familiar on Lower Sixth Avenue. In the café she nodded to many, calling out 'Hi honey' in a Bronx accent, embracing others, then returning to the table with an intensity and warmth that swept us up once again. We were with her daughter, a woman in her thirties with a long blond plait nearly down to her waist, and my husband, John Annette. After a while, Grace said, 'Let's go,' and we followed her out and down the street. More nods and hellos and at her apartment block she unlocked the big front door. She had lived there for years, and it was rent controlled so it was hers for life, but as we trailed up the stairs she said she couldn't live there right now. Knocking on her own door and calling out 'Hello?' as we filed in behind her, she nodded to two extremely languid, youngish men who were lying on the sofa and the chair in the living room. They called back, groggily, sleepily, though it was mid-afternoon by now.

In the kitchen we grouped around a tiny round table. There were four wooden chairs, one of which was missing a seat. Grace fixed this by piling phone books across the frame and then plopped herself down, a bit higher than the rest us. She smiled and leaned on the table. We took our cue from her and sat quietly, conscious of the men in the next room. I wondered why we were there.

Then, after five minutes or so of complete silence, Grace leaned on the table, stood up, and said, 'Okay. I just wanted to do that.'

Back on the street she said, 'I have given the apartment to those guys for now. They're not well. They're sick.' She shrugged. 'Come on.'

Had we just lived one of her short stories? In her art, families, emotions, obligations, and politics all crowd in on top of each other—as in her life—but 'it doesn't preach; it doesn't demonize or lionize; it doesn't nobly set out to illustrate a set of beliefs or ideals. Indeed, it often undercuts them with sly self-awareness.'

She understood how love, humour, forgiveness, and understanding, rather than a singular and unbending political stance, could be the medium of change. A self-proclaimed co-operative anarchist, that's the way to be.

And then, sometimes, a political lesson comes from the audience, the readers.

Ursula Owen commissioned Beatrix Campbell to follow in George Orwell's footsteps to write the 1980s version of *The Road to Wigan Pier*. It was a clever way to be part of the Orwell events of 1984—but also an important way to look at contemporary poverty and politics. As our blurb had it, 'This time the journey north has been made by a woman—like Orwell a journalist and a socialist, but, unlike him, working class and a feminist. Out of this investigation comes her passionate plea for genuine socialism, one informed by feminism, drawing its strength from the grassroots and responding to people's real needs.' *Wigan Pier Revisited* went on to win the Cheltenham Literature Festival Prize in 1984.

When we published the book Bea and I went on the road: and one of our stops was a crowded, very noisy working men's club in Wigan. We squeezed ourselves alongside the bar and then managed to get things quietened down for Bea to speak and for me to lay out the books for sale. Under a dartboard, against the clinking of the glasses and through the swirling smoke, Bea spoke to the crowd. She is a wiry presence with wild curly hair and a northern accent, and she caught the mood correctly. She was funny, honest, and hard-hitting, talking about the research for her book, getting people to talk about their lives and what needed to be done. Some of them, involved with the miners' strike of the time, were bitterly familiar with injustice.

Then it was opened to the floor. Before answering the first question, Bea began with a self-deprecating preface indicating that she was just a modest woman, not unlike those in the audience. Immediately a large woman rose up, interrupting, angrily pointing, 'If you—you who have written books, you who go on telly and the radio, you, who come here to talk to us tonight— if you say you are not important, what the hell does that make me? That makes me absolutely nothing.'

We reflected on it on the train home. Perhaps we had thought we were encouraging these women to talk about themselves as feminists? Ha! These women were way ahead of us: they knew all about hierarchies of power and they wanted Bea to own hers proudly. It was a profound lesson for us both, not least that we had to go to a working men's club in Wigan to get it drummed into us. Grassroots politics, power: there are so many ways to gain awareness and make change.

But power for individual women and for feminist presses—that is complicated.

Celebrity feminism—fame of authors, feminist businesses, and successful feminist books—was a concept that, for many, fought with the mood of the times. Even today, one of the insults thrown at the author of, among other books, the radical and bestselling *The Beauty Myth*, Naomi Wolf, is 'celebrity feminist'—and I am dismayed that it is feminists who hurl it. We can work out why men fear powerful women, but why do women fear them? Celebrity feminism *could* be seen as a force for good. We seem to be fine with groups of women standing up together—women in parliament; the Women's Equality Party; the Women's Prize for Fiction; the Fawcett Society; Virago, even—but the woman who is seen to put herself above others is bossy, a tall poppy, the one too big for her boots, with ideas above her station. But isn't that what we need? Women who *do* have ideas above their station? Modesty, likeability, and anxiety not to be too grand: these may be female qualities which help make friends, but we need more than that from our women leaders. It could be down to plain old jealousy but to my mind it's bigger and more complex than that. I think our anxiety is because though we women make up more than 50 per cent of the population, we still feel as if we were a minority group. Because we don't see enough women in positions of control, because it is not yet ordinary and an unremarkable fact that women have power, we are therefore highly critical of the particular women who are visible; we only approve of them when we feel they really represent us. When they don't comply with our views we seem to want to tear them down and say, that is not what I, as a woman, think; she doesn't represent me.

The obvious answer to this female problem with power is to have more women in power. Of course. We need more of what the British broadcaster Mishal Husain calls 'second women', explaining:

'While we owe a great deal to those who smashed glass ceilings and led the way . . . the follow-up is vital.' It means the first women were not one-offs.

We need women in power to be an ordinary, unremarkable fact.

Though of course sometimes it *is* plain old jealousy; women are human, after all!

Conflicting feelings about power and representation have existed within the women's movement from the beginning. In 1975 Susan Brownmiller published the hugely influential and revolutionary *Against Our Will: Men, Women and Rape*, one of the first books to locate the imbalance of power—rather than sex—in rape and to challenge the notion that it was a woman's problem to fix, that it was us who must change our ways, curtail our lifestyles. 'The ultimate effect upon the woman's mental and emotional health has been accomplished *even without the act*. To accept a special burden of self-protection is to reinforce the concept that women must move about and live in fear and can never expect to achieve the personal freedom, independence and self-assurance of men.' It was groundbreaking and became a huge bestseller.

However, it didn't please all.

'People in the movement were starting to say "We don't need stars,"' Brownmiller remembered in an interview more than forty years after publication. 'When I announced to my consciousness-raising group that I'd finished writing it, someone said: "Why don't you be the first feminist without ego who doesn't put your name on the book?"...Another time, when I was giving a talk on a college campus, a woman raised her hand and asked: "Why did you put your name on *Against Our Will*? All your ideas came from our movement, after all."...I said: what page did *you* write, sister?'

My younger self—the one back in that gymnasium meeting, the one over-schooled (bullied?) in what the 'correct' feminist answer was—wants to stand up and loudly applaud this bolshie, honest feminist. My guess, though, is that no one did that that day.

The phrase 'be the first feminist without ego' strikes me sharply, as it immediately catches the tension in feminist writing and publishing. Of course, as feminists, what we wanted was deep-rooted change; we wanted to hold up to the light everything that had been taken as received wisdom. We wanted to turn the balance of power in our private and public lives— and indeed many feminist presses and shops and organizations did that very thing and redistributed power and responsibilities and evened out pay and hierarchies. But that demand for a radical shake-up sat (and sits) awkwardly alongside individual creativity and is hostile to books that catch the mood or are brilliantly marketed—or both—and become bestsellers, with the result that their authors became famous and even rich. In our case it sat uncomfortably with some feminists that our success made Virago stand out in the eyes of the general public and often looked better and more successful than our sisters in publishing. Whereas some of the smaller presses—Onlywomen, formed before us, and later Sheba—were genuinely alternative and it was fair for them and their fans to contrast themselves with us, it was odd for us to see the Women's Press, formed in 1977, held in higher esteem by some feminists as an indie press that did not pursue commercialism when they were not independent but in fact part of Quartet, owned by Naim Attallah. And of course they too wanted and needed to turn a profit. This tells me a great deal about how people see what they want or need to see. That said, we had a good relationship with the Women's Press.

The conflict here—the contradictions of using traditional methods to sell radical ideas—caught Virago fair and square. We didn't protest it was otherwise; in fact, we acknowledged that paradox and, knowing exactly what we were doing, were happy to exploit almost any means to challenge patriarchal attitudes—we still do.

But the problem of celebrity feminism has dogged all the presses and feminist authors and bookshops. Lynn Alderson from the Sisterwrite bookshop collective, set up in Islington in 1978, recalls, 'We didn't do book signings as we thought it was a bit star-worshippy, we were a bit holier than thou at times. But it was very much frowned upon in the movement to be famous or stick your head above the parapet—we were determined not to have leaders and it was very difficult at times for those trying to do things publicly when all they got was criticism for it.'

All social movements need charismatic leaders, need key books or speeches or songs that become anthems, to galvanize and steer the course, and what is true about the second-wave feminist movement (and, I would say, much of the third and fourth waves too) is that authors ignited much of the change.

Successful authors become sought-after spokeswomen, icons, figures of significance. The second wave of feminism rose alongside the 1970s/80s new style of 'marketing' authors as personalities because newspapers, magazines, and television programmes were opening the doors both to 'lifestyle' pages and to 'women's issues' pages. The media wanted these women and the publishers supplied them: celebrity feminists, in all their contradictions, were the inevitable result. It might make some—including the authors themselves—uncomfortable, but before the days of social media it was almost the only way for us publishers to get our messages out beyond the Women's Liberation news sheets or magazines such as *Spare Rib*.

Then, as today, women authors famous for their feminism generally took their fame and fortune seriously. Susie Orbach, author of *Fat is a Feminist Issue*, co-founded the first Women's Therapy Centre; Naomi Wolf started courses on leadership for women; Margaret Atwood generously supports many charities and campaigns and, among other organizations, International PEN; Kate Mosse, a co-founder of the Orange Prize (now the Women's Prize for Fiction) works with it still; Sandi Toksvig co-founded the Women's Equality Party; J. K. Rowling founded the charity Lumos; Åsne Seierstad supports education for women in Afghanistan; Natasha Walter founded Women for Refugee Women; Maya Angelou was never afraid to speak out against injustice; Sarah Waters gives much of her time and support to LGBTQ+ causes; Deborah Frances-White raises money for charities that help refugees; Jessica J. Lee founded *The Willowherb Review* to bolster nature writing by emerging and established writers of colour.

I am sure it's an honour and a debt they are more than glad to pay.

PART TWO

# The Books

_____

*All that really matters is the authors
and their writing*

## CHAPTER FOUR

# The Virago Modern Classics

Virago salaries were not exactly extravagant—in fact they were, necessarily, paltry. Before I bought a house with Cathy Porter I had been living with a boyfriend who owned his own flat, but when we split up I had to find another spot. I first paid expensive rent for a shoe box of a flat—two tiny bedrooms and an even tinier corner kitchen with a slot meter that took fifty-pence pieces for the electricity—until I was offered a room on the top floor in a semi-squat in Stoke Newington, north London. I look back now and see that it was a seriously danger-ous choice: the electric wires had been rigged to avoid paying much, if anything, and there were faulty space heaters— one of which caught fire while we were at work and burned my friend's bedroom, full of books. Unsurprisingly, it was very shabby, as was the street. However, most compellingly, overrid-ing any common sense I should have possessed: it was virtually free. Ah, blissful, ignorant youth . . . From there, in the flowing skirts and dresses that I liked then, I would ride my bike the nearly six miles to the Virago offices which were by this time at the top of the Oxford University Press building on Dover Street in Mayfair.

One morning I was collected from that house and graffiti-ed street by a black Mercedes. Inside was the stately, beautiful, and marvellous Rosamond Lehmann, in her eighties, once again famous thanks to Carmen's revival of her novels as Virago Modern Classics. *Invitation to the Waltz*, a poignant story about a young girl's coming of age, was followed by *The Weather in the Streets*, a brave novel about the same character, now a young woman, unlucky in love, who has a secret abortion. It caused a stir in 1936, when it was first published, but had been well forgotten only forty or so years later. That day we were off to Granada television in Manchester, where this wonderful writer was to be interviewed. As I quickly climbed into the car, slightly ashamed of my place, the graceful woman who'd lived a fascinating life looked out of the windows and asked approvingly, 'Is this bohemia?'

Rosamond Lehmann was read and adored once again because of her place in the Virago Modern Classics list. The famous green-spined series is, I think, the key to Virago's high profile. It was an idea of genius that will ensure both Carmen and Virago go down in history.

To mark the landmark anniversary of forty years of the Classics we held an event at Foyles on Charing Cross Road in spring 2018 with Carmen, Donna Coonan, today's excellent Virago Modern Classics Editorial Director, and writers Tessa Hadley and Elizabeth Day. Rachel Cooke, herself a Virago author, of the ground-breaking *Her Brilliant Career: Ten Extraordinary Women of the Fifties*, chaired the event and asked Carmen to think back to when she first conceived of the idea.

Said Carmen: 'I wanted to celebrate women's lives—not just anguish and suffering. And the Classics presented a history of women . . . I thought, I'll do what Penguin did—we all loved Penguin Classics—but I'll do it for women . . . No one talked about women—the canon was male. I wanted to reclaim literary history.'

I think what the Classics achieved is even more than that. 'It's not too much to claim that Virago Modern Classics changed the course of English literary history,' says Margaret Drabble; a view shared by Philip Hensher: 'Virago changed English reading habits for ever.'

The first of the Virago Modern Classics was *Frost in May* by Antonia White, a poignant novel about a convent girl whose spirit the nuns try to break. Given to Carmen by the writer Michael Holroyd, it spoke deeply to her and also took her on to other forgotten gems. 'Antonia White, a novelist wonderful to know, courageous and wonderful, gave me other novelists for my list...others I found through the critic Elaine Showalter [author of *A Literature of Their Own: Brontë to Lessing*, which Virago published in 1978] and then the London Library...I would walk along the shelves looking for interesting things.'

'If one novel could tell the story of my life, there were hundreds more, and thousands of readers who would feel as I did...The Virago Modern Classics list was meant to be...ebullient, a library of women's fiction with Boadicea...waving the flag. I chose green because it was neither blue for a boy nor pink for a girl. I saw in my mind rows of green paperbacks with luscious covers on all the bookshelves of the world...It was common to think of the literary tradition that runs from Jane Austen through Ivy Compton-Burnett to Barbara Pym as a clever and witty women's view of a small domestic world. This was not a ghetto we accepted. The female tradition included writers of vast ambition and great achievement: mistresses of comedy, drama, storytelling, of the domestic world we knew and loved. I saw a large world, not a small canvas, with all of human life on display, a great library of women's fiction.'

They altered the way women's novels were perceived. They 'would unseat some of my deepest assumptions as a reader', remembers the writer Jonathan Coe.

The Virago Modern Classics as symbol, era-changing, and catching the mood of the time, ensured that Virago entered the public consciousness—and stayed. They have been effective on every front.

It's not that they have guaranteed a vast amount of money— though some of the titles, such as Angela Carter's *The Magic Toyshop*, and authors Elizabeth Taylor and Zora Neale Hurston have been hugely profitable; some have inspired films and certainly Margaret Atwood's novels, first appearing in paperback in the UK as Virago Modern Classics, became one of the foundations and an enduring part of Virago's success, financially and otherwise. The Classics have been a solid part of our backlist income for years but the series is so, so much more important than its mere monetary value.

The Classics were a Trojan horse, taking Virago into areas where people were frightened of a women-only list; they were a critical success with literati and reviewers, and a popular success with readers who loved the novels and sought out the next in the series; a scholarly success in challenging the hitherto mainly male canon; they were a feminist success in giving readers a female literary tradition. I think they have gone beyond the Penguin Classics, the series that inspired them, because no matter how apolitical or even anti-feminist the reader is, there is a clear understanding that this series is about the changing status of women. It is about the march of women. As Rachel Cooke said, 'It reminds you that we connect to the

women on whose shoulders we stand.' It shows, as Carmen—
and I too—believe: that fiction can change lives.

What was particularly fascinating about the series, even in
the early years, was its staggering reach. In the mid-1980s I
went to Belfast with one of our sales reps and was told by a
bookseller that they didn't want Virago titles because 'there are
no feminists here'. But, wait, they would happily take the
Classics. Women's Institutes would ask us to speak— about the
Classics. Libraries and teachers wanted posters and postcards—
of the Classics. Readers wrote to us in droves—when was the
next Classic? Bookshops grouped them together, making a
vibrant section of green spines, and told us that readers came in
asking for the next Classic. It was a high class club; a guaranteed
good gift; a signal. Tessa Hadley said that, as a young woman, she
would look at people's bookshelves to see if they had the green
spines, 'like looking through someone's LPs to see if they were
okay'. I know men who say they kept a VMC by their bed to
show women how intelligent, enlightened, and thoughtful they
were. They were a guide to an important, formerly hidden
world. Rachel Cooke remembered herself at university: 'It was
the '80s, the heyday of dreadful literary theory, and because of
the Classics I had an alternative view of English literature.'
Donna, from a younger generation: 'I realised that many of the
titles I loved bore the apple icon...and my teachers cham-
pioned many of the authors: Angela Carter, Willa Cather, Stevie
Smith...Virago has influenced my reading tastes—after all,
we've grown up together.' Elizabeth Day said of them, 'I was
reading for female experience' for 'a female narrative voice' and
'the right of a female to write angry and complicated women'.

Virago borrowed the idea of using paintings on the covers from Penguin and Alexandra, Carmen, and Lynn would spend hours poring over auction and gallery catalogues and visiting galleries to find the right image to match the novel. Women's faces, landscapes, details of famous and little-known paintings were chosen for mood, for colour, not to match the characters or even the location of the story necessarily, but the emotion of the novel. Alexandra, in the Virago documentary, smiles with pleasure at the memory of searching for the right image: 'To find the jacket was enthralling.'

They were all paperbacks, not just because most of the novels had appeared in hardback years before but also because it signalled a modern approach. The slightly larger trade paperback also had more gravitas than the small, cheaper, mass market paperbacks.

Just like the Penguin Modern Classics, each VMC had a new introduction by a current novelist or journalist who gave the novel its context and, just as important, gave the novel a champion who could talk about the book in the media. This was crucial for me when I was doing publicity as, except for some of the very early authors in the series—Antonia White, Rebecca West, Barbara Comyns, Molly Keane, Storm Jameson, and Rosamond Lehmann—the rest of the authors in the list at that time were dead, which meant I had to search for a way to publicize a book, beyond reviews, without a living author. As the series grew, we produced posters that highlighted certain groups such as Irish Virago Modern Classics. We also made Virago Modern Classics postcards. Carmen had a vast store of old postcards, one of which we copied to make Collector's Cards for many of the authors. We used them for correspondence and gave them away to readers. Alexandra and I wrote most of the copy for them; I should say sweated the copy: I remember us weeping in laughter and triumph as we tried to jam a whole life into about 200 words—with style and heavy use of the semicolon. Poor Charlotte Mew. I remember us finishing her little biography off dramatically— as she did herself—with a great dose from a bottle of Lysol.

Virago Collector's Card Number 11, Violet Trefusis, is a marvel:

One of the most exotic women of her day, was born in London in 1894, daughter of Alice Keppel, the mistress of Edward VII. At the age of 10 she met Vita Sackville-West; their friendship later grew into a passionate affair; perhaps the great love of Violet's life, and certainly one from which she never completely recovered. On its traumatic end in 1921 Violet fled with her husband to France where she was swept up by the Princess de Polignac and began to write her 7 novels—acutely observed comedies of manners. Famous as hostess and mistress of La Tour de St Loup near Paris and L'Ombrellino in the Florentine hills, she entertained all of society—Colette (who cried 'Violette? Ah non, plutot Geranium!'), Lady Diana Cooper, Nancy Mitford, Jean Cocteau, Rebecca West, Christian Dior, Osbert Sitwell, Poulenc...She died in 1971 and is buried in Florence under the epitaph 'She Withdrew'.

After *Frost in May*, also in 1978, came *Mr Fortune's Maggot* and *The True Heart* by Sylvia Townsend Warner; Christina Stead's *Letty Fox: Her Luck* and *For Love Alone*; soon followed by Stevie Smith's *The Holiday* and Margaret Atwood's *Surfacing*.

The series was an almost immediate success and the novels followed hot and fast as Carmen read feverishly to find the next book, helped mainly by Alexandra, and later by Lynn, but also by Ursula and Harriet—and by legions of suggestions from authors, readers, booksellers, academics, librarians, and the Advisory Group. It was a uniquely collaborative enterprise.

'The biggest contribution came from writers,' wrote Carmen. 'Each of them seemed to choose a writer they loved best to write about in introductions to our reissues and elsewhere: A. S. Byatt twinned herself with Willa Cather; Victoria Glendinning with Rebecca West and Vita Sackville-West; Polly Devlin with Molly Keane; Janet Watts with Rosamond Lehmann; Sally Beauman with E. H. Young; Anita Brookner with Margaret Kennedy. Germaine Greer wrote about Henry Handel Richardson. Jenny Uglow and Hermione Lee would turn their hands to any of them, though I always thought of Hermione as the champion of Edith Wharton. Margaret Drabble wrote about her friend Nell Dunn ... Paul Foot advocated Olive Schreiner, Penelope Fitzgerald Mrs Oliphant. Susannah Clapp and Paul Bailey were attached to perhaps my favourite Virago Modern Classic author, Elizabeth Taylor ... Rosamond Lehmann, my friend for a decade, who knew or recommended every writer of her time: May Sinclair, F. M. Mayor, Sybille Bedford, Rose Macaulay, Elizabeth Jenkins.'

When an author was suggested, Carmen, Alexandra, and Lynn would read almost everything she had written and then decide what was good enough for the Classics. For some writers, such as Antonia White, the deft and acute Elizabeth Taylor, and the great American writer Willa Cather—all of their books became Classics. All—or as many as we could publish, as in some cases other houses, mainly Penguin, had their most famous book in print. Sometimes an author was deemed to have written only one great book—Ada Leverson's *The Little Ottleys*, Elizabeth Jenkins's *The Tortoise and the Hare*, Dorothy Baker's *Cassandra at the Wedding*, *Olivia* by Olivia, for example—and that's what was published. The process of listing the ideas for authors, reading their works, reporting on them in great detail, and then choosing the titles to be published filled lever-arch file after huge lever-arch file.

People often say, dismissively, that these books were a cheap and easy option for Virago, but this is not true. Most of the novels were in copyright (and often huge efforts had to be gone to to find the estate) so advances (admittedly very small) and royalties were paid. Virago did save money, however, on not typesetting each book, but rather offsetting them from the original hardback, which gave the books' pages a period charm. We also paid the introducers a fee.

And then there was sometimes the problem of convincing estates and publishers who held the head contracts that Virago was the right paperback home for these writers. A. S. Byatt, writing about her beloved Willa Cather, remembers that 'Carmen Callil persuaded Alfred Knopf, who held the copyrights, that Virago was a respectable and honourable enough house to publish her.'

Initially, Rosamond Lehmann had been highly sceptical of a publishing house with a shrewish name. Her relationship to feminism was certainly a little bemused. I have a note from her thanking us for a pretty cushion we gave her and she writes, teasingly, in December 1984: 'Dearest Lennie . . . I hardly know how to thank you and all the wonderful Virago girls for my

lovely present. The essence of all that is feminine (not feminist!!)...Blessings and warmest love and thanks all around from
your grateful Rosamond' with eight kisses. Rosamond was
thrilled with her revival, claiming that with Virago she was
'reincarnated'. She told us that, over the years, she'd had so
many letters which said 'Oh, Miss Lehmann, you understand my
story.' She was deeply empathetic on the page and in person.

On that long drive to and from the television studio in
Manchester she discovered that I had recently met someone
new—John Annette, who was to become the father of my children and my husband—and when she and I were next together
a few months later, at a talk she gave at the ICA, she leaned
towards me at the lunch afterwards and, whispering in my ear,
asked how things were. When I answered positively she said,
'Oh good, an on-going situation, then!'

Carmen and Rosamond became huge friends: 'Anita Brookner
and I would go for dinner with her and we talked for hours
about love. She loved food, people, writing. They were two of
the greatest friends of my life.'

The curation of the Classics list obsessed Carmen who,
though she listened to others' views, particularly Alexandra's
and later Lynn's, was largely of the belief that it should be a
reflection of one person's taste—hers. And with these choices
she intended to challenge the notion of great. In an article for
the *Times Literary Supplement* in September 1980 Carmen wrote:
'Afflicted as I was with three years' study in English Literature
in the passionate Leavisite English department of Melbourne
University, I longed to put a bomb under Leavis's agonizingly
narrow selection of "great" novelists. [F. R. Leavis wrote *The
Great Tradition*, in which he created a canon of great novelists]

Many of his chosen masters remain favourites of mine . . . but the tendency to claim "greatness" for the few obscures the rich enjoyment to be found in the many. Leavis though has also exerted a positive influence, happily lacking that ovarian view of literature which dismisses so many women novelists; at least he claimed that novels matter, that they tell us truths about civilization, that they are forces for change.'

She had high standards, but they weren't always high literary ones—though they often were. She also loved and chose novels for their comic quality or for the way they revealed something about a woman's life—*I'm Not Complaining* by Ruth Adams, is a seriously good novel about teaching in a working-class area in the 1930s.

Carmen had a memorable *cri de cœur*: 'Below the Whipple line I will not go.' Poor old Dorothy Whipple was a popular novelist of the 1930s and 40s, and her prose was thought by Carmen to be dreadful. Many a novel fell into this category and did not make the grade—or the list. 'A considerable body of women novelists, who wrote like the very devil, bit the Virago dust when Alexandra, Lynn and I exchanged books and reports, on which I would scrawl a brief rejection: "Below the Whipple line."'

Dorothy Whipple devotees were rewarded for their loyalty many years later when Nicola Beauman, who wrote *A Very Great Profession: The Women's Novel 1914–39* for us, established Persephone, her own reprint publishing house, and proudly reissued Dorothy Whipple's novels.

Persephone was founded in 1998, but there were others who watched the success of Virago Modern Classics when they began and started similar lists, including the Women's Press, whose small reprint list included some excellent novels by Kate Chopin, and the Gay Men's Press, which had a nice line in classics. When Carmen became head of Chatto & Windus in 1982 she reinvented the Hogarth Press to do the same literary recovery work, for out of print novels by men as well as women, and latterly New York Review of Books has a very impressive list but, in my view, the political and cultural success of the Virago Modern Classics has not been replicated. Harriet would often say of Virago in general that 'we are more than the sum of our parts', and that is patently true of this list.

It was gratifying to see authors enjoy a second fame. Barbara Comyns, who Carmen discovered through Graham Greene's recommendation, turned out to be as wonderfully eccentric and quirky as her books; she reminded us of her heroine in *The Vet's Daughter*, who would levitate on Clapham Common. A tiny woman with a neat grey head, she was delighted but slightly bemused by all the attention.

Another author who was ironically amused by it all was the redoubtable Storm Jameson, author of *Company Parade* and *Women Against Men*, which became Classics in 1982. In 1984 we published her autobiography, *Journey from the North*, and I went to see her in Cambridge. She was ninety-three, and said she ate nothing but a few eggs a day and that she was surprised to be alive. However, she was studying physics, a subject new to her, to pass the time.

When in the 1980s we reissued Dame Rebecca West's absorbing, acerbic, truth-telling novels she was ensconced in a magnificent flat overlooking Hyde Park. Here was a writer who was first published in 1916, admired by George Bernard Shaw and a lover of H. G. Wells. Her sharp observations of the sexes remained with her in old age; she said in a television interview that Mrs Thatcher had been badly served by the male members of her party: 'Men would rather be ruined by one of their own sex than saved by a woman.'

Her sprawling Edwardian novel, *The Fountain Overflows*, about an impoverished genteel family, thought to be modelled on her own, is a favourite of mine, and Sarah Waters's too. At an event at the Edinburgh Book Festival, Sarah talked with me about Rebecca West and later she published the talk in *Harper's Bazaar*. Sarah's description of the author she admires is exactly what I think of Sarah's own work: 'She also had a genius with language—with image, metaphor and simile. She does what the very best writers do: she makes us see the world in a way that feels absolutely right, yet absolutely new.'

When in 1981 Rebecca West was chosen by the Book Marketing Council as one of the Best of British Authors, I wrote to her with the good news that her novels were going to be in major retailers right across the country. She was not especially impressed; she wrote back saying 'What *IS* WH Smith's?'

One who really did enjoy the limelight was the wickedly splendid Irish writer Molly Keane. She had already been much lauded for *Good Behaviour*, the novel she'd written in 1981 which begins with the death of an old, cranky mother, killed by her daughter with a rabbit mousse. That book was followed by *Time After Time* and *Loving and Giving*: all three published by Diana Athill at André Deutsch. However, she had a great tranche of novels published many years before, under the pseudonym M. J. Farrell, and the Virago Modern Classics went after those. Self-deprecatingly, Molly told us that she'd written these early novels for dress money and under a false name because no one in her hunting and shooting crowd would consort with a 'girl who wrote books'. When we asked Molly for a photo from the time of her writing as M. J. Farrell she gave us a very smart studio photo but bewailed her hair, saying she had always despaired of its thinness. She seemed to feel that girlhood pain all over again, but then she laughed. Always beautifully and carefully dressed, her slightly fey charm hid a deeply intelligent, spiky talent; we adored her, but I can see from her novels that she was not at ease. And nor did she find writing easy; it was 'The grims, absolutely the grims,' she told her fellow Irish writer Polly Devlin in an interview that formed the preface for the reissue of her 1932 novel *Conversation Piece*.

Many years after she died we published *Molly Keane: A Life* by her daughter Sally Phipps. She described her mother as having 'stiletto sharpness and infinite kindness', and remembered when she was first published in the Virago Modern Classics. Carmen (whom Molly called 'a tiny bombshell') and I went to Dublin for the launch of the Irish Classics list and we held a fabulous party in the famous Shelbourne Hotel with all the great and good. The morning after I went to Molly's room to wish her goodbye and she was tucked up in linen sheets with breakfast on a tray, a small woman smiling in a vast white bed. I observed how properly luxurious she looked—'Oh no,' she said, waving her hand across it all, 'comfort is for the old. Luxury is for the young! Off you go!' An immensely engaged woman, she sent me a note in December 1988, along with a copy of *Loving and Giving*, when I was in the latter months of my pregnancy with my first child, Amy. 'Thinking about you a lot—& full of Old Wives Progress—ask Alexandra to let me know at once which IT is, and how you are, & all about the

Labour Pains—duration of, and all Lurid Detail. Now I am so immensely old & after many bloody disagreements with my daughters—I wouldn't be without them for anything, life wouldn't be a thing if they weren't in it.'

Molly lived in Ardmore, in a small, highly decorated, comfortable house overlooking the estuary, and I went there when she was alive and then again with both her daughters when we published Sally's biography. As we stood looking out of the windows I was told that William Trevor, the great short story writer, had lived just across the water; I had a flash of thinking what extraordinary writers Ireland produces and how marvellous that these two had been neighbours. But no, apparently William Trevor did not like Molly's writing, and Molly felt the same about his novels, though thought his short stories were all right.

Molly's letter to me finishes with a little sadness about her writing: 'Actually I haven't picked up any prizes—so Unfair—However this last book seems to be doing very well.' (Salman Rushdie had won the Booker in 1981, the year Molly had been shortlisted for *Good Behaviour*.)

What we referred to as the Virago Irish Classics list included novels by Molly, Maura Laverty, and Kate O'Brien, as well as Elizabeth Bowen's non-fiction, and later works by Julia O'Faolain and Polly Devlin. There were also Scottish Classics: Catherine Carswell, Susan Ferrier, Naomi Mitchison, and much later Muriel Spark.

Unsurprisingly, Carmen developed the Australian Classics: Miles Franklin, Angela Thirkell, Henry Handel Richardson, Christina Stead, and later Shirley Hazzard; a couple of Canadians joined the list: Atwood in the early days and Margaret Laurence.

One of the greatest sorrows for me was that we invited Margaret Laurence, author of *The Stone Angel* and the inspiring *The Diviners* to London and she said yes. I was going to meet another one of my heroes; but then, sadly, she wrote to say she was too ill to travel and she died soon after.

There were Victorian Classics: Mary Cholmondeley, Charlotte M. Yonge, Mary E. Braddon, Mrs Oliphant, Mrs Humphrey Ward, Rhoda Broughton, and George Eliot's ghost story *The Lifted Veil*. There were Modernists: Djuna Barnes, Gertrude Stein, and H.D.

The Americans. It seems astonishing now, but some of America's most important women writers were almost completely unknown in Britain in the 1980s, and this section of the Virago list has some truly great and acclaimed writers: Willa Cather, Edith Wharton, Eudora Welty, Grace Paley, Charlotte Perkins Gilman, Zora Neale Hurston were published in the 1980s and 90s and became yet again highly regarded and studied. Many Americans have been added since, including Nora Ephron, Mary McCarthy, Helene Hanff, Patricia Highsmith, and Elaine Dundy.

Elaine Dundy, author of *The Dud Avocado*, later wrote an autobiography, *Life Itself!*, which we published with a photograph of her doing a beautiful swan dive, epitomizing her avidity for life. She came to London to work on the book with me (I was by then Publisher and her editor) and we sat in a hotel she loved on Jermyn Street to edit the memoir. It is quite a story—from Park Avenue in New York to Paris to London in the 1950s, though ending, oddly, with a passion for Elvis Presley. In London she had met and fallen in love with Kenneth Tynan, the *enfant terrible* of theatre reviewers. She sent a telegram

to her parents: 'Have married an Englishman. Letter to follow.'
By the time we were editing this part of her story, in the main
lobby of the hotel, Elaine was a bit deaf and so her explanation
of why she had to leave Kenneth was shouted out to me and the
other guests: 'He liked spanking and I tried but I just couldn't
do it.' *The Dud Avocado*, which I love, has the same surprising
frankness and insouciance. That marriage failed, not just
because of the S&M but because Kenneth Tynan wanted to be
the only creative person in the relationship.

Eudora Welty also managed to come to London to meet us and
some of her admirers; Alexandra arranged a lunch at Mon Plaisir in
Covent Garden that included Hermione Lee and Salman Rushdie,
who gave us a quote—'impossible to overpraise'—for her new
novel, *Losing Battles*, which we first published on the frontlist.

Edith Wharton, who was in her time more famous than her
contemporary Henry James, wrote acute observations of society, and Willa Cather rivals William Faulkner for her descrip-
tions of solitude and landscape. At last these writers, deservedly,
were seen in the UK as major writers.

However for many years, other than the Harlem Renaissance
writer Zora Neale Hurston, whose fabulously stirring and
romantic novel *Their Eyes Were Watching God* remains a bestseller,
we did not have many Classics by women of colour. We have
published the wonderful writer Bessie Head, and from America
Dorothy West and Paule Marshall, and Attia Hossain from
Pakistan (aunt of the award-winning Kamila Shamsie) among
others. Donna Coonan is very alive to this and has recently
published Gayl Jones's *Corregidora* and has re-introduced Ann
Petry's *The Street,* a novel Virago published to muted success in
1986. The publishing and reading world is at last changing.

Lesbian novelists—Radclyffe Hall, Mary Renault, Sylvia Townsend Warner—or novels about lesbians have been key to the list. Our edition of *The Well of Loneliness*, with its glorious cover of two lovers by Gluck, would have introduced many lesbians to Radclyffe Hall's important novel, banned in the UK in 1928 when Jonathan Cape first published it.

The English novel of the 1940s to the early 1960s has proved to be the most successful part of the list, led by Elizabeth Taylor, E. M. Delafield, Daphne du Maurier, and Barbara Pym, followed by Nina Bawden, Nell Dunn, Stella Gibbons, Winifred Holtby, Elizabeth Jenkins, Rose Macaulay, Shena Mackay, Sylvia Townsend Warner, and Mary Webb—among so many others. Lynn Knight, who became Editorial Director of the Classics in 1988, remembers the pleasure of helping to shape the series: 'people forget how many of the writers we take for granted today were unavailable then'.

At the heart of the Classics is a commitment to a female literary tradition. Then, as now, the female imagination was much argued over.

We had particular trouble with one famous critic over this issue: the novelist Anthony Burgess, then the dominating chief fiction reviewer of the *Observer*. He seemed to have made it his business to decide which female novelists could be said to have risen out of their 'ghetto'. But his 1979 review of Virago's publication of Dorothy Richardson's four-volume *Pilgrimage* has gone down in history—both Virago's and his.

He wrote: 'Lovers of literature of either sex, unconcerned with sexism, must be grateful for [Virago's] recovery of a great fictional masterpiece. Or, God help us, mistresspiece . . . By no stretch of usage can Virago be made not to signify a shrew, a

scold, an ill-tempered woman, unless we go back to the ety-
mology—a man-like maiden (cognate with virile)—and the
antique meaning—amazon, female warrior . . . It is an unlovely
and aggressive name, even for a militant feminist organization,
and it presides awkwardly over the reissue of a great *roman fleuve*
which is too important to be associated with chauvinist sows.'

The fact that his editors did not challenge and cut his outrageous slur tells us of his power but also of the time. Burgess was
reflecting what some thought—Virago was a separatist company that appropriated to its cause works and authors which
were not feminist. Of course, this entirely misses the point of
the Virago Modern Classics, which Carmen repeatedly said was
to 'demonstrate a female literary tradition'. Dorothy Richardson,
who wrote in a stream of consciousness style before James
Joyce or Virginia Woolf, more than justifies her inclusion in the
list. But the deep irony here is that *only* a feminist press would
have republished this long out of print work and caught the
attention of the likes of Burgess.

Today, Donna Coonan defends the world sometimes deni-
grated as the women's realm: 'I take the view that a small canvas
is not necessarily an unambitious one. What is seen under the
microscope can reveal much about the world in which we live.
And what skill it takes to write observantly, feelingly, with wit
and perception, about the everyday . . . Relationships, families,
children, love—these are not marginal; on the contrary, they
are life itself.'

By the early 1980s the Classics—each carefully numbered—
were nearing one hundred titles. It had become a hugely famous
part of Virago and that made for some anxiety within the office.
I look back now and see that whereas Carmen had originally

been Managing Director in charge of finance, publicity, sales, rights, and marketing, alongside some editorial acquisitions, and Ursula had the Editorial Director's realm, as Carmen became more and more editorially involved the balance of power shifted somewhat. The balance of the list was also unequal and that made some of us uncomfortable. The point of Virago was not only to look back, surely? Our detractors and our competitors were quick to point this out. The Women's Press's slogan at one point was 'Live Authors, Live Issues'. In our catalogue of this time our editorial note works hard to claim prominence for our new titles. I remember feeling dismayed when talking to the press and at events when people expressed surprise that we did anything but reissues. We also had a vibrant, original frontlist!

We complicated the situation by publishing even more reprints: starting in 1981, the Non-fiction Classics list; a Virago Travellers list; as well as keeping the original Virago History Reprint list in print. Later we started Lesbian Landmarks, a list overseen by Alison Hennegan which published novelists Nancy Spain, Han Suyin, Christa Winsloe, Maureen Duffy, Clemence Dane, and Gertrude Stein.

Then because of the success a decision was taken to give all Virago books, not just the reprints, a green spine. Even though we had a different logo for frontlist titles, many booksellers and reviewers understandably saw everything as Classics. It was a frustration but also, of course, a great triumph. In only a few short years Virago green had come to mean something beyond the publishing industry: it had reader recognition and loyalty.

Over the last few years Donna has emerged as one of the most inventive Classics editors. She has added 200 new novels,

including the writers Patricia Highsmith, P. L. Travers, Barbara
Pym, Mary McCarthy, Muriel Spark, and Janet Frame, and
introduced the beautiful Virago Classics hardbacks and a new list
of children's classics by Nina Bawden, E. Nesbit, Noel Streatfeild,
Rumer Godden, and Joan Aiken among others. Her curation of
the Virago Modern Classics' fortieth-anniversary editions won
plaudits and prizes. *Rebecca*, in its proper place as a Classic since
2003, alongside all of Daphne du Maurier's titles, celebrated its
eightieth anniversary in 2018 and the special edition reissue hit
the bestseller list. I think Donna has splendidly honoured the
tradition of the Virago Modern Classics.

By 2020 the Classics list will have published more than 700
titles. I have listed so many of them here because only by naming—and publishing—them will these authors avoid the fate of
once again being forgotten.

## CHAPTER FIVE

# 'Fuck the Patriarchy!'
## Non-fiction

I am on a platform at the Bradford Literature Festival with the extraordinarily brave and powerful Egyptian-American activist Mona Eltahawy, author of *Headscarves and Hymens: Why the Middle East Needs a Sexual Revolution*. The topic—which, not uninterestingly, we are sharing with two men—is How to Be a Feminist. It's 2017.

A young woman in a hijab lifts her hand and asks a question about her struggle to get a commitment to equal opportunities in her office. Free of any head covering (very intentionally, we have already learned), red-haired Mona waves her heavily braceleted arm in the air and to a loud laugh and huge cheer from the audience—and me too—shouts 'Fuck the patriarchy!'

The mic then comes my way. I, feeling conspicuously less than rousingly radical but, you know, I recognize office life, say: 'You *can* make a difference, but you must choose your battles.' Thinking back to Adrienne Rich and also to June Eric-Udorie, a new young Virago author—more of whom later—I add, 'Take care of yourself. Learn what is important to you.'

Somewhere between these two options—fuck the patriarchy or keep plugging away for what you know is right—is how most women find themselves responding to sexism and inequality. We need rage and inspiration, we need realism and practical solutions, and we need to know our histories, literary and otherwise.

Virago's non-fiction books come from that intersection, where women authors search and explore, report from the front line on how it is, or uncover hidden histories—with as much style, aplomb, and energy as Mona's exhortation—to produce literary biographies, polemic, history, humour, and memoir.

In the 1970s the universities, polytechnics, and colleges were under pressure to change and we saw as a result the rise of women's studies, black women's studies, and lesbian studies. In 1975 in the UK there were forty-eight women's studies courses and by 1981 the number had tripled, to around 150.

What is striking about this is that the majority of these courses were in adult education classes—not least because there were fewer feminist academics in the universities then. Many scholars and academics came to Virago with their ideas and Virago worked in tandem with them.

Each year the Virago list expanded and in 1979 Virago published thirty-four titles (fiction, Virago Modern Classics, and non-fiction) including, with the Bristol Women's Studies Group, *Half the Sky: An Introduction to Women's Studies*. Its chapter breakdown is optimistically wide-ranging: Growing up Female; Education; Bodies and Minds; Marriage; Work; Creativity; and Setting up Courses.

And the following year came *Alice through the Microscope*, edited by the Brighton Women and Science Group, which looked at science as a man-made discipline, and then with the Cambridge Women's Studies Group we published *Women in Society* in 1981.

The introduction to *Half the Sky* shows how the new courses first had to explain, even validate, their case: 'Women's studies comes out of research inspired by an increasing interest in what it means to be a woman... One part of the modern feminist movement is an increased interest in women as a subject of study... [The other part] is dependent on the work of earlier feminist writers... on completing the record... correcting the bias.'

Fascinatingly, the hierarchical change inherent in this new discipline is highlighted: the authors observe that the divisions between teacher and student tend to break down as all can contribute from their experiences. Everything was up for revision on this new frontier.

I recognize the late 1970s' almost apologetic explanation of what feminism means as the authors write, 'By feminism we mean both an awareness of women's position in society as one of disadvantage or inequality compared with that of men, and also a desire to remove those disadvantages... In talking about female oppression we do not wish to imply that all women are apathetic or worn-out [*sic!*] or that no woman anywhere has any kind of decent life. Female oppression is... about how society is organised... [We take] two approaches to the question of inequality... "plain equal" or "equal but different".'

Feminists, often, were attempting to persuade women who did not feel the movement had anything to offer them that feminism was a way of understanding all of our lives.

However, there were many women eager to learn more, particularly about women's history. Barbara Taylor, the historian and author of *Eve and the New Jerusalem: Socialism and Feminism in the Nineteenth Century*, which we published in 1983 to awards and praise, recalls that in around 1977 she and another feminist historian, Sally Alexander, later author of our *Becoming a Woman: And Other Essays in 19th and 20th Century Feminist History* (1994), began co-teaching classes in women's history and feminist theory and found a 'host of feminist predecessors—feminist radicals like Ray Strachey, Sylvia Pankhurst, Maud Pember Reeves. Sally's acute understanding of these women ... probably taught me more about late nineteenth early twentieth century feminism than anything else.'

We published many historians in response to this new hunger. As well as Cathy Porter and Sheila Rowbotham we had Janet Todd on seventeenth-century professional women writers including Aphra Behn in *The Sign of Angellica*; Judith Walkowitz took on the morals of Victorian England in *City of Dreadful Delight*; Jill Liddington, with Jill Norris, published *One Hand Tied Behind Us* on suffrage history, and Jill went on to write books for us on the peace camp at Greenham Common, and on northern suffragettes. One most fascinating book was drawn from a decoded lesbian diary. *I Know my Own Heart: The Diary of Anne Lister*, edited by Helena Whitbread, is now republished in the Virago Non-fiction Classics as *The Secret Diary of Miss Anne Lister*. The diaries inspired the splendid 2019 television series *Gentleman Jack*.

Historians, journalists, and writers were realizing that the stories of ordinary lives, particularly some British lives that were hidden from the mainstream media, was where the truth of women's experiences resided. Ursula Owen commissioned Amrit Wilson's book about South Asian women in Britain, *Finding a Voice*, which won a Martin Luther King Award in 1978. In the reissued, expanded edition published by Daraja Press forty years later, the writer and activist remembers how a visit to a woman in her home gave her the urgency to start: "'People should know," she said, "that we can speak, we have feelings and that we have thoughts. Write what you and I talk about, what we think." That night I started writing the chapter on Isolation. The words poured out... Suddenly I knew I had to be... the narrator of a complex collective experience.' She recalls that on publication some middle-class South Asian men ridiculed her book, while some middle-class English women responded with apparent feelings of guilt, and that her accounts of racism were challenged by 'many white figures of authority, teachers, administrators, social workers', but the overwhelming response to the book was from young Asian women who embraced it as their own. The British writer and actor Meera Syal writes of the succour it gave her: 'For the first time, here was a book that collated the presence and experiences of Asian women in Britain with clarity, compassion and forensic care. It was affirmation that our lives mattered... that we were now part of the story of Britain.'

Have times changed? I think speaking about the truth of one's community can still be dangerous. More recently, the *Washington Post* reporter Souad Mekhennet, in her book *I was Told to Come Alone: Behind the Lines of Jihad*, challenged the simple 'black and white' narratives. A Muslim woman of Turkish and Moroccan descent who grew up in Germany, she searches for the answers to why, for some, faith is used to encourage acts of terrorism. It is a brave and necessary book in which she shows that at times she is held in suspicion by both the jihadists she seeks out and her own colleagues. It takes courage to stand up and speak.

I think of the memoir *A Woman in Berlin*, by a German woman who wrote of the searing experiences of life in the city as it was sacked by the Russian Army in her diary of April–June 1945. She published it anonymously in English in 1954, and in German with a Swiss publisher in 1959. But German readers were not ready to face the truth of this period and the author was disparaged for her 'shameless immorality'. Women were not supposed to talk about rape. The book was relegated to obscurity and forgotten until it was taken up by the women's movement and, after her death, finally published in Germany by Eichborn in 2003; her country was at last ready to listen. I published the book with an introduction by Antony Beevor two years after that. Even though there was speculation by this time that the writer was a journalist named Marta Hillers, we honoured her original decision: the author on the cover is Anonymous. I feel sad she didn't live to see her book recognized as a significant testimony of war.

A deeply personal story can move people to change their views, to recognize their biases.

*The Art of Starvation: A Story of Anorexia and Survival* by Sheila MacLeod was one of the first memoirs about anorexia. Now we are all more knowledgeable about this condition but when it was published in 1981, and became the first Mind Book of the Year, it was in the vanguard of books about the pressures on women and the female body. The author is also a novelist and her description of the moment she saw the beauty of a plum and felt she could eat once more has stayed with me to this day. It named a secret and brought it out into the open.

I would say the same about *Desert Flower*, the memoir by Waris Dirie that I published in 2001. Dirie, originally a Somalian nomad, lived an almost fairy-tale story, complete with tigers and bandits, ended up on fashion catwalks around the world and was one of the faces of Revlon. But she decided that she could no longer hold her secret: female circumcision, as it was then called. She gave an interview to an American women's magazine and for the first time talked of the brutal practice that she had suffered at a very young age. At this time, very few feminists were addressing female genital mutilation, excepting some such as Alice Walker and Pratibha Parmar. Western feminists were, on the whole, cautious about interfering with the rituals of another culture. Waris spoke out, she became a UN spokeswoman, and set up the Desert Flower Foundation to raise awareness and eradicate FGM. She told Western feminists they were wrong to stand back: FGM was a human rights issue. I went to a press conference where she was interrupted endlessly by a Somali man who we later learned was disparaging her for the betrayal of her people by speaking her truth. There is greater awareness of and action against this practice now, thanks to the huge bravery of campaigners like Waris.

Though editors and publishers are the traditional gatekeepers, deciding what gets published or, just as importantly, what *doesn't* get published, in many cases publishing houses such as Virago are also closely aligned with readers; therefore peace rallies, environmental demonstrations, unjust laws such as the homophobic Section 28, women's marches, anti-racist rallies, Black Lives Matter, reform of the Welfare State (*Radical Help* by by Hilary Cottam), transgender rights—all intersect with our publishing. Sometimes we feel we must put a book together at great speed to respond to a sense that something needs to be done quickly; that an urgent women's response is required to challenge government policy or plans but also to encourage women to take a stand. Such was the case with *Over Our Dead Bodies: Women Against the Bomb* in 1983.

'We are beginning to think the unthinkable—that there could be a nuclear war in our lifetime' read the shoutline on the back of the book. Edited by Dorothy Thompson, a historian active in the peace movement, the collection of essays included historians, novelists, politicians, philosophers, women in the peace camps, and women working in arms factories. The introduction is not only galvanizing, as if delivered from a platform to a crowd, to wake us up to the nuclear threat, it also entreats women to step up and take responsibility for themselves, to trust their own judgement: 'We often feel that we are unfitted by our education and training to form an opinion on questions of defence strategy and weaponry...[we] give in with too much humility to "experts".'

In the same vein, we decided to hold a rally in the name of this book and its message at Central Hall in Westminster, with proceeds from the event going to the peace movement. And so on 16 April 1983, from 3.30 to 7.30 p.m., we filled a hall with 2,000 people who thrilled to the twenty-four performers and speakers on stage: Angela Carter, Julie Christie, Jill Craigie, Greenham Common Women, Harriet Harman, Diana Quick, Sheila Rowbotham, Spare Tyre Theatre Company, Fay Weldon, Susannah York—among others.

The organization of it all was, well, as I wrote in a letter in the month before, 'absolutely thrilling, heady...and hell. I've just got to organise the order in which the speakers and performers will appear, arrange the loud-speakers, confirm the catering arrangements, arrange a first-aid brigade, help organise a staffing rota that consists of about 80 people, make up passes for the people working on the 14 bookstalls, tell the MCs what to say, publicise the event...We've sent out 8,000 leaflets...' The whole office was deeply involved and it was a huge success. But frankly, it was a little ambitious for a book launch.

Virago published—and continues to publish—many anthologies. The great benefit of an anthology on a difficult, shifting topic is that it acknowledges there is no one answer, that many voices, dissenting or agreeing, is the way to tackle a subject, and it is also a way of encouraging busy, notable names to write for us. Not to say that feminists are particularly humble, but an anthology that shows differences of opinion and experiences is also a great antidote to the single, absolute, male view.

When in the early 1990s the notion and naming of dissent seemed to degenerate into sneering at 'political correctness' I asked Sarah Dunant, then a commentator on the BBC 2 *Late Show* and famous for her quick understanding and large red specs, to untangle the subject. She edited *War of the Words*, a collection of pieces that looks at what happens to debate when people who try to right the imbalance of power—whether in literary canons, speech, or laws—are disparaged as being politically correct.

Vehement feminist disagreement over pornography was best explored through an anthology: *Sex Exposed*, edited by Lynne Segal and Mary McIntosh, was commissioned by Ruthie in response to the raging arguments of the time.

Sometimes the anthologies were great fun and revealing: *There's Something About a Convent Girl*, edited by Jackie Bennett and Rosemary Forgan, included pieces by Marina Warner, Carmen, and Germaine Greer, who wrote, 'I think one of the reasons why I was never properly domesticated is because I was actually socialised by a gang of mad women in flapping black habits.'

Ruthie and Ursula's interest in psychoanalysis brought us Alice Miller, Dinora Pines, Jessica Benjamin, Juliet Mitchell, Melanie Klein, Marion Milner. I later added to this list with Susie Orbach, Kate Figes, Susanna Kaysen's *Girl, Interrupted*, and Lisa Appignanesi's book about the history of female 'madness' in *Mad, Bad and Sad: Women and the Mind Doctors*.

As well as working on the Classics and publishing frontlist fiction, Alexandra drew on her background and interest in art to publish, among others, books on women engravers, Pre-Raphaelite women artists, and *Life with Picasso* by Françoise Gilot.

I think back to that journalist asking after Virago's first year of twelve titles: would there be enough books? In the 1980s and 90s, as well as a young adult list we had an education list, a Virago Pioneers list (short biographies of trailblazing women), a poetry list, and a history list, alongside a small health list. A feminist publisher has many obligations, and we had huge ambitions to mirror the feminism and issues of the day. Looking back over the catalogues I can see how we editors have always picked up the mood of the times.

The leading feminist theorist Lynne Segal wrote for us on women, men, and straight sex; social and cultural historian Carolyn Steedman on working-class culture; linguist Deborah Tannen on how men and women communicate (or don't); the late Rozsika Parker, psychotherapist, on the experience of maternal ambivalence in *Torn in Two*. We had books on birth— the novelist Kate Mosse's first book was *Becoming a Mother*; we had books on living with Aids, on fashion, on religion, on alcohol, on friendship, on gardening, on women travellers.

Today the same mirroring is going on. Sarah Savitt, Virago's current Publisher, has introduced feminist graphic novels and, understanding that some of the most vocal feminists are now in powerful positions, she has brought us the television writer Lauren Graham of *Gilmore Girls* fame with *Talking as Fast As I Can*. She has also tapped into the rise of smart women comedians with the spot-on *The Guilty Feminist* by Deborah Frances-White, who came to fame through her hugely successful podcast.

In the early days we accepted unsolicited manuscripts—the slush pile—and once a month or so the editors would attend to the teetering tower. Very little came from the pile, unfortunately, but what we have always noticed is that these manuscripts reflect a dawning of women's new understanding about their lives. I remember in the 1980s Ruthie commenting that we were getting a striking number of what were then called incest stories. Child abuse was a secret that women were bringing out into the open. We published several books on it, one of the most striking by a Canadian, Sylvia Fraser. She wrote *My Father's House* almost like a detective story as she searched through memory and evidence to uncover the secret abuse.

We try hard to look beyond our borders and lives, crucial for Western feminism, thus *Opening the Gates: A Century of Arab Women's Writing*, edited by Margot Badran and Miriam Cooke; Alicia Partnoy's memoir, *The Little School*, about being one of the 'disappeared' in Argentina; and *Islam and Democracy* by Fatima Mernissi. Åsne Seirstad's book telling the truth about women's lives in Afghanistan, *The Bookseller of Kabul*, became one of our all-time bestsellers, selling over 750,000 copies.

Her Virago editor, Antonia Hodgson, went on to publish Åsne's powerful investigations of Serbia, Chechnya, and Syria.

But Virago woman is not only an activist. I think of the outrageous wit and wisdom of Stevie Smith in *Me Again: The Uncollected Writings*; the fabulously eccentric *Acorn* by Yoko Ono; the story of the famous American trumpet player Billy Tipton, a woman who lived her life as a man, in *Suits Me* by Diane Wood Middlebrook; *Treasure: The Trials of a Teenage Terror* by the late, clever humourist Michele Hanson; delicious cartoons in *I'm Not a Feminist But...* by Christine Roche; the wild and passionate story of *The Bolter* by Frances Osborne.

Received wisdom about some of our great women writers has been challenged, not least in the dramatic *The Haunting of Sylvia Plath* by Jacqueline Rose and in Lyndall Gordon's extraordinarily perceptive biography of Emily Dickinson, *Lives Like Loaded Guns*, which dismantled the sentimental legend of the reclusive poet. 'Lit crit' was key to Virago from the start: Elaine Showalter's *A Literature of Their Own* was one of the first Virago books and opened up the very idea of a female canon.

'Inspiring women' could almost be a non-fiction and fiction category on its own. Maya Angelou, who was a legend in her own time, has become even more influential since her death in 2014. Her memoirs are studied; her wit and wisdom are tattoos, and her poetry, particularly 'And Still I Rise', is quoted by artists, singers, politicians, and sportswomen.

We've had some very big personalities in Virago covers.

But sometimes inspirational women are quiet—and young.

With great pleasure I have watched the fourth wave of feminism emerge. Wanting to engage quickly with what younger women were thinking, in 2015 we published *I Call Myself a*

*Feminist: The View from Twenty-Five Women under Thirty*, edited by Victoria Pepe, Rachel Holmes, Amy Annette (my daughter), Martha Mosse, and Alice Stride with the shoutline 'Young feminists—whether you call yourself one or not—this book is for you'.

One of the contributors was June Eric-Udorie who came to mind when I was on the stage at that literary festival back in Bradford. Aged seventeen at the time of our publication, she had already run a successful petition to get the study of feminism added to the A-level politics curriculum in the UK and the following year was one of the BBC's 100 Inspirational and Influential Women. She went on to edit a book for us about intersectionality: *Can We All Be Feminists?*

We launched *I Call Myself a Feminist* in March 2015, at the WOW (Women of the World) festival at the Southbank Centre in London. A woman in the audience, who said she was twenty-five, told us that when she had told her friends where she was going, they asked her, 'Do you hate men?' I felt like holding my head in my hands: after all these years, is that still what some women think about feminism?

This woman wanted to know what to say.

Wise June just nodded and said you don't have to take on everything that's wrong with the world; try not to feel overwhelmed; do what *you* need to do. Choose your battle. Learn what matters to you.

Fuck the patriarchy!

Just let me count the ways...

## CHAPTER SIX

# What Stories Can Do
## Fiction

I first met Margaret Atwood on the page. I remember, at seventeen, pulling from the library shelf a slim, home-made-looking poetry book entitled *The Circle Game* and then earnestly telling my English class at my high school in St Catharines, Ontario, that we should read and support this writer because 'she is Canadian and going to be important'. A beautiful little volume, it gave me a sense of private discovery. I learned later that Margaret had made the cover herself—with red Letraset dots.

I met her again on the page at Queen's University in Kingston in the mid-1970s in a relatively new course: CanLit. There were so few Canadian Literature books—or at least those deemed worthy of study—that it was only a half-year course. I read Atwood's *Survival*, a non-fiction book that came to define Canadian writing at that time as being, in part, a literature of us against the elements, of survival, metaphorical and real. 'A country needs to hear its own voice,' she wrote, and indeed it was extraordinary to begin to hear it. We learned that CanLit had themes: mild anti-Americanism, immigration, nature, survival, self-deprecating humour, and, above all, the search for self-identity. Canada was then obsessed with the search for what was Canadian. In the early 1970s, referencing the saying

'As American as apple pie', a CBC Radio programme ran a competition asking listeners to finish the sentence 'As Canadian as . . .' The winner proved our humour: 'As Canadian as possible under the circumstances.' The Canadian writer Mavis Gallant, who lived most of her life in Paris, said a Canadian is 'someone with a logical reason to think he may be one'.

We also studied Atwood's *The Edible Woman*; a funny, prescient novel about a girl who unwillingly commits herself to marriage and then finds she can't eat. We read Michael Ondaatje, Margaret Laurence, Alice Munro, Robertson Davies, Anne Hebert among others. I was aware that this surge of activity was partly down to the small presses: Anansi, Coach House, and also an older one that styled itself as 'The Canadian Publisher', McClelland & Stewart. The idea that Canadians could write and get published, and that there was a creative industry in my own country, opened my mind to new possibilities.

Atwood, especially, was a giant in my literary landscape, so when only a few years later she was there in the Virago offices, in the flesh—though actually not very tall or big—and looking to me to accompany her around Britain to her publicity interviews, I was, frankly, overwhelmed. I had worked with some famous authors already, but this one? It was inconceivable to me that I would eventually be her Virago paperback editor and publisher—and friend.

Margaret Atwood immediately understood and heartily approved of Virago (and I expect she knew how to deal with a starry-eyed young Canadian too). 'Virago felt like home to me, as many Canadian writers of my generation had been involved in similarly small ventures . . . [Carmen] was a wild colonial girl, like me, only wilder. In her hands the Old School Tie publishing network was about to become macramé.' We got down to business—just as we have been doing ever since; Margaret has been with us since 1979 and we've published nearly thirty of her books. She is central to Virago. Though we share her fiction and non-fiction with Bloomsbury and Vintage, gratifyingly to my younger self, we are her sole UK poetry publishers.

We have been Margaret's main UK paperback publisher since Carmen first brought her books to Virago. She licensed the paperback rights from André Deutsch for *Surfacing*, *The Edible Woman*, and *Lady Oracle*, and published them as Virago Modern Classics. Liz Calder at Jonathan Cape then became Atwood's UK hardback publisher so we bought our paperback licenses from Cape until Liz moved to co-found Bloomsbury. Atwood followed her there in 1989 and we made a paperback arrangement with Bloomsbury, where Alexandra became her hardback publisher.

Initially people in the UK didn't know quite what to make of this savvy Canadian writer. Canada was thought to be wild, snowy, and empty; Margaret Atwood's childhood in the backwoods accorded with that vision but Canadians were also supposed to be a bit dull and here was a woman who knocked that annoying notion on its British head. That dry wit of hers still flummoxes some British interviewers, whom I see approach her gingerly. Formidably clever and very funny, she, rightly, expects the most of others. It is something I have learned to step up to.

When we first launched her books in 1979 I was aware that at home she was commanding audiences of 2,000—just for her poetry readings. Now, forty years on, that is the case worldwide, but back then we were still introducing this writer to the

UK, so Margaret and I slogged up and down the country, mostly by train, seemingly leaving no interview, bookshop, or event untried or unvisited. One of the many things I love about Margaret—or Peggy, as she is called by her friends and publishers—is just how game she is. I often quote her to younger writers, particularly when they need consoling. When things on our endless road trips were not going quite to plan, if we had bad hotels or late trains or when interviewers were clueless, I would apologize and she would just laugh and say in her low drawl, 'Never mind, it's all material'—for a novel or short story, I would imagine. On reviews that didn't please us she would say she would prefer the reviewer to review the book that was written, not the one the reviewer wished was written, but, oh well.

There was—and still is—a 'Do It Yourself' quality about her. She didn't mind sharing taxis with large display cases (dumpbins) and boxes of her novels—she would tell tales of dragging her books on a sleigh through ice and snow to readings in northern Ontario; she didn't mind readers asking odd questions because she told us she'd even been asked if her hair was naturally curly; she left the choice of covers to us: 'I am sure you know what you are doing in your market'; she didn't mind long publicity hauls with terrible food and indifferent hotels—she'd done them all her working life.

What she did, and does, want is careful attention to the things that matter. I don't know another mind as capacious as hers; she has a forensic brain, one that can hold the smallest business detail, read across all genres, manage a family, involve herself with Canadian politics, enjoy being funny—silly even—for charity events, support many causes, and all at the same time as developing profound ideas. No boundaries, genres, boxes, classifications, or categories can contain her; nothing is beneath her notice and everything is of interest to her.

Unafraid of new frontiers, she was one of the first authors on Twitter and one of the first to write fiction online on Wattpad, and then there is her great invention, the LongPen machine—created so that authors can sign books remotely. She was at the forefront of warning us about climate change—in fact, reversing her literary thesis about the elements being something people have to defend themselves against. Her most famous novel, *The Handmaid's Tale*, and its sequel, *The Testament*, warned long ago of the consequences of an authoritarian government that, among other things, controls women's reproductive rights. As she said in a brilliant essay about witches, 'When times are tough... those in authority start looking around for someone to burn.'

All this, at the same time as writing more novels, essays, short stories, children's books, and poetry.

Atwood's trajectory has mirrored the women's movement. Even before the remarkable effect of *The Handmaid's Tale* and *The Testaments*, which has made her rock-star famous, she was a voice that we listened to. She is in my 'inspiring women' pantheon because she has the knack of seeing and naming, writing in 1982: 'Why do men feel threatened by women? I asked a male friend. They're afraid women will laugh at them. He said, "Undercut their world view." Then I asked some women students...Why do women feel threatened by men? "They're afraid of being killed," they said.'

She's never shied from uncomfortable truths. *Cat's Eye* was likened to William Golding's *Lord of the Flies*—showing the particular cruelty girls can inflict on each other; *The Robber Bride* has at its core a dastardly woman, Zenia, who steals the men of her 'friends'. Both were a challenge to the notion of sisterhood, or that women were better than men and she got some flak about being 'anti-feminist'. But we women know the many truths about female friendships; yet again Margaret is right in fearlessly showing the full gamut of female experience in her novels—women's lives are the motor of her fiction.

Over the years, each new Atwood manuscript has been received by Virago with deep curiosity and great excitement. Where other writers, even literary ones, might be predictable, Atwood never is. Her fiction gives the reader exactly what I remember her saying she desires in novels: surprise and pleasure. Of course, she does so much more than that too, but those two elements are firmly within all her work. Her novels are wide-ranging; she's written thrillers, speculative fiction, historical fiction, contemporary and satirical novels but they are always recognizable, such that she's earned her own adjective: 'Atwoodian'. I remember the startling and terrible chill of reading *The Handmaid's Tale*, staying up all night unable to stop turning the manuscript pages until the very end; I remember the compelling, shivery reading of *Alias Grace*—the word '*Murderess*. It rustles, like a taffeta skirt across the floor'—and coming to work the next day and telling the office: now she's written an historical novel! Very few literary writers were doing that then. The same could be said for her prescient speculative fiction, the *Oryx and Crake* trilogy that followed the magnificent, sprawling *The Blind Assassin*. Wonderfully, *The Blind Assassin* won the 2000 Booker Prize. Margaret, Bloomsbury—Liz Calder and later Alexandra Pringle—along with her agent, Vivienne Schuster, and one of us from Virago had trotted to the award dinner with her a few times by then. Three times nominated—for *The Handmaid's Tale*, *Cat's Eye*, and *Alias Grace*—and three times disappointed. I remember on that glorious night in 2000 Nigel Newton, CEO of Bloomsbury, saying, 'I am glad we won, but I am even happier we didn't lose,' and we all knew what he meant. She finally got what was deserved—and just brilliantly, again in 2019 with *The Testaments*—but Margaret has never been short of prizes; she's been much garlanded and heaped with over 130 honours around the world, from the Order of Canada to *Ms.* magazine's Woman of the Year, from the Edinburgh International Book Festival Enlightenment Award to the PEN Pinter Prize.

On a long train ride from London to Glasgow (in the days when that journey took nearly eight hours) as part of one of our tours, I told her a story.

The summer before my final year at university I went on a rubber raft ride through the whirlpool rapids beneath Niagara Falls and the trip ended tragically. A 30-foot wave tipped us over and three people out of the nearly thirty of us on the ride sadly drowned. Margaret remembered the incident: the accident had been headline news. She listened carefully to my description of fighting the waves, determined to stay alive, and then when I had finished, she asked, 'May I have that?' Her version of my unbelievably lucky escape from death appeared a few years later as a short story in *Bluebeard's Egg*, called 'The Whirlpool Rapids'. There are my thoughts, perfectly remembered, though Margaret took no notes.

To find myself on Atwood's pages was a surprise, and a deep pleasure.

She is terrific company; such good conversations, and we have all had so many laughs with her and her late partner, Graeme

Gibson. She's got a tremendous sense of humour and she's splendidly generous. Her contribution and importance to Virago is incalculable, beyond the over four million copies of her books we have sold, in itself an astonishing contribution.

Ultimately, what I really treasure is her seriousness—maybe it's a Canadian trait—and her belief in the written word: 'The writer retains three attributes that power-mad regimes cannot tolerate: a human imagination . . . the power to communicate; and hope.'

Unlike Virago non-fiction, where we actively seek out a woman's point of view, in fiction we look for talented women writers. We have never had an ideal feminist novel in mind; that would be an overly prescriptive brief, for a propaganda novel and not a great work of fiction. We've welcomed our authors taking a feminist slant on genre fiction—most particularly crime fiction, publishing Sara Paretsky, Barbara Wilson, Sandra Scopottone, Amanda Cross, and the early crime novels of Sarah Dunant and Gillian Slovo. One of Virago's first big novels was a feminist generational saga, *Stand We at Last* by Zoe Fairbairns.

We also published contemporary fiction writers including Tatyana Tolstoya, Lisa St Aubin de Teran, and Nina Bawden; Lucinda Montefiore acquired an early Barbara Kingsolver and Ruthie bought Ali Smith's first collection of short stories, *Free Love*, which we still publish alongside her novel *Like*. Alexandra launched Lucy Ellmann's career with *Sweet Desserts*, which won the Guardian Fiction Prize; Ursula Doyle brought us the magnificent and angry novel *The Woman Upstairs* by Claire Messud, and Paula McLain's *The Paris Wife*, which told the Hemingway story from his wife Hadley's point of view. Today's excellent Virago editor Ailah Ahmed is taking us further afield: to

Greenland with *Crimson* by Niviaq Korneliussen, about LGBTQ identity, and to America's past with C. Pam Zhang's *How Much of These Hills is Gold*, a Western-style novel about Chinese-American sisters during the Gold Rush.

Gillian Slovo and Sarah Dunant both eventually found the constraints of the crime genre too binding. Gillian went on to write marvellous big sweeping novels including *The Ice Road*, about the siege of Leningrad. We stood holding our breath the year it was shortlisted for the 2005 Orange Prize alongside Shirley Hazzard's *The Great Fire* and Margaret Atwood's *Oryx and Crake*, which Andrea Levy won for her novel *Small Island*.

Sarah Dunant, who I have now published for over twenty-five years, moved to provocative thrillers, including *Transgressions*, which included a bold and controversial rape scene. That gave us both some tough media coverage to handle and was a bonding moment, though we've always had a rewardingly intense and honest relationship—one I value. Most surprisingly, Sarah then suddenly turned to historical fiction and *The Birth of Venus* launched her on an outstanding and bestselling path of novels about the lives of women in the Italian Renaissance, which she followed with two novels about the Borgias. Over the last few decades feminist and social historians have opened up vast reams of research that illuminate previously unknown ordinary lives, particularly those of women, and Sarah, a historian before she became a novelist, acknowledges that none of her historical novels could have been written even twenty-five years ago: 'The research into courtesans, convents, women as healers, vision-aries, artists and musicians had not been done ... Inevitably, some of what historians found was tantalisingly fragmentary: like watching salmon swimming upstream—the odd glimpse as they leap out, the sun catching their scales, before plunging back into the deep. But put all those glimpses together and you can start to see the shape of the shoal under the water.'

Her great skill is to put those very glimpses together to create characters who might well have trodden the dirty streets in Rome, smelled the fetid canals of Venice, mixed oil paint in Florence, howled to escape a convent in Ferrara, danced in heavy velvet at court, saw beauty in frescos—set against a perfectly rendered backdrop. Sarah has always been keenly alive to the beat of politics, rumours, and ideas that affect our individual worlds and she is scrupulously historically accurate. I think of Sarah like a little ferret—down she goes and then up she comes—grinning with the prize—the truth. Combine that scholarship with her beguiling and visceral powers of description and we are there, on the ground, in that time.

This imaginative truth-telling enlarges our contemporary world and gives us new understanding of women's lives from earlier times. As Sarah says, 'One of feminism's great achievements is the way it has changed not only the present, but also the past.'

Some readers believe that truth lies only in non-fiction. But to Sarah and to me and so many, it's through imagination that we understand veracity, authenticity, and one another. I hold George Eliot in esteem for many things but especially for her view that 'art is the nearest thing to life; it is a mode of amplifying experience and extending our contact with our fellow-men beyond the bounds of our personal lot'.

Though, interestingly, Marilynne Robinson says she does not read much fiction, she does write profound novels that accord with George Eliot's belief in the power of fiction and echoes

Eliot when she says art is 'imagining—generously—life that is not your life', adding 'beauty gives people hope'. Like many, I adored Marilynne's beautiful first novel, *Housekeeping*, and so I made it my business to visit Ellen Levine, her long-time agent, every time I was in New York to say IF Marilynne ever wrote another novel and IF her UK publishers were not keen, I was.

I was not poaching, I was merely making my passion known. Swooping in and poaching an author by offering a huge amount of money, sometimes even before there is a book ready, is a not uncommon fact of publishing but I just don't think it's fair. Of course, if a publisher does a bad job, or even if they don't but the author still wants to leave an editor and a publishing house, that's absolutely fine—it might well be a good career move. Authors' decisions like this have happened, and more than once, for me, as one would expect in a long career such as mine. No good comes of publishing a writer against their will. When an author does come free from a long-term relationship with a publishing house, I would think everyone who is interested would jump in and take part in an auction for their work.

With Marilynne I was breathtakingly lucky. As twenty-eight years had passed between *Housekeeping* and the time when she began writing a new novel, her UK editor, Robert McCrum, had moved on and so eventually pages of the new novel came to me. It was such a delicate fragment that I really could not predict what it would become but as I said to the meeting that decided on acquisitions, anyone who could write *Housekeeping* must be able to produce something special. That fragment turned into the first of three novels: *Gilead*, *Home*, and *Lila*, masterpieces all and, respectively, winner of the Pulitzer, the Orange Prize, and the National Book Critics Circle Award. Marilynne was awarded a National Humanities Medal for 'grace and intelligence in writing' by President Obama, who has proclaimed himself a fan and made himself a pen-pal of hers. She has gone on to become one of the most respected thinkers in America today, looked to for the wisdom that is demonstrated in the essays that we also publish. She too believes in the enlarging and enlivening power of the written word, that 'culture and education are basically, at their best, meant to make us aware'. Her fiction does not conform to the usual plot-driven or character-led novel; I think of it as akin to stepping into a river that sometimes roils and sometimes meanders, one to which you give over, knowing she will hold you and take you places you've not been before. Marilynne has told me that when she taught creative writing at the Iowa Writers' Workshop she tried to get her students to unlearn what they knew, to start afresh, in the belief that 'we have learned what looks like learning', not what is real thinking and real knowledge. How lucky are we to have this thoughtful—and surprisingly funny—writer on our list. A writer in whose great works we meet awe, each time anew.

'She stimulates the mind and satisfies the heart' is praise I would apply to all of the storytellers I have mentioned here, but that particular quote belongs to a review of a Linda Grant novel by *Scotland on Sunday*. There are certain novelists who I think of as writing from the headlines; that is, taking a measure of what's going on in our world and helping us make sense of it all. Linda is such a writer. She first came to Virago in 2002 with *Still Here*, a story about architecture, cities, families—and unbridled lust in a forty-nine-year-old woman and I have published all seven books of hers since. She writes exhilarating, intelligent, humorous, and deeply humane novels that, even when they are telling bleak or sad stories, restore the reader. Her themes are the big important ones that define our lives: identity and immigration, love and loss, family and clothes, generosity and connection, and her people are deftly drawn, intelligent, and satisfying character sketches. Linda is like one of those street artists who cleverly and accurately pounce immediately on the characteristic that makes us the individual we are, she picks up on nuances and foibles to create real and memorable people. Readers and reviewers recognize her ability and reward her with praise, and prizes too. What I especially like about her novels is her understanding that, despite all, we mostly try to do our best, that even if today was awful and disappointing, tomorrow we'll put on our new dress, paint our face, lift our chin, and try again because that's what it is to be human. That is what a story can do for us.

Linda's novels are very speech-driven, and dialogue moves the plot along. That is a feat that few writers pull off.

I have had long and fascinating talks with Sarah Waters about dialogue and I often send new writers to study her books to see how she does it. Sarah's first, rollicking, sensuous novel, *Tipping the Velvet*, a Victorian lesbian story, was acquired by Sally Abbey for the Virago V list in 1998, and since Sally left I have been Sarah's editor. Sarah says she has increasingly realized that dialogue—the way her people speak, and what they say—is where she can reveal the truth about her characters. Of course dialogue in books does not reproduce how people speak in real life; creating the illusion that it is real is her genius.

In some ways she picks up the thread of early feminist authors who took genres such as crime or science fiction and joyfully twisted them into new feminist stories. Sarah has borrowed from the sensation novel, the ghost story, the war novel, the crime novel—but she has done so much more than mere genre-busting: she has subverted those forms and made them her own. And what extraordinary, delicious novels she has created by revealing worlds most had only intuited before. Sarah explains: 'The very patchiness of lesbian history, I was trying to say—the very leanness of the lesbian archive—invites or incites the lesbian historical novelist to pinch, to appropriate, to make stuff up. I wanted the novel not just to reflect that, but to reflect on it, to lay bare and revel in its own artificiality.' She has made lesbian stories 'ordinary': 'To me, lesbian stories are the norm, not the aberration'.

From the glory of Victorian music halls to a quiet London home with a beguiling lodger; from women in Millbank Prison to hidden lesbian lives in the Second World War; from a sensational, breath-taking swindle to a haunting in a decaying country house—reading a Sarah Waters novel is a deep and intimate pleasure. She recognizes that reading, listening, telling, and being told stories is a basic need: 'Storytelling makes us human.'

On publication of Sarah's second novel, *Affinity*, one of the reviews said, 'Such a brilliant writer that her readers would believe anything she told them.' It's true. We will follow her anywhere because she understands the transforming power of a story.

### PART THREE

# The Politics: Office and Otherwise

---

*'Tell all the truth but tell it slant'*—Emily Dickinson

CHAPTER SEVEN

# The Dramas

Back to the office and the chronology of Virago. In 1982 Carmen was offered the prestigious Publisher's job at Chatto & Windus, one of the companies that made up the consortium of Chatto, Bodley Head, and Cape. She decided she wanted it— and to take Virago too. The working shareholders of Virago were Carmen, Ursula, and Harriet, and the latter two did not want that move. Us younger women—Alexandra, working part-time, Ruthie, who had joined us that year from *Spare Rib*, Kate, Lynn, Katrina Webster, office assistant appointed the year before, and I—were not part of the conversation (though Kate and I were by then Sales Director and Publicity Director) but we were well aware of the battle.

A company needs capital to publish and grow, and Carmen's view was that Virago had reached its limit as an independent, and so selling Virago to the CBC group would be an essential and savvy business move. Carmen, Ursula, and Harriet had been working together for nearly ten years and though they had respect for each other there was real tension and this disagreement ratcheted up the divisions.

Over the years people have always asked me about the rifts at Virago, which continued until 1995 when we shareholders (which by then included me) sold the company to Philippa Harrison at Little, Brown. The disagreements were a fact of

Virago's life for less than half the time that we have been publishing, but in media lore they are legendary. In the BBC 4
Virago documentary, Alexandra says of the passionate arguments and debates, 'You have to realize we were like family.' We
felt strongly about the imprint we had created and in which we
had invested our money, but even more importantly our lives.
We identified deeply with Virago—all of us still do. Harriet
Spicer once said that she felt there was a sort of blessing/curse
of Virago that would never let you go, and that we who have
worked there, never want to let it go—'Whatever happened,
no one ever wishes they hadn't worked there'—because to us
there are no jobs like it. Even now, when Virago is part of
Hachette, a major international corporation, it is unusual in
publishing, and probably in most industries too, in the way it
provides those who work for 'her' with meaning and purpose,
at the same time as being high-profile, political, and creative.
I think it could be described as a vocation.

Ursula was extremely articulate and loudly passionate, not
afraid of expressing anger. Carmen's feminism was instinctive;
Ursula's was too, but hers also grew from the politics of socialist feminism and academia. Initially, these forces had been com-
plementary: their vision for Virago—to be a mainstream feminist
publishing house—was in accord, as was their respect for
authors and their ability to bring writers, readers, press, *et al.*
along with the Virago mission. But even by the time I got to
Virago there was tension between them. Jealousy, opposing
personalities, widely differing styles, money—I wasn't around
when it started and I cannot say what initiated it, but curt
words, silences, and angry memos became a not exactly unusual
part of everyday office life. Harriet, an important shareholder,

sat somewhere between the two women: clever, calm, committed to justice and the cause; when she decided to be mediator, she was highly effective.

By the time Carmen was offered the plum job at Chatto & Windus our offices were at the back of the Oxford University Press building in Dover Street, Mayfair. With a staff of eight we had outgrown the Wardour Street room. In our new spot we had four small rooms off a central space, an attic floor reached by an old metal-gated lift.

Even though we weren't quite open-plan any more, and Carmen had her own little office, the walls were paper-thin and the space was small. Negotiations with lawyers began to be part of the background noise. The heated conversations were about whether or not Virago should be part of Chatto in the group, something Harriet and Ursula strongly opposed, and finally it was agreed by all that Virago would remain a separate company. The three women sold the company and all their shares, as did, of course, the other shareholders. Carmen, Harriet, and Ursula honourably gave Kate Griffin and me (as directors) some of their redeemed share money. On 19 February 1982 Virago, with a turnover of well over half a million pounds and more than 160 titles, became part of Chatto, Bodley Head, and Jonathan Cape Ltd. We had a farewell lunch for Carmen in our offices and gave her a wine decanter etched with 'Thank you for setting the world on fire'. Soon after that we left Mayfair and took up residence above Chatto & Windus at 41 William IV Street, near Trafalgar Square, as part of the newly named Chatto, Virago, Bodley Head, and Cape (CVBC). Sadly Kate left at this point, as our sales would now be handled by a central 'service' part of the company, as it was rather demeaningly called.

Our new offices were terrific and light, and again at the top of the building, this time in what had been a flat above Virginia and Leonard Woolf's Hogarth Press. I got my first solo, though extremely tiny, office, which had formerly been a loo; I had to slide in sideways between the wall and my desk, and my chair was where the toilet had been. The bathroom down the hall had a large white bathtub, which was handy for keeping the wine cool when we had parties—of which there were a fair few. Carmen continued to work with Alexandra and Lynn on the Virago Modern Classics, though Alexandra, as Editorial Director, was now in charge of that part of the list, and in February 1983 we celebrated the publication of the hundredth Classic. Carmen became our Chair and met us monthly for board meetings, but she was no longer our Publisher and no longer a daily presence in our office. Harriet and Ursula became joint Managing Directors and though the rift between Carmen and Ursula only slightly abated and we never lost the anxiety of survival, daily office life did take on a different, slightly calmer tenor.

But those battles, particularly between Ursula and Carmen, who have barely spoken for decades, but also between us all, remain part of our history. The media love a so-called cat fight. Clashing personalities and stressful times produce friction, and sometimes for a productive, creative good; disagreements are part of any organization, particularly small owner-operated ones, but they are of especial interest when the combatants are women. It's far from the only example of sexist opinions and interest in us but it is a very telling one that feels prurient and almost sexualized. There are boardroom bust-ups all the time but the demeaning coverage of women's disputes has an extra edge—an almost gleeful joy at what is portrayed as women failing. It is enraging.

Virago has had many owners, and after this period with Chatto, Virago, Bodley Head, and Cape we had three more. Many times I would feel that we were at the perfect size, with the right turnover and appropriate number of titles, but sadly it's not long before a static company is one in decline. Growth—even incremental—is essential for publishers, idealistically powered or otherwise, if we want to pay our staff, printers, and, of course, our authors. And once an author has broken through to success, naturally they will expect their advances to rise. A publishing house needs money to draw on to pay advances on books and authors: money that will not be recovered until the book is published, often many years after the initial advance is paid, and even then we may not get that money back. The finance of a publishing house, as with most creative industries, is dependent on a small part of the output to make the profits: in most houses, approximately 20 per cent of titles make serious money; most of the other 80 per cent will break even or lose money. The trick—and one that is only ever a practised guess—is to know which ones will make up the 20 per cent. Many small independent publishers can't survive once they run into the problem of lack of proper capital underpinning and of cash flow—which can, ironically, come as a result of success, such as one of their books winning a big prize. Bob Gavron, one of Virago's original guarantors, had a favourite mantra: 'Cash is king'—it was one we all learned too. I used to travel to work with a neighbour, an economist fascinated by the quirks and flukes of the publishing industry. When I explained the finances and how arbitrary was success, he would wave me

off at my Tube stop with 'Hope you hit an oil well today.'
Sometimes it does feel as serendipitous as that.

Our initial years with CVBC were good; our sales rose—
from a turnover of £600,000 to £2 million—we were more
visible, we were financially secure, and this was the period
when we published some of our most successful books, including those by Margaret Atwood and Maya Angelou. We were
publishing about sixty titles a year and we took on new editors,
but then things began to sour. Whereas before we had controlled our own overheads and could adjust accordingly, we
were now tied to a percentage of the overall costs of CVBC,
over which we had no control, and it began to hurt us. Ursula
wrote, 'By the end of 1986 the group situation was grave and
affecting Virago's financial situation; the end of year accounts
registered our first loss.'

Cash flow began to be a problem and CVBC shut down part
of the Bodley Head as a cost-saving measure. We began to feel
anxious: though we were high-profile, we were also the smallest of the group. Might they try to fold us into another company—Chatto?—to help reduce overheads?

In the summer of 1986, barely four years after joining the
group, we began to talk about a management buy-out.

Though this period of Virago must rank as one of the most
anxious in many ways, it was also exciting, and because we
five—Carmen, Ursula, Harriet, Alexandra, and I—were all
united in our desire to save Virago it was also a relatively tran-
quil time between us. We met often to discuss and to galvanize
ourselves: we believed ourselves to be planning secretly, only
to discover that several times we had talked so loudly in res-
taurants that the news of our plans were known before we were

ready to spring. Bob Gavron, who once again agreed to invest, lined us up with the venture capital arm of the bankers he used for his printing business. Rothschild Ventures agreed to back us with the proviso that each of us put in money of our own. I had no capital at all, a small mortgage, and a modest salary, but my bank manager agreed to loan me £10,000, which I was to pay back in monthly instalments of £224. We produced business plans: working out staffing, number of titles, overheads, premises, and cash flow. We learned the language of the City, such as 'it's important who you are in bed with', and conversations with Tom Maschler and Graham C. Greene, the two major shareholders of CVBC, were looking positive.

And then on 7 May 1987 Tom and Graham solved the cash flow problem by selling us all, the whole of CVBC, to Random House US. The *New York Times* reported the sale, writing that our company had been losing money since 1982—the year we joined. They also relayed some hitherto unknown battles that now left the boardroom and hit the press: 'The author Graham Greene—who is on the board of Bodley Head, with whom he has been associated for 30 years—wrote a letter to *The Times* suggesting that his nephew [Graham C. Greene] "is living in a fantasy world".'

Overnight the picture changed. Not only were we suddenly under our fourth ownership, but now we were up against an American giant. New personnel were appointed: Simon Master, long-time publisher at Pan, was brought in and to him fell the job of 'handling Virago'. He tried to persuade us to stay—things were all different now, properly capitalized, and we would have a happy home with the new company—but for us, the die was cast and, if anything, the urgency now seemed greater: we desperately wanted to go. Simon relented and the deal was struck. In July 1987 we and Rothschild Ventures bought ourselves out from CVBC/Random House. There were two riders: they would retain 10 per cent of Virago, and we would stay with them for sales and distribution. Rothschild had some serious stipulations too: ratchet clauses that would kick in and escalate if we didn't pay back their money and dividends as agreed.

Thrilled, proud, scared, determined, we moved to a warehouse in up-and-coming (but still a long way from being up) Mandela Street in Camden Town. Jeremy Dawson of Rothschild's, who had been appointed to oversee their investment, came to see us in our new home and to meet the rest of the staff. Afterwards he clapped his hand theatrically to his forehead: 'I've bought a company that runs on tummy waters!' 'What?' we said. He'd asked editors how they took decisions, how they decided what books to publish, and had been told 'it was a gut decision'. Just like others from outside our industry, he was often frustrated by the capriciousness of publishing, the precariousness of the decision-making, and the unpredictability of readers' tastes. At the same time as he'd been working with us, he'd been conducting a management buy-out of a pork-pie factory and he would compare us to them, seemingly longing for more straightforward people, product, and process. But he grew to love Virago, and publishing too, even suggesting books and ideas for us to publish. I believe the pork-pie management buy-out went bust.

Our offices were one floor below MTV (which was then a new concept: a twenty-four-hour music channel) and they'd outfitted their offices with neon lights, purple carpets, and flash studios. We'd occasionally see young music stars in big cars in the narrow street outside. When we first moved in, the front door of the building was just a large wooden building-site door; we had an industrial lift and poorly lit concrete stairs; the street was also dimly lit. It was a scary place after dusk. However, our office had lots of glass partitions and lovely wooden floors; we'd put it together cheaply but it was functional, nice looking, and it was proudly ours. We suddenly had lots of space and set about hiring staff to fill the jobs that CVBC had carried for us: an accountant, a bookkeeper, and a receptionist.

Our staff had joined the National Union of Journalists when we were part of CVBC. In our independent set up it now fell to us directors to do the salary negotiating and at these periods a management vs staff division was sharply felt. We've never had a steep hierarchy but neither have we ever been a co-operative, and even though we all thought unions were the right thing, it wasn't at all easy for either side around wage-negotiation time. We tried to be honest and fair, but we directors were not always thought of that way. I wonder if a hierarchal structure can ever be otherwise? I know that Writers and Readers Co-operative didn't always feel fair either. We got through negotiations and pulled together again.

We increased our editorial, publicity, and marketing staff, and, excitingly, got a few computers, which were just entering the working world. We had one large desktop computer in my publicity and marketing area of the office—for about five of us to take turns on. I remember Becky Swift, Jane Parkin, Melanie Silgardo, Arzu Tahsin, Julia Hobsbawm, Smita Patel, Jo Tracy, Lucinda Montefiore, Karen Cooper—among so many others—working so hard, but also taking such delight in the enterprise.

Surrounded by books and piles of manuscripts, we wrote leaf-lets, made phone calls, sent postcards, typed pages of editorial notes, designed covers, went to bookshops, conferences, and author events, and publicized and sold our books. We organized roadshows where we would take authors out to bookseller presentations beyond London: Manchester, Bristol, Edinburgh *et al.* We had great fun.

In my expanded role as Marketing Director I oversaw a team of publicity people but I had reached the end of my interest in this side of publishing and before we began our management buy-out I had thought seriously of leaving it all behind. However, the chance to own part of my beloved Virago and to learn about that aspect of business was utterly beguiling.

Now on the other side of the buy-out, I was itching to do more and Ursula suggested that, with Ruthie, I could start edit-ing by launching a new list for young people, which we called the Virago Upstarts. Publicity and marketing prepares one well for editorial choices as, after all, much of publishing is thinking about how best to present a title and author and to be highly aware of the market. We had early experience of this at Virago as Carmen had moved from publicity to editorial, as had the esteemed Liz Calder, who was at this point Publisher of the new independent, Bloomsbury. Both Carmen and I agree (though wouldn't we?) that coming from publicity is a great background for editorial. As Carmen says, 'The book is never just about the text, it's about publishing, marketing, seeing the book as a whole thing.'

But I had to learn how to edit on the page. I had some great instruction from Ruthie until I was confident to rely on my own instincts and we had some terrific successes on our new list, such as *The Young Person's Guide to Saving the Planet*, which sold 50,000 copies in the first two months; I remained Marketing Director, and worked on the Upstarts on the side. But my heart and passion was now in editorial. Then Alexandra was head-hunted by Hamish Hamilton to be Editorial Director in 1990 and the next year Ursula left to work for the Labour Party. Harriet, who now became sole Managing Director, suggested that I become Publishing Director. I didn't think twice.

## CHAPTER EIGHT

# Disrupting the Old Stories

'Tell all the truth but tell it slant.' Emily Dickinson's line that I love tells me there are many truths, some of which are difficult, some of which are best expressed obliquely, but also that people find it easier to hear and digest truth if you come at it a bit sideways.

I am impressed with the young women of today who seem to speak out without anxiety of consequence, who feel able to state their truths, their feminism, boldly, in the confidence that they will be taken seriously, that they will find sympathy and consensus—among many men as well as women. I and my generation might have written as angrily, marched as passionately, and argued as strongly, but we were in different times. In the 1980s feminism was a frightening word for many women as well as men. Often feminists would explain that feminism was pro-woman and not necessarily anti-men; that feminism was liberating for all; that it was right and just that over 50 per cent of the population deserved visibility, representation, and equal opportunities. However, there were those who were just downright hostile, believing—as a result of the feminism of the 1970s—that women needed pushing back before they got the upper hand and started to run the world (as if!). Femininity also concerned many women. Can feminists have a good time, shave their legs, wear make-up, and like pretty clothes? The answer is undoubtedly yes, and please, let's worry about more important things, but these anxieties occupied many then.

In my view, using traditional means to impart new ideas—such as converting the mainstream to seeing women's literature and women's stories as central to human experience—might mean one has a better chance of success. I think, absolutely, that labels matter and that one must always feel able to name oneself, but I am also persuaded that there are many ways of presenting ideas. Zoe Fairbairns, one of Virago's first writers, tells a wry story about this, though: 'In the mid-80s, I was once invited to speak at something called a Women's Activity Day. The organisers explained that they didn't want to use the word "feminist" as it was too scary for what they called ordinary women. "Ordinary women don't like extreme, aggressive feminists," they told me, "so we decided to invite you instead." I didn't know whether to be flattered or offended.'

The idea for a Feminist Book Fair and Booklist began as a way of both subverting and copying some of the ideas used in the trade. Creating a list of best books around a theme had already been done by the Book Marketing Council, run by Desmond Clarke. Following a fairly successful Best of British list in 1981, which included our Rosamond Lehmann and Rebecca West, in 1983 he created the Best of Young British Novelists. When Bill Buford, editor of *Granta*, produced an issue devoted to the list—Twenty Under Forty—this group of new writers, including Ian McEwan, Kazuo Ishiguro, Salman Rushdie, Rose Tremain, and Pat Barker—made headlines, launched careers, and sold thousands of books.

Both lists were made up of twenty writers and in both cases only six were women. (Also noteworthy: when the Best of

Young British Novelists was recreated ten years later it again managed only six women out of the twenty writers chosen.)

A group of us thought, why not use the same method to promote feminist books? Though, as we were feminists, could we have a hierarchy of best? That taxed us a bit until we came up with a Selected Booklist. Following another more left-wing model, the Radical Book Fair, which for years was held annually in Camden Town Hall, we decided to hold a fair too. We gathered booksellers, publishers, and editors around the table and planned the launch of the First International Feminist Book Fair, to take place from 7 to 15 June 1984. Egged on by one another, we got even more ambitious and decided we'd have Feminist Book Week, with events up and down the country. We got a grant from the Greater London Council and hired Carole Spedding, who had been a co-founder of Sheba, and publisher Gail Chester to work part-time from offices in Room 306, 38 Mount Pleasant, London WC1. Bolstered by very frequent meetings of volunteers, booksellers, and interested publishers, we eventually created not only a huge three-day fair at Jubilee Hall in Covent Garden, but also sixty-five events in fifty-seven towns throughout Britain and Ireland. It was an astonishing feat; it felt like we'd left the margins and were centre stage. Our Booklist booklet announced: 'It is indicative of the power of the movement that 1984, the most pessimistic of years, sees the First International Feminist Book Fair: an event that has the confidence, strength and audacity to call for a celebration.'

The emphasis on internationalism and intersectionality, as it would now be called, was particularly strong. When I look at the list of exhibitors I see we had ninety-one publishers, bookshops, collectives, distributors, and magazines from around the world. I list them all to show what effect feminism was having on the printed word.

From the UK alone came the Anarchist Feminists, Blackwell's, Battle Axe, Black Women Talk, Bloodaxe Books, Bookmarks, Bookplus, Brilliance, Central Books, Centerprise, Change, Dizzy Heights, Dorling Kindersley, Gollancz, Falling Wall Press, Fontana, Feminist Review, Allen & Unwin, Granada, Harper & Row, Harvester Press, Heinemann Education, Hutchinson Education, Journeyman, Lawrence & Wishart, Letterbox Library, Macmillan, Manchester University Press, Methuen, Nicholas Treadwell Gallery, Norton, Onlywomen, Pandora, Penguin, Pergamon, Pluto, Quartet, Routledge, Sangam Books, Scottish & Northern Book Distribution Cooperative, Settle & Bendall, Sheba, Silver Moon, Sisterwrite, Sphere, Third World Publications, Trevor Brown Associates, Triangle Translations, Virago, The Women's Press Bookclub, The Women's Press, Women in Publishing, Workers Educational Association, Writers Guild, Writers & Readers, Zed Books.

Events all over the country involved not only British writers such as Susie Orbach, Pat Barker, Eva Figes, Michèle Roberts, Michelene Wandor, Sara Maitland, and Zoe Fairbairns. There were also visits and appearances by writers from overseas, including Marge Piercy, Valerie Miner, and Lisa Alther from the USA; Urvashi Butalia from India; Frances Molloy from Ireland; Nawal el Sadaawi from Egypt; Dacia Maraini from Italy; and Manny Shirazi from Iran.

After our first year the fair was picked up by feminists around the world and continued to occur annually, hosted thereafter in Oslo, Nairobi, Montreal, Barcelona, Amsterdam, and Melbourne, into the early 1990s.

Urvashi Butalia and Ritu Menon set up India's first feminist publishing house, Kali, and Urvashi had been very involved in the planning of the London fair. She and Ritu had a stand in the hall. Remembers Ritu: 'I will never forget the sheer ebullience...also the solidarity of women in print. Alice Walker, Toni Cade Bambara and Alifa Rifat, Barbara Smith, Ellen Kuzwayo, Gert Brandenberg, Suniti Namjoshi and Madhu Kishwar—the whole surge and potential of the international women's movement, it seemed, was there for all of us to see...How Covent Garden buzzed with the excitement of hearing these amazing women speaking of things in a way that had never been heard before...books that presented not just one woman's experience, not one particular society's foibles, not exceptional situations, but a whole new perspective based on a shared history of inequality. I realised then what it meant to be at the centre of opinion-making.'

Zoe Fairbairns recalls 'it was about the people who read books getting together with the people who write them'. She goes on to ask and answer the question that invariably raises its head once politics and money meet: 'Was this a genuinely radical movement, or was it just the mainstream capitalist publishing industry spotting a gap in the market and cashing in? It was both. The feminist organization Women in Publishing were strongly active in running these events, as were feminist booksellers, librarians and writers. But it was a commercial operation too.'

Of course the feminist, independent, and radical bookshops supported the books and the list, and organized events, but we went further: we managed to get WH Smith to back the promotion with stands of books labelled 'Feminist Book Week'. That would be a surprising coup even today, to be frank, but in

1984 it was just short of revolutionary. It was almost totally down to Michael Poultney, who was the book buyer of Smith's, a quietly political man who I knew through work but also as a result of another political publishing group I was in at the time, Book Action for Nuclear Disarmament. That group also organized a promotion and a list the following year, launching Peace Book Week with twenty-four hours of reading on the steps of St Martin-in-the-Fields in Trafalgar Square.

Michael chose a small list of books—mostly novels—and promoted them in the largest shops; the signs in those WH Smith windows proudly proclaimed Feminist Book Week. I remember standing in Kensington High Street amazed by the Smith's window, and I am still grateful to him. It does show yet again how feminism has always had allies who are prepared to put themselves on the line.

One could of course say that the larger publishing houses and even WH Smith were not moved by radicalism but saw the commercial potential of feminist books—and that probably is right. However that is to diminish the courage of individuals who felt strongly about feminism and were trying to use their positions within traditional companies to effect change.

Kate Griffin, Virago Sales Director until 1982, echoes this: 'I remember the booksellers who became passionate Virago champions, mostly women, recognizing in our books their own stories. These included special fans within the conventional booksellers such as Blackwell's and Heffers, as well as those within the thriving and hugely supportive radical book trade and included the extraordinary wholesalers Pipeline Books, and Scottish and Northern, who stocked every Virago title. Without such book trade individuals—in the UK and throughout the world—

who invested both emotionally and commercially in the enterprise, Virago could not have achieved the success we did.'

The launch of the fair coincided with the opening of the radical bookshop Silver Moon Bookshop at 68 Charing Cross Road.
It wasn't the first London feminist shop. In north London, at
190 Upper Street in Islington, Sisterwrite Co-op had been going
since 1978 alongside their café, Sisterbite. Lynn Alderson, who
had been at other important radical bookshops, Housemans in
King's Cross and Compendium in Chalk Farm, before she became
part of the collective, recalls that their bookshop was a mecca:
'If you went looking for the Women's Liberation Movement, as
I had a few years before, you would find it.'

The location of Silver Moon was significant: a feminist bookshop and café in central London, on the famous Charing Cross
Road, the bookshop street. Run by Jane Cholmeley and the late
Sue Butterworth, and stocking only books by women, it became
another important centre and meeting place for lesbians and
feminists but also for women who just wanted to know what
this movement was all about. Virago held many an event there
over the years, the most famous for us was a signing session for
Maya Angelou in the late 1980s, which saw a queue spooling
out of the door and down the street.

We also attempted to get into bookselling ourselves and
opened a beautifully designed bookshop on Southampton Street,
near Covent Garden, but we closed it before our management
buy-out in 1987. Best to leave bookselling to booksellers.

The First International Feminist Book Fair was, on the whole,
an exhilarating commercial and political success. However, we
on the organizing group got two things staggeringly wrong: we
weren't a very diverse committee and we held our fair in a hall

that had no disabled access. I write that sentence with some amazement at our naivety and ignorance. It shows how far we have come that it's highly unlikely that either of those things would ever happen now. Despite the glory of the event, the week that followed, and the subsequent international fairs, I can't forget three searing moments.

First: Looking down maybe fifty steps to where a group of women in wheelchairs with placards are gathered at the bottom. The stairs lead up to the hall of the fair. The shame of this is compounded by the fact that our author Adrienne Rich, who suffered from rheumatoid arthritis, had to be carried up those stairs for her attendance. Even now I feel deep mortification for our culpability in her discomfort.

Secondly: The poet Audre Lorde utterly silencing the marvellous opening-night party of authors, publishers, and booksellers when she broke through the talk and laughter with a long, angry speech about the outrageous lack of many women of colour on the committee. I remember feeling the absolute rightness of her argument and the hot distress of being publicly shamed in equal measure. Later she dubbed the fair 'a monstrosity of racism', 'which distorted and deflected what was good and creative, almost visionary about having such a fair'.

Third: Standing with Rosa Guy, a Virago author, on a balcony watching two long lines of women come into the London venue where she and other international authors were to speak. One line is all women of colour, the other all white. We were asked to give women of colour priority over white women to hear some of the major writers of colour from around the world. The result of which was that we soon had two separate queues. I remember Rosa, a black American writer and a veteran of the

Civil Rights Movement, sighing deeply beside me at what was now segregated lines. 'I thought I would never see the day again.' Thankfully, everyone who came that evening got in; there was enough room for all.

These episodes were hugely painful for the committee but I saw then that that was what the fair also should be about. Feminist concerns about marginalization within the book trade were matched by feminists of colour's concerns about marginalization within the feminist book trade and indeed feminism in general. It was a sobering lesson.

The poet and novelist Jackie Kay also remembers the power of Audre Lorde at the time of the fair: 'In those early days of the black feminist movement — of the Organization of Women of African and Asian Descent (OWAAD) and the Black Lesbian Group (BLG)—Audre's words were a breath of fresh air. We had only just found each other. We were only just hearing each other's stories. Some of the fifty or so members of the BLG had never met other black lesbians before. We'd come from all over the country, from Glasgow and Glossop to London, and the two things converged—discovering each other and reading the work of Lorde.'

Jackie, who was part of Sheba, accompanied Audre Lorde to interviews and talks: 'There was a fervour that greeted Audre. She had the aura of a superstar. To hear her was to be aware that you were in the company of somebody who would become legendary. You knew that her words would reach an ever-widening audience . . . A framed poster of "A Litany for Survival" signed by Audre hangs in my kitchen. It has come with me from house to house since she first gave me the poem when she came to stay in 1984 and I was twenty-three.'

I find it fascinating to note what happened between some of the high-profile black American women writers and UK feminist publishers around this time: we found each other. Alice Walker was published by the Women's Press, Audre Lorde was with Sheba. Toni Morrison, who had been published in the UK by Chatto since the 1970s, was now enthusiastically published there by Carmen.

And in 1984, Maya Angelou came into our lives at Virago. *I Know Why the Caged Bird Sings* had never been published in the UK despite it being well known in America since its publication in 1969. Maya Angelou told us that her memoir had been sent to British publishers in the 1970s but they had all turned it down, saying no one would be interested in the story of a young black girl growing up in the American South. She loved us for taking a chance on her, characterizing us as her small and feisty 'English' publishers. As we grew to know her, we came to understand that she highly prized courage and loyalty. 'I've got your back' was something she said often.

We published all seven of Maya Angelou's memoirs, her essays, volumes of poetry—and a cookbook—over the next few years. She came often to Britain and we watched as the country fell deeply in love with her: she captured every size and shape of heart—old, young, ignorant, wise, proud, and shy. When I first took her around the UK I saw that it was as if people were thirsting for her: they drank deeply of her words and felt lifted by her spirit. They flocked to her, at times weeping, literally wanting to touch her hem, at other times shouting with the pleasure of seeing a six foot tall woman dance across a stage unashamedly, outrageously sexily, head tipped back with a huge, infectious laugh. 'My mission in life is not merely to survive,

but to thrive; and to do so with some passion, some compassion, some humour, and some style.'

She was in the mould of the people who inspired her: she
was a preacher with a sermon, writing and speaking, as she
said, with 'the rhythms and imagery of the good Southern black
preachers', and she was a teacher with a lesson: 'I speak to the
black experience, but I am always talking about the human condition.' We are more alike than unalike was her very powerful
mantra.

Maya Angelou believed in poetry; she trusted in it and she
used to say that she knew from a young age that you could live
by its strengths. The grandmother who raised her and whom
she called Mama, said to the little Maya, 'Sister, Mama loves
to see you read poetry because that will put starch in your
backbone.'

She had hundreds of poems (po-ems she used to call them,
in her slow, rich, deep voice) at her fingertips and could—and
would!—sing or recite them at a beat.

And even in a most terrible time, after being raped by her
mother's boyfriend at age eight—after which she became mute
for years—she wrote that poetry was her saviour. In *I Know Why
the Caged Bird Sings* she tells how the splendidly named Miss
Flowers beguiled her back to speech: 'She opened the first page
and I *heard* poetry for the first time in my life. Her voice slid in
and curved down through and over the words.' That sensuous
quality, that appreciation of the nourishment of the written
word is what I loved about Maya Angelou and her writing.

This child, with little formal schooling, brought up in Stamps,
Arkansas amidst the poverty and segregation of the Deep South
had been, by the end of her life, at age eighty-six in 2014, awarded

more than seventy honorary doctorates and honoured by two presidents; she wrote and performed her poem 'On the Pulse of Morning' for President Clinton on his inauguration and was given the Presidential Medal of Freedom by President Obama. She was justifiably proud of those facts, happy to be called Dr Angelou.

Ursula Owen learned about *Caged Bird* from a feminist magazine, read it and immediately knew it was for us. She made a small offer for UK rights to Maya Angelou's US publisher, Random House. Within days I received a short, crazily typed letter, full of xxx and crossings outs, from the English upper-class memoirist and 'muckraker', as she was known in America, Jessica Mitford, telling me that she was going to make it her business to tell the British about her great friend. Though from vastly different backgrounds they had met in America, I would guess through the Civil Rights Movement, and we were to discover that they were utterly devoted to each other. Maya Angelou claimed that Decca (as Jessica was called) once came to her rescue, literally facing down the Ku Klux Klan with the words 'I am Maya's mother.'

I photocopied Jessica Mitford's letter and sent it to all the literary and feature editors with review copies of the book. It had the immediate effect Decca had intended: the British wanted to know more.

Maya Angelou came to London to meet us all. I always say that 'came to meet us' is just too tame a description: in our tiny office, this elegant, tall woman with a big heart and large laugh recited her famous poem— 'Phenomenal Woman'—just for us. It was obvious that we would invite her back for the launch.

So it was that fifteen years after the US publication, in 1984 we published *I Know Why the Caged Bird Sings* in a Virago paperback. We printed just 8,000 copies.

I remember thinking hard about how to launch this extraordinary book and 'phenomenal woman', and decided that we needed to reach both community and television audiences. Maya Angelou's first UK event was at a community centre in Paddington, in a space for about a hundred people. Her now-famous bravura performance on stage was unknown to me and others in the UK back then and we were utterly bowled over as she recited poetry, sang songs, encouraged, danced, laughed. Afterwards, I sold all the books I had brought with me. One man hissed 'capitalist publisher' at me as he purchased his copy, but the event is one that I treasure deeply. After, it was very late and we fell, exhausted, into a taxi to take us back to the Basil Street Hotel; it had been recommended to her by James Baldwin, who loved the place. Maya Angelou taught me so many things, but one stark lesson was that after a performance a woman needs food and drink! It took all my powers of persuasion to get the hotel kitchen even to give us miserable little sandwiches. Not preparing for after the show was a mistake I never made again . . . Both of us now relieved, eating crisps and sandwiches, and drinking whisky (Maya's favourite), we toasted the beginning of a great success.

Her appearance on television the next day took Maya Angelou to another level. *After Noon Plus* on Thames Television was an important daytime programme hosted by an amazing woman, Mavis Nicholson—maybe the Oprah Winfrey of the UK at the time, a woman not afraid to ask bold questions. She and Maya liked each other immediately and when Mavis asked Maya about being raped as a child, Maya told her the story openly, honestly, simply. Those watching in the studio cried and then applauded as Maya turned the story to show she was a woman unbowed. She said then and would often say to audiences: 'You may not control all the events that happen to you, but you can decide not to be reduced by them.' Immediately, the switchboards were jammed as viewers rang in: 'Who is that amazing woman?' Our first print run sold out and we quickly did another cautious 8,000 which again immediately sold out. Today, the Virago edition of this first volume has sold nearly a million copies and it is on courses, required-reading lists and remains, to my mind, one of the world's great autobiographies. We've now sold over two million copies of her books.

Maya Angelou was prominent in the Civil Rights Movement—as an activist and a campaigner working with Martin Luther King—but arguably her greatest contribution to campaigning for equality and change came through her writing. She was part of the Harlem Writers Group and she dedicated her artistic energies to inspiring justice, dignity, unity, and pride in oneself—what she called self-love. Maya's fierce belief was that each of us has a deep worth—a simple yet profound fact. Her activism was in her prose: 'History, despite its wrenching pain, cannot be unlived, but if faced with courage, need not be lived again.'

Maya Angelou had a fondness for jokes and stories and songs—sung by anyone; a delight in good food and excellent whisky; she adored driving big cars and wearing fabulous clothes (on one of her first trips, her shoulders were draped in a fur coat), and on her hands flashed large, gold jewellery. She was proud of her success; she had more than earned it. She had been born into a brutally mean and segregated America in 1928. After the birth of her son, when she was just seventeen, she endured many hard years of struggle as a nightclub dancer, cook, and performer before she became a civil rights activist working with Martin Luther King and, later, the writer we came to love.

She had a great generosity to her friends and loved a party where we could dance—which we did often. She had a special hip-rolling move that I and others tried to learn; I too love to dance. One of Decca Mitford's great friends was the broadcaster Jon Snow and on one of her visits to London—this time to direct a play at the Almeida, *Moon on a Rainbow Shawl* by Errol John—Maya rented his house, a little cottage in Kentish Town, for over a month. That house became the stage for many an evening performance; drinks and singing with the likes of Salman Rushdie (who gave a very passable rendition of 'Waltzing Matilda') and discussions with Christopher Hitchens; Helena Kennedy was a regular, as were all of us Viragos: Ursula Owen, Ruthie Petrie, Harriet Spicer. A memorable sight and sound was Decca and Maya singing with gusto—gloriously and badly and very loudly—their favourite tunes: 'Right Said Fred', followed by 'Bang, Bang Maxwell'. Maya often encouraged Decca to sing a very sweet old ballad about Grace Darling, a girl who saved drowning sailors near Bamburgh on the Northumbrian coast in 1838, and about whom Decca wrote a book. Maya always joined her on the line that she loved for its particular oddity: 'Grace had an English heart'.

Other remarkable singing moments took place at Hay-on-Wye—a festival that she loved, particularly when we could stay at the very grand Llangoed Hall with its expansive halls and rolling lawns. Peter Florence, the director, an actor and a Welsh poet at heart, could rise easily and gracefully to her banter and songs. He had the audacious idea on one visit to have Maya Angelou sing with a Welsh male voice choir, and they came along—in shorts and T-shirts—for an afternoon rehearsal in one of the large, beautiful rooms of the hotel. The sun poured in across the polished wooden floor and we clustered around the grand piano in pleasurable anticipation. The idea was to sing 'Swing Low, Sweet Chariot' together. A nod to Maya Angelou and her 'backing singers' and they began—and clashed and stuttered and stopped dead. Bewilderment.

'Ah,' said the pianist to Maya, 'you sing it like that.'

'I do,' said Maya, arching her eyebrow. She was not the one to change her style—slow, swinging, jazzy.

That evening, under lights, in the big tent, with the men in smart suits and Maya in a long glittering dress, the men showed their worth and sang along—in Maya's way. The choir finished with the famous Welsh song 'We'll Keep a Welcome' and we all cried.

There was lots of crying around Maya—sometimes because we were moved, which was often, and sometimes we cried with laughter—and sometimes, away from Maya, we cried in frustration and fatigue. She had many Virago publicists: first me, and then others including Sarah Baxter, Julia Hobsbawm, Susan Sandon, Fiona McMorrough, and Susan de Soissons, and she did take us all to our limits. Maya had a saying, 'When I come, I bring my all', and there was no doubt that she expected it all back too. When she came to London I would put my life on hold: it was Maya time, she took priority. Though my husband, and later my two children, admired and enjoyed being with her. They called her Auntie Maya, and Maya asked to be my daughter's godmother. When she learned that my son, Zak, was a baseball fan she sent him a ball signed by Hank Aaron, a black player, who with Babe Ruth remains one of the most famous players in baseball history.

I have a sweet letter from August 1987 that came with some pretty silver earrings. On Basil Street Hotel notepaper, in her firm round hand, she wrote, 'These earrings appear to be abbreviated ballet slippers. Giving them to you might seem to imply that I am encouraging you to stay on your toes. Perish the thought. You do not need that encouragement. Thank you and all your V Pressing sisters. Joy! Maya.'

Coming off a train at Victoria with Maya Angelou and our entourage (she always had a companion from the US travelling with her and generally more than one of us from Virago went when the publicity tour was extensive) after a successful but very long trip, I remember feeling absolutely drained, almost unable to drum up the last bit of energy to get us and all our stuff from the station to the hotel when, as if by wishful, magical summons, Jon Snow appeared on the platform. Cool and calm, broadly grinning, welcoming and pushing a luggage trolley, he picked us up and whisked us off. Jon understood, as we did, that she was special, a one-off, a woman who pushed us, not just to publish her well, but to be better ourselves: to be more open, more generous, to respect oneself, and she did inspire one to do one's best—to go beyond one's best, even.

An example. One Sunday afternoon my family and I went to see Maya Angelou at a hotel in Covent Garden and we found her in a beautiful plush red sitting room with Alice Walker, who happened to be staying at the same place. Maya, knowing from me that my daughter, Amy, aged about thirteen at the time, had a nice voice, suddenly asked if she would sing for us all. I was stricken. Would Amy want to do it? Could she do it? I knew she could sing, but under those circumstances? While I was debating whether I should intervene, Amy stood up, moved to the back of a chair, where she rested her hands, took a deep breath, and sang out in a clear soprano 'My Ship' from *Lady in the Dark*. Amy couldn't have been prouder.

We all remember her words. After her death, Alice Walker said, 'I envision Maya as a kind of General of Compassion, offering an army of words of encouragement.' Michelle Obama thanked her for words that were 'clever and sassy', and powerful.

In the month before she died I went to visit Maya Angelou in her home in Winston-Salem, North Carolina. Miss Lydia Stuckey, her beloved assistant of some years, made us pancakes for brunch and ribs for supper, and we drank large glasses of cold white wine. It was a Sunday and they wanted to watch a religious programme with a Baptist preacher, followed by reruns of Oprah Winfrey shows. 'Ope', as Maya called her, and Maya were devoted—Maya referred to her as her 'daughter'; over the years they came to each other's aid and celebrations. Oprah had thrown huge parties for Maya's seventieth, seventy-fifth, and eightieth birthdays. Most memorable for me was a party that lasted three days under marquees in the grounds of Wake Forest University in Winston-Salem, North Carolina, where Maya Angelou was Reynolds Professor of American Studies (for more than thirty years at her death), which culminated in a Sunday-morning service with twenty golden harps, songs by Maya's church choir, and Jessye Norman singing 'Amazing Grace'.

Now Maya was eighty-four, she was connected to an oxygen tank to aid her breathing, and she wore dark glasses to protect her weak eyes. I said I was sorry, thinking she was in some pain, and she shook her long index finger at me, 'No!' She did not want pity. 'I never complain,' she reminded me fiercely. On the table were large yellow legal pads covered in her elegant, looping handwriting. I knew that she always began her books in this way, and tantalizingly we talked of what she was writing about. Memories of people she'd known she said: Jimmy Baldwin, Malcolm X, Martin Luther King. A roll call of men who had changed the twentieth century—as had she. I knew that it was James Baldwin who in many ways was the catalyst for Maya's memoir-writing. In the desperate days after Martin Luther King was assassinated (on Maya's birthday, 4 April) Baldwin had persuaded Maya to dinner with the cartoonist Jules Feiffer and his wife, Judy. Both were civil rights activists. They told stories all night, and soon after Bob Loomis from Random House rang and invited Maya to tell her story. Convinced he was put up to it by Baldwin, she demurred until finally he said, 'Well, it's hard to write a good autobiography.' 'I'll start tomorrow,' came her answer.

Sitting in her kitchen we talked too of the Obamas, whom she deeply admired, when I noticed she had a photo of them near the table. She asked after my children and my husband, and wanted to see photos of them. After a while I said a lingering goodbye. As my taxi sped through the countryside back to the airport I sat up straight—with starch in my backbone.

Though the black women writers making a mark in Britain were on the whole American, our list at the time also included black British women, particularly poets, including Grace Nichols, Jean Binta Breeze, Merle Collins, and Amryl Johnson. Grace Nichols's slim but boisterous and poignant volume, *The Fat Black Woman's Poems*, was first published in the same year as the Virago edition of *I Know Why the Caged Bird Sings*; it remains a bestselling collection and is on school curriculums. It tells of being a West Indian woman who is now in the cold UK, thinking of food and warmth. We went on to publish more of Grace's work, including novels. Ruthie Petrie was Grace's editor and she commissioned an important book for Virago that was published in 1985. *The Heart of the Race: Black Women's Lives in Britain* by Beverley Bryan, Stella Dadzi, and Suzanne Scafe 'describes Black women's celebration of their culture and their struggle to create a new social order in this country'. We also published Melba Wilson's *Healthy and Wise: Black Women's Health*.

In the 1970s and 80s the feminist houses (like the traditional ones) were largely white and largely published white authors— even if we were conscious of needing to be more inclusive. I remember that in doing the publicity for *The Heart of the Race* I was really finding my way; the literary and media world was changing, but slowly, and I very much needed to be guided by the authors. Even though white feminism could hardly be called mainstream or at the centre of things, it was my world and it was time to step out and learn. And writers of colour were telling me why. The late Toni Morrison told a story about being on an American talk show and being asked when she was ever going to write about white people. 'You know you can only ask that question from the centre of the world ... He's patronizing; he's saying, you write well enough, you could come on into the centre if you wanted to ... And I'm saying, Yeah well, I'm gonna stay out here on the margin, and let the centre look for me.'

The world was beginning to tilt; voices from the margins were breaking through.

Says the memoirist and journalist Yasmin Alibhai-Brown, 'I remember the day Salman Rushdie was described as a British writer and how that made me feel ... he was the first and the best and he ... changed the literary terrain so others could grow.'

When Salman Rushdie won the Booker in 1981 it wasn't just the fact that a British Asian had won the prize that was important, but also that his novel, *Midnight's Children*, in so many ways, began the thirst for literature about life beyond these shores.

Prize lists for novels are a great barometer of society. If I look to the Booker, the Women's Prize for Fiction (previously the Orange and Baileys), and even the Best of British lists—which, though driven by marketing, were selected by writers—I see a very gradual change of subject matter and of visibility for British authors of colour since Virago was founded.

In fifty years of the Booker Prize, nine writers of colour have won, three of them women: Kiran Desai, Arundhati Roy, and (co winning with Margaret Atwood) Bernardine Evaristo, the first black British woman to win the prize.

The shortlists over all the years are not much more cheering: only thirteen women of colour and only four are British: Monica Ali, Zadie Smith, the late, much-loved Andrea Levy, and Evaristo.

The Women's Prize for Fiction, set up in 1996 to celebrate, honour, and recognize the voices of women overlooked by prizes such as the Booker, is an international prize with diverse longlists. There have been only five women of colour winners in twenty-four years: Andrea Levy, Zadie Smith, Chimamanda Ngozie Adichie, Kamila Shamsie, and Tayari Jones, three of whom are British.

When *Granta* took up the Best of Young British Writers, the number of women writers of colour were, in 1983, only Buchi Emecheta and in 1993 none. The 2013 list, however, featured seven women of colour.

Perhaps it feels reductive to make lists of prizes and recommendations, and to tally and highlight writers, but such things are hugely important: they make the headlines, indicate a nation's taste, significantly influence readers' choices, and, not least, often launch writers' careers. The conversation around race and writing has powerfully shifted but in my experience, and in using these lists to see the clear evidence, it is a recent occurrence: mostly taking place only since 2000.

And, of course, one could quite correctly point out that publishing does not have many people of colour in powerful positions.

Over the years there have been many initiatives to try to correct this imbalance. GAP—Greater Access to Publishing— playing on the obvious (gap in the market, bridging the gap, mind the gap)—was set up in the late 1980s by Margaret Busby—the writer and founder of the publishing house Allison and Busby—with the late Ros de Lanerolle, the then Managing Director of the Women's Press, and others, including me, and it did feel very much up against the grain.

Even though there were many small black publishing houses at the time—Akira Press, Karia Press, Karnak House, Black Ink, Inky Fingers, Arawadi, Black Womantalk, Zora Press, and the long-established New Beacon Books and Bogle-L'Ouverture— the mainstream houses were not multi-cultural. We went out to the UK book trade under the banner of Toni Morrison's statement, 'It's not patronage, not affirmative action we're talking about here, we're talking about the life of a country's literature.'

Margaret and I wrote a piece about our group for the *Bookseller*, pointing out the success of black and Asian writers but noting that 'the desire for a multi-cultural list does not seem to have extended to a multi-cultural staff'. We formed to act as a campaigning and information group; to alert career guidance people to the possibilities of jobs in publishing; and to create a register of African, Caribbean, and Asian people experienced in different aspects of publishing.

We ran a day-long conference (funded by the Greater London Authority) and encouraged the trade to think harder about how to encourage applicants of colour. GAP was followed by other initiative in later years, particularly Diversity in Publishing Network (DIPNet), founded by Elise Dillsworth, then an editor at Virago, and now a literary agent, and Ellah Wakatama Allfrey. Similar encouraging and lobbying groups continue today, including Sharmaine Lovegrove's radical work with her imprint, Dialogue, at Little, Brown. But none of us are there yet.

In 1991 we published the paperback of the novel *Joy* by the black American writer and actress Marsha Hunt. As she said, because 'publishers want to make money and the consensus was until publishers can see the fiscal advantage of signing up black British-born writers, they won't bother', she decided to set up a prize with backing from *Saga* magazine and help from the Book Trust. Dear Margaret Busby was a judge, as was Steve Pope, co-founder of X-Press. I too was a judge, as Virago promised to publish the first winner—female or male. Marsha set the rules, that 'the author had to be a writer born in Great Britain or the Republic of Ireland having a black African ancestor', which ironically attracted criticism from the Commission for Racial Equality and opened a discussion about what exactly is black British writing. Marsha ran the prize for four successful years and launched four new writers.

The first winner was Diran Adebayo for *Some Kind of Black*. We stuck to our promise and he was Virago's first living male novelist. (He later moved to the Abacus list at Little, Brown.) His novel was remarkable, a wild urban ride through London. It was 1996 and a long way off from the list of recognized black British writers that publishers can produce now.

A year later our author Patricia J. Williams delivered the Reith Lectures, which we published as *Seeing a Colour-Blind Future*. She spoke about understanding and probing 'the distance between the self, and the drama of one's stereotype', which is 'the question at the centre of our resolution of racism'.

The drama of one's stereotype; the injustice could hardly be better expressed.

Racism, like sexism, is still far from being eradicated, however the writers telling stories and the gatekeepers deciding who gets to tell them is changing. The conversations are shifting.

Stepping outside one's culture, learning the limits of one's knowledge, is a challenge to editors, particularly white Western ones. We can get it wrong. I was reminded of Waris Dire's insistence that the fight against FGM went beyond culture when we published Masih Alinejad's *The Wind in My Hair: My Fight for Freedom in Modern Iran* in 2018. Masih is now exiled from her beloved Iran for speaking out against the enforced wearing of the hijab. But she says, 'We don't want to be saved by Western feminists . . . we are brave enough.' She rails against Western women who visit her country and cover their heads, which she says is mistakenly out of respect, as all that does is 'legitimize the discriminatory law'. It makes it worse. 'You should stand up for your own values, for your own dignity', not justify a discriminating law.

Similarly, a contributor to our anthology *Fifty Shades of Feminism*, Sayantani DasGupta, calls for a sisterhood of solidarity rather than 'saving'.

Thirty-four years after the first Feminist Book Fair, I am fascinated to attend a new Feminist Book Fair in November 2018, at the Barbican in London. Stalls with feminist books occupy the downstairs floor and upstairs there are talks. Joanna Bourke, feminist, historian, and author of our book *Rape: A History from 1860 to the Present* and Lola Olufemi, black feminist, former Women's Officer of Cambridge University Student Union, and author of a book for young people, *Feminism Interrupted: Disrupting Power*, share a stage with others to talk about After #MeToo. Though one might think this 'After' is suspiciously like the 'post' in post-feminism, we *are* having conversations with more nuance and awareness of intersectionality. Joanna points out that looking at a problem historically can give us hope because 'things don't *have* to be the way things are, history shows we can change things'; though it also tells us that the battle is a serious one, as 'things are deeply embedded in media, in law, in art… but because history forces us to think structurally—we can't just say women are women are women'. The definition of woman has and will continue to change.

As does the defining of people of colour, for although publishing houses are no longer only male, white, and Oxbridge, editors of colour and from working-class backgrounds are still rare. Lola Olufemi said, 'The feminist pundit class is not attuned to race and class.'

Diran said to me, when we published him, 'White people like talking about racism—because then it's about them.' I hear him in my mind as I witness and enjoy the fact that one of the bestselling books of 2017 was Renni Eddo-Lodge's *Why I am No Longer Talking to White People About Race*.

She went on to win the much-welcomed Jhalak Prize for the Book of the Year by a Writer of Colour, founded by Sunny Singh, Nikesh Shukla, and Media Diversified, the previous year.

The old, tired narratives are being seriously disrupted at last.

## CHAPTER NINE

# Beyond Borders

We had a little run-in with boundaries in the late 1980s. We received a manuscript from an agent who told us she was representing a British Asian author who had written some remarkable short stories for young people. We read and loved them, and decided we wanted to publish the collection in the Virago Upstarts series. The author's name was Rahila Khan. Could we meet her? No, said the agent, who also hadn't met her; she was apparently keeping the fact that she was writing fiction a secret from her family, and she didn't live in London and could never get away from her home. So we corresponded by letter: agreeing the cover image, the cover copy. Rahila Khan provided us with a full biography, which we printed in the book: 'Born in Coventry in 1950. She has lived in Birmingham, Derby, Oxford, London, Peterborough, and Brighton. In 1971 she married and now has two daughters . . . [in 1986] her first story, 'Pictures', was broadcast on BBC Radio 4's *Morning Story* and since then five more have appeared on the programme.' It was frustrating, but the many reasons provided to explain not meeting seemed credible.

Then the agent rang to say she had news about the author, and could we meet for lunch? Ruthie and I went off in great expectation: finally we would learn more. We arrived at the restaurant to find a slightly nervous agent. She had at last met

Rahila Khan; or rather, she had met the person who wrote under that name. (And, it turned out, at least one other too.) *His* name was Toby Forward, and he was an Anglican vicar. Maybe he believed and felt he had just proved that it was easier to get published as a British Asian woman than a white man. Most surprisingly, this had never been done to us before.

Outraged, we went back to the office, sent out a press release, asked for the books in the shops to be returned to us, and pulped all his stock in our warehouse. I now see this was a little extreme. We could have probably just laughed it off—and then pulped his book. But we felt enraged by his duplicity. Possibly naively but in good faith we had taken 'her' story as the truth about the author and had presented his book as fiction by a British Asian woman to young people. We felt that we too were part of the misrepresentation—and we did not like being duped.

The press release set off fireworks. I was asked to go on Breakfast TV, BBC Radio 4, *World at One,* and it was all over the press. I protested falsehoods, talked about authenticity and 'literary blacking-up' (today I suppose I could have talked about cultural appropriation); the media attacked us for sexism and lack of humour; the tabloids had a go at us with headlines about feminists defrocking a vicar. Oh, not a time I would like to live through again . . .

Aside from thoughts on racism, lies, and feminism, a conversation and questions about the text emerged. Does it matter who wrote it if a book is good? Our answer: well, it also depends how you are presenting the book. Question: what about the Brontës—they published under false, male names? Answer: they had to. Question: can you tell the difference between male and female writing? Answer: no. Question: is it true that female writers of colour have an easier ride than white men in getting published? Answer: no, look around you. Question: did the Reverend Toby Forward have the last laugh on the feminists? Answer: nobody agrees on that one! Question: is it okay for a vicar to dissemble? Answer: hmmm . . .

A few years later, Toby Forward, under his real name, wrote another young person's book and in it there were two rather nasty characters. One was named Lennie and the other Miss Goodings.

Writers reveal who they are by the way they conduct themselves with readers and with the writing community.

Angela Carter was what I call a good citizen writer: she went out of her way to help other writers. Virago published Angela's *The Sadeian Woman* and *The Magic Toyshop* in the Classics, but the way I got to know Angela better was through her discovery of the writer she brought to us: Pat Barker.

Angela Carter loved to talk: she was famous for long, winding, wandering, fascinating telephone calls and, when they came my way, I loved them too. I feel she would have taken to email and possibly even Twitter; she was a sociable soul with voracious curiosity and always wanted to know what was going on, to be part of it. She was clever, witty, and eccentric in her dress and manner which gave her a slightly distracted demeanour— but she was actually bull's-eye sharp with bracing, sometimes lacerating, observations about people, literature, and politics. Instinctively and fiercely moral, she wasn't afraid to veer from the feminist party line. She was also funny, laughed often, and was good at—and obviously enjoyed—swearing.

She felt deeply connected to us at Virago—particularly to Carmen—but she was so kind and attentive to me too: sending me a little cloth doll for my new baby girl with a note, 'Bravissma! Welcome to Amy.' Her own relationship to being a mother seemed joyful. Perhaps coming late to motherhood, and certainly because she was more than supported in his care by her partner Mark, she appeared at ease and her adoration of her little boy, Alex, was palpable. When he was very young he drew a wild-haired picture of her on his small blackboard and Angela suggested it was a perfect representation of her—and it was— for our cover of *Nothing Sacred*, a collection of her brilliantly sharp political and cultural pieces from *New Society*. She knew herself.

Her relationship to Mark Pearce, who was eighteen years younger, was of great interest and mystery to us younger women at Virago. We knew the story: that they had watched each other for weeks, she from the window at which she wrote at her home in Bath and he from across the road, where he was building an extension on a house. She ran over to him one day to ask him to help fix a burst tap—and he never left. Tall and lean, dark and bearded, very handsome, he was shy and rather unsmiling. I know him now as a passionate, talkative man working with refugee charities, but back then he was almost completely silent. At parties, when we would find him standing quietly at the side of the room, Alexandra and I would try, out of politeness and, admittedly, deep curiosity, to engage him in conversation. Though he didn't actually rebuff us, and he was obviously kind and adoring of a very voluble Angela, who could be the life of a party, he made it clear that chat was not for him. She described him as 'like a werewolf'; we thought of him as a man from one of her stories.

The ICA arranged a Literary New York weekend of talks and invited the great American writers Grace Paley and Susan

Sontag—and also Angela Carter, among others—for a Saturday panel in the 1980s. I can see them on the platform: little, round, talkative, and generous Grace; sharp, unswerving (and unnerving) Susan Sontag, her famous lick of grey-white hair across her dark head; and Angela. Attentive, she cocked her head, listening, assessing, and presenting a slightly diffident, amused demeanour that disguised what I knew to be someone with decided opinions. As usual, she spoke slowly and searchingly, laughing a bit when arguing—her deflection.

The wide-ranging conversation eventually settled, fascinatingly, on what could be judged as literature. Voices of writers—working-class writers and writers from ethnic minorities—from beyond what was regarded as mainstream culture were at last reaching the big publishing houses, but Susan Sontag was cautious and wary: boundaries needed to be drawn. She argued, uncompromisingly, for upholding the calibre of quality literature; if these new stories were to be regarded as literature they had to reach a certain standard. Grace, in turn, felt particularly strongly that this cultural change was important and that news from the margins was exciting and potentially transformative; that literature would be broadened and very much for the good. Angela, I felt, sat somewhere between the two.

In the end 'testament of experience' was the compromise description offered by Sontag. Both Angela and Grace indicated they felt that was patronizing. As, frankly, I thought it was. The canon was then—as now—under scrutiny from feminists and Sontag's stance felt uncomfortable and unbending. Virago's entire *raison d'être* was founded on the belief that this old-style exclusion from and protection of what was deemed 'literature' needed re-examining and challenging. Who gets to tell the stories?

What voices are admitted? Who decides what is great? The compromise—or put-down—of 'testament of experience' upheld the notion that there was only one standard by which to be measured.

We in the audience were fired up by the conversation and of course in awe of the three astonishing women. But what I also remember with great pleasure was that afterwards Grace came off the stage, hugged me, and referred to me as 'like a daughter'. Nodded Angela: 'Lennie is daughter to us all.' Happy me.

Angela—as with so many writers—had to supplement her income with teaching creative writing, and after one session with the Arvon Foundation she wrote to Carmen saying that she'd found a writer we would like. It was Pat Barker. Pat had been writing for years but without success: 'I set out in a very tepid, tentative sort of way writing short, middle-class novels which weren't published.' Angela encouraged her to tell a story in her own voice, to tell an authentic story. The result was the absolutely searing *Union Street*, a story of working-class lives, brilliantly written, one that should have satisfied Susan Sontag. Angela not only worked with Carmen on the editing, she was also extremely helpful to me in talking about publicity for Pat. We had long, long phone calls where she suggested writers we could send the book to, reviewers we could buttonhole, and events Pat might do. At Virago, Carmen decided to present this novel as an important new female working-class story. The male working-class voice had been praised, with the likes of Alan Sillitoe's *Saturday Night and Sunday Morning* and *Billy Liar* by Keith Waterhouse in the late 1950s, but it was our contention that the women's perspective had been overlooked. Here was an honest, true, woman's voice taking up the stories of silent women from the margins—in a provocative and impressively written novel.

One of the people we sent the manuscript to was Jennie Lee, fierce Scottish Labour MP and one of the founders of the Open University. She was also a miner's daughter and the widow of Aneurin Bevan, architect of the welfare state. She, we thought, would be a perfect champion of the book. We sent it, and I rang her to see if she had read it and would like to give us a quote for the cover. No! She was appalled and very sharp with me: this is not my working class! We'd had books in my home. It was not like that. This is not my working class. It was an early indication of what we might be up against with our publication.

*Union Street* is a tough novel about unforgiving, hardscrabble lives in the shadow of the Tyneside mines—each chapter is the story of a woman from a house along Union Street: they are orphans, women on the game, miners' widows, mothers. The saving grace for the women is their community and, for some, literacy. Pat knew these lives and she also knew these women were not well represented.

By far, reviewers and readers responded well to what was for many a new literary landscape. We did get strong reactions— some found it just too graphic and bleak—and others didn't give it its literary due. Pat says: 'Regional, working-class voices are very, very marginalized, and there's a tendency either not to review the work or to review it in slightly different terms . . . whether its authentic sociology, rather than looking at your themes or the way you've treated your characters'.

Susan Sontag, neatly depositing this sort of subject and writing in the 'testament of experience' pigeon-hole, would be chastened by Pat's description of writing her later novels, comparing them to a particular sort of middle-class novel: 'All those bloody dons sitting around talking about the theme of the book. Frankly, I think it's a doddle compared to writing about semiliterate or illiterate people . . . It's money for old rope compared with what you have to do when the character can't possibly do that.'

*Union Street* won the Fawcett Society Book Prize in 1983 and was a runner-up for the Guardian Fiction Prize but Pat's success created another problem: 'I felt I had got myself into a box where I was strongly typecast as a northern, regional, working-class, feminist—label, label, label—novelist. It's not a matter so much of objecting to the labels, but you do get to a point where people are reading the labels instead of the book.' And after writing three more remarkable, plain-speaking, bold novels, she left Virago to write books about war from men's points of view. And though she continues to champion the voice of the marginalized her review profile changed, especially after she won the Booker Prize for *The Ghost Road*. We can thank Pat for being one of the writers who pushed at the boundaries and opened up new territories for literature. *Union Street* is now a Virago Modern Classic.

Angela Carter was alive to who won the prizes and who got the big reviews. I never felt she resented Pat's success but she did take a wry view of 'the boys' for whom she was a great advocate and who then found greater success than her. I remember phone conversations about Salman and Ian and Ish (Rushdie, McEwan, and Kazuo Ishiguro). She was a writer who took a great interest in other authors, reading widely and supporting them generously. It was an outrage to many of us—publishers, readers, reviewers—that her work was not properly or fully recognized in her lifetime. Gore Vidal said drily that death is a good career move—and, tragically, in Angela's case it was true. Only after her death did the world catch up with her particular outrageous, imaginative genius.

When Angela was dying, she continued a project that she had started for Virago: editing fairy tales that she had collected from around the world. As a child she had been enthralled by Andrew Lang's compilations of tales, twelve books in various colours—a fact I delighted in as I too had loved them growing up—and she wanted to make a series like his. She had already translated *Perrault's Fairy Tales* but these new collections were about women. We published *The First Virago Book of Fairy Tales* with a blue jacket and the second was to be in red. Of course we said to her that she must not tax herself, fully expecting her to abandon the project but no, she told others that 'I am just finishing this for the girls.' Though we asked another writer, Shahrukh Husain, to finish the endnotes, Angela did complete the book. *The Second Virago Book of Fairy Tales* was published post-humously, in a deep claret-red jacket, with an introduction by the critic and novelist Marina Warner, a slightly modified version of the special obituary she'd written for the *Independent*. Marina wrote, 'She gave of herself—her ideas, her wit, her no-bullshit mind –with open but never sentimental prodigality ... She had the true writer's gift of remaking the world for her readers.' Both books were illustrated with woodcuts by Corinna Sargood, one of Angela's oldest friends, who also created brightly coloured illustrations for the jackets. I later put the two volumes in one and renamed it *Angela Carter's Book of Fairy Tales*, and it remains one of Virago's bestsellers. How I wish Angela could enjoy the fact that we have now sold 100,000 copies of her book.

Before her death I wrote to Angela, and Edmund Gordon asked me if he could include it in his highly perceptive biography of Angela. Reading it over twenty years after I wrote it was a strange but good experience. I still feel a deep sense of loss.

> 11th February 1992
>
> I want to write & say thank you to you—for many things. For giving me such delight as a reader; for all the support & encouragement you've given me & Virago; for the wonderful books you've published with us. I was talking to a friend this weekend & I mentioned your name & she said she didn't go in much for hero worship but you were her heroine—& I guess that's another way of saying what I feel too. Except that heroes are usually distant & cool, until you get close to them & then they have lead feet (or whatever that expression is!) and that's not you. You've been such fun; & such a tonic and such an interesting, good, generous human being. I feel very privileged to have had the chance to work with such a rich, rewarding writer—who also understands about being a mother . . . I send you & Mark & Alex love. From all accounts the three of you are dealing with this horribly sad & difficult time with great spirit and dignity & that is a tribute to you & Mark. You are a wonderful woman, Angela.

Angela Carter was important to so many Virago writers, including the generation that followed her, particularly Ali Smith and Sarah Waters, who responded to the virtuosity of Angela's fiction writing. There is something thrilling and freeing about Angela's wildness, that told these writers that fiction can do anything, go anywhere.

Sarah Waters has talked—so interestingly—about one novel being a conversation with another novel, in the sense that all writers and novels exist because of the writers who precede them. Sarah is conscious of her forebears—Angela Carter being one—but also Jeanette Winterson. There have been novels about gay men, but Sarah has broken new ground in telling lesbian stories for the mainstream. She hasn't done it single-handedly and her rise in stature has coincided with societal changes at a time when novels, as she recalls in a new afterword to *Tipping the Velvet*, twenty years after publication, 'seemed to show grand narratives being prised open and made to reveal—or forced to accommodate—feminist stories, queer stories, lost stories, radical stories'. But it is undoubtedly true that what she has done in her outstanding, absorbing novels is make lesbian lives an ordinary part of fiction—and thus an ordinary part of the written and the real world. She's brought in voices from the margins, hidden histories out of the dark, and helped make a new British literary tradition. Her subject matter has been provocative, mysterious, and bold, but what really sets her apart from the many is her extraordinary storytelling.

Sarah, intensely modest and private, shows me what superb writing can do for readers. She excites passionate followers who feel that she and her books are part of their lives. As the first port of call for the many who contact Sarah via Virago, I see that she gives people—particularly gay and lesbian readers—great enjoyment but also courage. Sarah says that her own coming out would have been different if she'd had novels such as hers and if gay authors then had the prominence they have now. People write movingly about what her books mean to them.

Fans send pictures of their tattoos—lines from her novels—or ask her to sign copies for their lovers and their wives.

Overwhelmingly, most correspondents just want to say thank you for the novels. As many authors do, Sarah writes back to everyone, and it is so rewarding for me to be the go-between for reader and author. I see over and over again how books touch and change people's lives.

I go back to Grace Paley: 'There's an idea that there's this great mainstream, which may be wide but is kind of shallow and slow-moving. It's the tributaries that seem to have the energy.'

When novels come from the margins, beyond the boundaries, they are often met in publishing with a perception that such stories will only be read by the people represented in the books. Certainly that was the talk in certain quarters regarding novelists of colour until writers like Toni Morrison and Zadie Smith blasted that theory and showed how good stories cross any boundaries. The impetus for writing these novels often comes from writers feeling frustrated by the dearth of stories reflecting their lives: Toni Morrison famously said she couldn't find what she wanted to read so she wrote her own novel, and Sarah Waters has said because lesbian history had been so little known she decided to make her own.

Writing from the margins, knocking barriers out of the way is one thing; finding a publisher who believes in the writing and is determined to find an audience for it is another.

All books are positioned in the market by their title, their jacket, their category; they need to indicate the sort of reader they are appealing to and, not surprisingly, publishers often make them echo a book that has done well in the same area—see all the Dan Brown and The Handmaid's Tale lookalikes.

And yet, and yet, successful books constantly come out of the blue, and find a new readership.

Maggie Nelson, who with *The Argonauts* wrote an utterly uncat-egorizable, outrageous book that could not be pigeon-holed and 'positioned', said: 'I have always believed in a way, you invent your own readers—and that people can read more complicated books than they are credited for.'

As publishers we do know that people hunger for 'the next thing', but still we are more likely to be drawn to wanting to repeat a recent successful formula. I understand this and do it myself. But I have a very strong suspicion that we, the gatekeep-ers of culture—the editors, the publishers, and the booksell-ers—do not accord enough respect to readers. We underestimate the market. Toni Morrison was an editor at Knopf in America before she became a writer and she railed against this thinking: 'Acceptance of the "given-ness" of the marketplace keeps us in ignorance.'

Readers have always demonstrated their desire to stretch themselves and to try something new. This, to my mind, is par-ticularly important for us at Virago, as we already have the con-fidence of our audience. Our success proves that readers can be taken further.

I laugh that publishers now say confidently of unusual, bold books they are launching, 'for readers who like Maggie Nelson's *The Argonauts*'.

But it gives me hope; there is life beyond boundaries.

## CHAPTER TEN

# Up, Down, and Up Again

Independence is damn hard. Of course we always knew it was going to be, but our independence, at first glorious and a relief, became extremely tough. After six years we had a financial crisis leading to horrible redundancies, a vacating of our premises, and, finally, two years later, a boardroom battle that nearly killed us—and Virago too.

But first, festivities: in 1993 we marked our twentieth birthday in some style with a large party at the Barbican in London and with readings, window displays, and events around Britain. We also put on a fabulous show called *Her Infinite Variety*, drawn from Virago titles and written by Ursula Owen, Sally Alexander, and Jean McCrindle, which launched at Conway Hall on 20 June and toured the country. The readers included Juliet Stevenson, Sheila Hancock, Fiona Shaw, Harriet Walter, Abigail Thaw, Meera Syal, and Francesca Annis; it was spectacular.

Any celebration of Virago and our authors seems to invite articles that ask if we are necessary and bring out dreadful puns: 'Taming of the Shrewd behind a Write-on Success' in the *Scotsman* demonstrates my point. 'A Woman's Place is on the Shelf' in the *Daily Telegraph* does too. But the birthday articles—all written by women—tell a tale of where feminism was about to go.

Catherine Lockerbie, then literary editor of the *Scotsman*, betrays suspicion of success: 'Promotional paraphernalia from balloons to bookmarks . . . so much conspicuous consumerism; whatever happened, sisters, to the idealism of Virago's origins?' Even she, a real Virago fan, notes that the list ranged 'from classics to the newest of poets, from travel to crime to car maintenance. This is feminism as your flexible friend . . . the words "inspirational" and "financially viable" set side by side in the birthday blurb'.

The *Guardian*'s Catherine Bennett sees something more sinister or dismissive about feminism in general. Is feminism still necessary, she seems to ask, observing that, 'Today women reign over Random House . . . women editors thrive . . . frightening men with their formidable group, Women in Publishing (WIP).'

In the *Daily Telegraph*, E. Jane Dickson, under the subtitle 'Do we Still Need A Feminist Publishing House?' agrees, writing 'Virago has become a victim of its own success . . . female frontrunners in the bestselling and the literary stakes are no longer a novelty but the norm, rendering the positive discrimination of a women-only press at best obsolescent and arguably retrograde.'

Only in the *Independent* Natasha Walter, almost anticipating her own Virago book *Living Dolls*, wrote what I think was the truth of the time: 'Virago is the feminist movement in microcosm, in that its achievements have been enormous and not big enough.'

To us at Virago it was clear that at the same time as the world moved on—somewhat—the conversations about women's writing and about feminism were undoubtedly undergoing revision, and that our job was far from over. Driving over to the Barbican in the days before the big party to check out the room, we were faced with a billboard for a DIY company: a towering wall of locks, chains, and bolts was topped with the words 'Lock Up Your Daughters'. What? I wrote an article for the *Independent* they titled 'Call me old-fashioned, but that advertisement's sexist: Lennie Goodings defends her right to be offended by images that insult women'. I used the words 'old-fashioned feminism'; I could already sense the chill of post-feminism in the air when it was beginning to feel that talking about the rights of women was unfashionable and anachronistic, where 'politically correct' was the ultimate put-down. Even our own birthday celebrations risked masking an insidious complacency about women's position.

But we had a grand party!

It was the last celebration for a fair few years. I couldn't have predicted that we would fall but rise again to celebrate our thirtieth birthday, again in style and again with all the Viragos, but in much altered circumstances.

So what happened?

At the end of 1990, three years after our buy-out, Ursula Owen left to work with the Shadow Arts Minister Mark Fisher on the development of the Labour Party's arts and media policy (though she remained on the Virago board), and Alexandra Pringle was lured to Hamish Hamilton to become their Editorial Director. Harriet became sole Managing Director and made me Publishing Director in 1991, overseeing five editors. Susan Sandon's role expanded to Publicity and Marketing Director. We were cutting our titles back a bit, from 110 to 87, and had increased our turnover to £2.5 million. Outlook good.

But the changes of this decade were far from just internal.

Every publishing house is umbilically connected to the bookselling landscape, and since Virago was founded in 1973 the selling

of books has undergone a revolution. People often point to publishers and the way the conglomerates have grown and swallowed
independent companies, as evidence that publishers have utterly
changed the industry. While that is not untrue, the real and seis-
mic change has been in the way books are sold. In the 1990s the
rumblings of change erupted into a full-scale disruption that
forever altered bookselling with the demise of the Net Book
Agreement. Since 1900, publishers and booksellers had lived
happily with this agreement, which guaranteed every bookseller in the UK sold a title at the same price; that is, the one
fixed by the publisher as the recommended retail price. Though
that price was decided by the publisher, market constraints kept
the prices reasonable and similar across the board. This meant
that if a book became a bestseller, every shop in the land bene-
fited, thus helping keep hundreds of bookshops viable. Those of
us who opposed the ending of the agreement were wildly against
taking this benefit away from the booksellers who were paying
rent on the high street, who depended on bestsellers to support the shop, the new voices, and the slower-moving titles.
Discount wars, we said, are only for the big guys. The deep-
stocking bookshops would be hurt, take fewer titles, or close,
and the knock-on effect would be that publishers, without a
varied and wide range of outlets, would struggle to launch new
voices and to keep slower-selling authors in print. The result
would be an impoverishment of talent and variety, and a drift
towards a monolithic, polarized bookselling culture where the
big books are huge and the smaller ones are almost invisible.
And the price of books was already low, compared to what they
cost to produce and to other forms of entertainment.

The other side argued that, above all, the customer must have price benefits and this way they would get cheaper books and buy more, and that price-fixing by the producer was wrong. The courts ruled in favour of the end of the agreement. Range, quality, and a diverse offering came a decided second to price. Booksellers now decide the price. In itself that would not have had such a profound effect if the UK had put something like America's Robinson–Patman Act in place. Their federal law which stated that publishers offer the same price terms to cus tomers at a given level of trade was designed to protect small retail shops against unfair competition from chain stores. But the UK did not.

Today we are living in the wake of that judgment. Amazon dominates because they can sell cheaper than any bookseller, thanks to their size and because, as an online business, they don't have the high street rents and rates. The supermarkets take an extremely narrow range of books and sell them cheaply. The resulting struggle of bookshops on the high street has lead to the closure of hundreds of independent bookshops (500 in the twelve years after the end of the agreement). Fewer shops has meant a smaller range of books because the concentration of a few big outlets narrows what is offered to the public. I think that quality books have suffered: I believe a vibrant book industry needs a healthy and varied multiplicity of bookselling outlets, both online and on the high street.

The Net Book Agreement began to rock on its foundations in 1991, was effectively finished by 1994, and completely wiped out in March 1997: the period during which Virago struggled with independence.

Sisterwrite closed in 1993 and, as Lynn Alderson remembers, 'things had changed a great deal over that time. My last experiences of the shop had been of a rundown place with little energy or enthusiasm. But, to be fair, there wasn't the same women's movement to support it any more. And, everyone was selling feminist books, and many other things had changed, the big chains had been able to dominate the trade once compulsory RRP [recommended retail price] ended and they could discount books. This meant the end for many small bookshops. The whole political climate had changed beyond recognition.'

Virago has been tied to the ups and downs in health of all of the independent bookselling sector including Daunts and Foyles and of the smaller chains (now gone) of Ottakars, Books Etc, Dillons, and Borders. But most particularly we've been affected by Waterstone's: the fortunes of Waterstone's has been a bellwether for us and other upmarket, literary publishers.

Tim Waterstone's launch in 1982 of his first shop on the Old Brompton Road in London, followed by hundreds of others across the country, was transformative for quality imprints such as Virago. For the UK, it was more than a chain of bookshops—it was a cultural institution and an exciting change on a large scale. Tim believed in literature: he filled his windows with literary novels, piled them high on tables and floors, and prized literary authors. The shops were open late, seven days a week, and staffed by people who loved and knew their books. For almost ten years we gloried in being stocked in quantity and on the high street in Waterstone's.

Then, in the early 1990s, it changed. First it was policy: their commitment to huge backlist stocking underwent an overhaul and the streamlined result had a devastating effect on us, as we depended heavily on backlist sales—in some years, they accounted for as much as 50 per cent of Virago's turnover. Other publishers also found their backlist income sorely dented, but unlike them we did not have a large and bestselling frontlist to buoy us up.

Then it was change of ownership: Waterstone's was sold to WH Smith and pursued an entirely new direction, until it was bought by a consortium including Tim Waterstone, then sold to HMV Group in 1988. It was the same year that Amazon.co.uk came to town and Waterstone's, according to another bookseller, Tim Coates, lost its way: 'They decided to take on the supermarkets and Smith's by discounting prices and celebrity biographies. It was a strategic error. What they should have done was take on Amazon by offering something Amazon can't—the lovely, serendipitous experience of being in a really good, big bookshop.'

The owners of Waterstone's have, since 1993, bought Dillons, Ottakar's, and Hatchards. They had some decidedly shaky years, even worrying many of us that they might go under, but they did at last prove the pleasures of book-buying in person instead of online after they were sold to Alexander Mamut in 2011 and the Russian billionaire hired James Daunt as MD. As the owner of a small, highly successful chain, Daunt knew the particular nature of selling books. He applied many of the same principles—owner mentality, attention to community, the importance of 'hand-selling' books, and careful curation of stock—to the huge chain he now ran, and turned it around. In 2018 Elliott Advisors, a private equity company, bought a major share of Waterstones. That same year Waterstones completed its buy-up of the high street by purchasing Foyles.

James Daunt understands that the book trade, especially the upmarket publishers, need a high-street shop window as well as online sellers: 'You cut Waterstones out, and [literary publishers] go bust . . . So I didn't want my supply—the talent, the nurturing, the world I'm in—to just get severely buggered around.'

Under the management of Daunt, we are once again back to the philosophy that originally propelled Tim Waterstone. Excellent, inviting bookshops, attentive to the market but also to the neighbourhood and community in which the shops sit, as if they were a local indie, passionate about literature—and protecting themselves and guaranteeing their survival by once again turning a profit. Though of course controlling overheads meant cuts too.

Amazon's revolution of bookselling—which includes making a huge success of ebooks—has also been of major benefit to Virago book sales today.

But it wasn't like that in the early 1990s, and we were severely affected by the bookselling struggles. The high-street problems knocked us hard at the same time as we, a politically inspired publishing house somewhat at the mercy of the state of feminism, watched as feminism was morphing into post-feminism.

In October 1993 Bob Gavron and Carmen and Harriet put more money into Virago and bought out Rothschilds. Then, less than a year later, poor trading conditions hit and it was suddenly a perfect storm.

Did the bookselling world change too quickly for us? Were we not publishing enough of the right books? Had we neglected the Virago Modern Classics? Was our staff too big for our turnover? Did we have premises that stretched our budget? Were we let down by not having our own dedicated sales team, instead depending on Random House to sell our books for us? Did the money required to buy out Rothschilds cut too deep? Were we publishing too many books? Had we been too slow to realize we needed to reinvent our business for new times?

Yes, yes to all of these things.

The upshot was, though our turnover was not at all bad, we weren't making enough profit and once again—for the third time in our history—survival looked precarious. Our resources were limited; we had little or no cushion. We weren't alone: Penguin made many people redundant around this time.

The problem with trouble, obviously, is finding a solution all agree on. When things are going well any cracks can be papered over, but when they are going badly those cracks become deep fissures, and that is what happened with us. As Margaret Atwood says wryly, 'In my experience, the smaller the cheese the fiercer the mice.' Everyone tried hard to find solutions: Ruthie wrote reports; Harriet and I did new projections. We planned to cut back our frontlist from 90 to 70 titles and to prune the backlist. But then in 1994 we took a very tough and terrible decision: we made many people, including Ruthie Petrie and Lynn Knight, redundant. That sentence still makes me feel ill, even all these years later, even though because of their magnanimity, after some bad years, we are on friendly terms again. I still feel the chill of making the decision as to who can stay and who we could no longer afford. We just couldn't sustain the number of editors we had.

Publishing houses and businesses rise and fall all the time but when it's a feminist press everything is called into play—particularly feminism, but also independence.

As the *Independent on Sunday* noted: 'The setback raises questions about the future health of both feminist and independent publishing in a trade increasingly dominated by conglomerate publishers, where many bookshops are tending to follow the American trend to specialise in discounted bestsellers...This hits all publishers, but particularly Virago with its large numbers of existing rather than new titles.'

Authors Ruthie and Lynn had worked with were, of course, furious, and wrote angry letters. Commentators said that we'd outrun our innovative image and couldn't maintain our identity.

I was quoted, saying exactly what I feel now when I look back on this time:

> We are a literary and political publishing house, mainly in paperback; that's not a big money-maker. If you are a literary and a political publisher you have to shift, you have to keep taking the political temperature...at the same time as some things have gone wrong with feminism – it hasn't been the answer to all things as we thought it was; it needs redefining – at the same time, what's going on with the position of women in the world is in some ways worse...

I think we did get too big for our turnover. That was obvious to Bob Gavron, by this point our major shareholder at 40 per cent, and he became part of the team to pull us back into profit and success. I do remember us explaining to him the 80:20 ratio—that most publishing houses were dependent on 20 per cent of their titles carrying the rest—and him saying why couldn't we just publish that 20 per cent? He admired Carmen, who was holding nearly 15 per cent of shares, and as the creator of the Virago Modern Classics, which were an obvious lower-budget target for renewed success, and our flagship. He insisted she come back into the fold for fortnightly meetings. Then we had to get out of our lease at the beautiful old piano factory in Camden Town, where we'd moved after Mandela Street, to hunker down at the top of Random House building near the river on Vauxhall Bridge Road. Random House still owned 10 per cent of us and Gail Rebuck, who had since 1991 been the CEO of Random House, thankfully was happy to help us out.

Happy was not a word any of us would use, even remotely, to describe this time. Carmen, who had left Chatto & Windus just before this, was not at all happy to be pulled back to publishing and to Virago, and to be frank Harriet and I were not wildly happy to have her back either. We had deeply uncomfortable meetings, to which Carmen would come with her new puppy. We had endless strategy talks, putting the Classics to the fore of the list and getting a brand-new design for them. Said Harriet at the time, 'In challenging times you have to focus . . . Carmen is great at making you look hard at what you are doing and prodding you into activity.' The word 'prod' makes me wince at the memory of it. Though I do know that Carmen was trying her best, it was painful for us all and in February 1995 she decided it was too much. Carmen sent us a note saying she was resigning and wanted to sell her shares. Bob asked his wife, Kate Gavron, to be chair of the board. She was also chair of Carcanet, another small press that Bob had invested in, and Tim Waterstone was asked to become a non-executive member, joining Ursula, who was still on the board. There was talk of inviting Alexandra—who had left Hamish Hamilton and was now a literary agent at Toby Eady's—back onto the board, as she was part of our history, even though she had sold her shares by then, and not long after that is what happened.

None of us had the solution, all of us had plenty of opinions, and none of us agreed. It was an awful time. Harriet said she would resign. There was a search for a new CEO and Publisher, which included serious talks with Kate Griffin and with others. I resigned—Ursula and Kate Gavron wanted that. I believe that Carmen did too—until, that is, we decided to sell, at which point, as she says in the Virago documentary, 'I wanted Lennie to have Virago.'

Before any resignations were effected and before Carmen's shares were sold she came to the AGM on 28 September 1995, dressed, maybe deliberately, in pinstriped waistcoat and trousers, and delivered a paper and a devastating but actually sensible ultimatum: we must sell the company.

We agreed.

The media had another lovely time of it: cat-fighting, the death of feminism, Virago had outlived its use, ad nauseam.

Some people saw it for what it was.

Jan Dalley at the *Independent*, whom we knew and who had worked with Carmen at Chatto, wrote: 'Reports of the death of feminism are always warmly received, and at the news that Virago Press is to be sold, the press trumpeted that "sisterhood is too fragile for strong individuals" and "Virago has finally sold out on the feminist dream". Virago's first generation of readers may well feel that something of their youth has also died. It is true that the bidders in the Virago sale—initially thought to be Bloomsbury, Little, Brown and Random House—smack of corporate takeover and faceless suits. But in this case, the suits are more likely to be from Nicole Farhi or Agnès B, for the main players include Liz Calder (of Bloomsbury), Philippa Harrison (of Little, Brown) and Gail Rebuck (of Random House). No sign, though, of the headline that runs: Female moguls battle for women's dream.'

Bob began helping us build a portfolio for our sale. Eventually our buyers were narrowed down to Philippa at Little, Brown and Liz at Bloomsbury: both known to us all and both very close friends of Carmen's. We told one another that what mattered was Virago; we must find a home that would guarantee at least another ten years. We spoke about Virago as if she was her own woman—which, I suppose, she is. We talked about the Virago in the room. We wanted her to stay alive; on that we were as one.

But only on that.

I favoured Little, Brown; I liked Philippa's ideas and energy. I had had talks with her and knew she saw the point of continuity, and I thought Little, Brown could take us further. Bloomsbury, a much-admired British independent, felt to me just a bigger version of us and they were also beholden to City money. Though Little, Brown was owned by Time Warner and an American company was not ideal, they seemed to be operating independently in the UK. I felt we would be an asset to them, adding to their literary list, which at that time was Abacus. I worried what sort of weight we would have and what kind of imprint we would be at Bloomsbury.

The same price was agreed with both bidders. Bob and Kate Gavron would not use their majority vote: 'We'll leave it to the girls to decide,' said Bob, who absented himself. Carmen said she would not choose between her friends and flew to France.

We had a board meeting, which Alexandra attended as by then she had rejoined the board, but as she didn't have a vote she then went back to her offices.

That left Harriet, Ursula, Random House, and me. Harriet and Ursula voted for Bloomsbury; Gail, voting on behalf of

Random House, and I voted for Little, Brown, but our joint 18.4 per cent share vote did not beat Harriet and Ursula's combined 25.7 per cent. Virago was going to be sold to Bloomsbury.

For a moment we sat and digested this news.

Then suddenly Harriet stood and said that it was completely ridiculous that the woman who started this company was not going to vote. She left the room to ring Carmen in France.

A few minutes later she came back into the room, white-faced.

'Carmen votes for Little, Brown.'

We gasped.

We went back into the office, where the staff was waiting, with the unexpected news. All shell-shocked, we went home and got ready for new lives. Five of us—two editorial assistants, a marketing assistant, the Rights Director Gill McNeil, and I—eventually went to Little, Brown. The other four took redundancy; two of them, Melanie Silgardo and Fiona McMorrough, then set up their own companies.

There was much and immediate approval from the book trade, but between us Viragos there was real discord and it was broadcast to the press. Alexandra and I did not speak for over a year, though we are friends again now. I think Carmen and Ursula have exchanged very few words since. Harriet, though disappointed in her vote, was impeccable, before she left, in answering the due diligence queries of Little, Brown, such that to this day the then Finance Director speaks of her with great admiration. There was nothing wrong with our books.

On 2 November 1995 Philippa Harrison announced: 'The Virago list is close to my heart...Little, Brown will provide a home which will both honour Virago's past and bring in a new and different 90s vision...With the extraordinary changes in

the publishing scene in the last decade, Virago needs the help
today that a larger, well-capitalised structure and a really strong
sales and marketing force can offer it.'

We became an imprint of Little, Brown and, contrary to much
press speculation, it was not the end of Virago—or feminism,
for that matter—but the beginning of a new era.

I arrived at Little, Brown in January 1996. Unlike the fresh-
faced thing I was back in 1978 when I first climbed the stairs at
Wardour Street, now I was world weary and wary too as I passed
through the 8-foot-high doors of Brettenham House on Lancaster Place on the north side of Waterloo Bridge. The boardroom
battles that had spilled into the Sunday papers and split the
board over whose bid we would accept had left deep scars.
I knew I wanted to be with Virago, wanted to go on working
with our authors, knew that I loved publishing, but I felt as if
I had been through a long sickness and now needed some good,
constructive, positive air to breathe. Philippa Harrison said she
loved nothing better than to help fix broken things; I know that
is how she saw Virago—and I dare say to some extent, me.
Philippa re-confirmed me as Publisher of Virago. Sarah White
and Tamsyn Berryman returned to their jobs as editorial assistants, and we began to integrate. The other Viragos took jobs
within Little, Brown. I remember saying to Philippa after a few
weeks that coming to Little, Brown was like coming out of a
dark and twisted wood to a little clearing where the sun shone
through the trees. Once again we were talking about books and
not internecine politics. It was such a relief.

I found out later that Philippa had asked people such as Hilary
Hale, the crime editor extraordinaire, to keep an eye on me,
to make me welcome, and indeed I was swept up by her and

Richard Beswick, then Head of Abacus, who easily could have taken against this upstart younger sister imprint but instead welcomed Virago and the strengthening we brought to literary publishing at Little, Brown. They and others took me to lunch and offered friendship and an inside track of how to function in what was, to me, a very large company. The Sales Director, David Kent, set about a deep learning of the list—an invaluable and important task that almost immediately got Virago's backlist performing once again—and Charlie Viney, Export Director, improved our sales abroad. Little, Brown was about ninety people and I was the only full-time senior Virago person from the old team. I could feel from the start that Virago was cherished and there was not going to be any sense of asset stripping or changing the fundamental nature of the press.

But it was very different from being independent. There were so many systems for us to learn: print confirm, low-stock assessment, copy-editing and printing schedules, and new people: cover designers, marketing people, publicists, and all the international staff too. It was head-achingly confusing at times, but I could feel Virago being strengthened and helped—and this was even before we began to add new titles to the lists—with a team who recognized Virago's reputation, and individuals who loved our books and wanted the list to flourish.

There was, however, a need to reassure Virago authors that this was the case.

Letters went out and meetings were convened. I remember particularly one slightly awkward meeting with Philippa, Margaret Atwood and her husband and agent, and me. I remember a long talk I had with Maya Angelou on the phone. There were many such meetings and phone calls with authors and their agents. The message was: Virago was still very much in business. Yes, now an imprint in a large company owned by an American company, yes, that was true, but Virago—now in a new guise with Lennie as Publisher as continuity and a link with the past, and Philippa as passionate fan and Managing Director of Little, Brown—is here to stay.

Margaret Atwood remained loyal to Virago and the following year we published the paperback of *Alias Grace*—which turned out to be her most successful novel until her Booker winner, *The Blind Assassin*. Many more of Maya Angelou's books followed too. To me it seemed we might have the ideal situation: a continuation of idealistic publishing backed by the might of the conglomerate, helped by people who truly believed in Virago. Of course there is nothing guaranteed in such an arrangement; I know that. But I also knew very well that a business, whether financially underpinned by independence, or by a conglomerate, or by a family-owned group, can never be certain of success. I would define success as continuing to publish what we want, by the authors we admire, and selling lots of books, but I also know that publishing is capricious, dependent on markets, reputation, and people.

So many other small independent presses have since sold to Little, Brown or its now-parent Hachette: Piatkus, and then Constable & Robinson, with its Corsair list; Quercus, Bookouture, Rising Stars, and Jessica Kingsley.

Lots of people have helped Virago remain vibrant. Those people—editors such as Sally Abbey, Ursula Doyle, Donna Coonan, Imogen Taylor, Victoria Pepe, Jill Foulston, Ailah Ahmed, and assistant editor David Bamford, and the splendid Virago Publisher Sarah Savitt—and particularly the bosses—Philippa

Harrison first, of course, and later David Young, Ursula Mackenzie, David Shelley, and Charlie King—have supported Virago, as well they might, as we are a good thing commercially. But it's because Virago means something else to them too. Ownership by Time Warner ended, thankfully, when they sold Little, Brown to Hachette in 2006. Things got even better. When I went to my first board meeting with the Hachette CEO, Arnaud Nourry, I introduced myself wondering if he knew that he now presided over a feminist imprint. His eyes lit up and he reached out to shake my hand as he said, in his French accent, 'Ah, you publish the books that matter.'

When we began publishing under the auspices of Little, Brown it was right smack in so-called post-feminism. Suddenly it was all about individual empowerment, not women's rights. And women could look and act exactly as they wanted: this was 'raunch culture', as later coined by the feminist Ariel Levy. The word feminism was not fashionable. Irony ruled.

To work alongside me, holding the reins of the old Virago, the loyalty of the authors, and the knowledge of the list, we needed a younger editor who understood this generation.

Sally Abbey joined us as Senior Commissioning Editor and in 1997 began a new series: Virago Vs, books that were to 'avoid political correctness at all costs'. I must admit, I really wasn't sure about that copy line. However, one of the things that I know about publishing is that you need a range of voices and talents, and that one taste should not dominate publishing choice. A good editor must be given her head. You must trust them. I certainly recognized there was a sea change in how young women viewed feminism, and I loved the style, spirit, and humour of Sally's list. Though I did feel uncomfortable that Virago was appearing to agree that feminism was boringly, dully politically correct, it did mirror the times; many thought feminism was passé.

The Virago Vs reflected bold women's writing and views: Jennifer Belle's fabulous novel *Going Down*; *Tongue First: Adventures in Physical Culture* by Emily Jenkins; *Like Being Killed* by Ellen Miller; and the wonderfully named *In Search of an Impotent Man* by Gaby Hauptmann. The Virago V that outlasted the series, and the one that Sally will, correctly, be most proud of discovering, was Sarah Waters's first novel, the extraordinary, game-changing *Tipping the Velvet*.

Fiction had always been at the core of Virago's publishing—but mainly as Virago Modern Classics. The frontlist fiction, until we came to Little, Brown was not as plentiful. But now we were able to acquire more authors to make us an even better player in fiction publishing: Sarah Waters, Linda Grant, Sarah Dunant, Marilynne Robinson, Rachel Seiffert, and new work by Shirley Hazzard, to join the writers we'd been publishing for years including Gillian Slovo, Michèle Roberts, Nina Bawden, and, of course, Margaret Atwood.

The Virago Modern Classics underwent yet another revamp. We acted on sales reports that said the green spine was old-fashioned and listened to a bookseller who said 'they look like you need to have a university degree' to read them. It was deemed that de-branding would bring in more readers, so we kept the apple logo but took away the green. Twenty-two years later, readers were utterly thrilled to see that as part of the Virago Modern Classics fortieth-anniversary celebrations Donna Coonan ushered in those green spines once again.

It didn't take us long to get Virago back on her feet, but there is no gainsaying it: we have this in our story—a failure to stay independent, again, and to keep all our staff. This I have felt keenly, even though as I write this history I can see, more clearly, how many factors beyond us were in play and what we were up against in the publishing, bookselling, and political landscape. It wasn't the first time we'd left independence for the security of a larger company, but this one feels personal to me.

I don't regret our management buy-out for a moment and I am sure the others don't either. In my view it's hard, if not almost impossible, to grow an activist press within a corporate publishing house because the aims are just not the same. The activist press, while of course wanting to make a profit in order to survive, does not put profit as the almighty first. It takes time to grow and it will take decisions that are not always based on making money. Sometimes, of course, so do large publishing houses, but not so often. Our management buy-out years gave us time to grow and become an even stronger name to reckon with; it was good to have tried independence again, even if we couldn't maintain it for a long time. But we picked ourselves up; we very much leaned on others who cherished us; we did some re-inventing. Donna Coonan has been able to work full-time on the Classics, adding a dramatic number of important novels to the list; the larger company gave us national and international might, we had some great bestsellers and I learned how to negotiate the way for a feminist press inside a large company.

Then, as the world turns—feminism came round again.

That's the bigger picture. How one deals with the lows on a personal level is slightly different. It took me a long time to take pride in the Virago that I and so many others at Virago and Little, Brown have built. Blame, from self or others, is not especially helpful when it comes to getting down to finding solutions, but it is natural, particularly around something as precious—and precarious—as a feminist press. We blamed and were blamed—by each other and by the media. We had to fend off the idea that Virago having a downturn meant the end of women's enterprises and point out again and again that women not agreeing over something we cared deeply about was natural. In the midst of all this noise and bitterness and disloyalty, I am not sure we ever acknowledged the idea that trouble or even failure in business is far more normal than success. We felt we must carry the mantle of feminism and women in business, and because our earlier success was so glorious there was just so much at stake.

All successful business people talk about having failed in some ways and begun again. Did we think because we were feminists that option wasn't open to us?

Turns out, it was.

Eight years later, in May 2003, we marked our thirtieth birthday with a glorious celebration at the Chelsea Physic Garden. Gratifyingly all the old Viragos—every one of them—came to the party: Carmen, Ursula, Harriet, Alexandra, Ruthie, Lynn, Kate among so many others, including the sadly now late Becky Swift, were there, alongside the people—Philippa Harrison, David Young, Ursula Mackenzie—who had helped get us back on the road. And, of course, our authors and agents.

Mark Bostridge, biographer of Vera Brittain, interviewed me for the *Independent on Sunday* under the headline 'The Apple Bites Back'. He characterized me as having 'survived a mauling' but he also told of our success: doubling our turnover to £4 million with 600 titles in print and, pleasingly for me, spoke of my passion for editing: 'Talk to any of her authors, and one quickly gains an impression of a kind of individual who's all too rare in modern publishing: the committed editor.'

That evening I was hopeful but anxious. Though people moved around the party with some wariness, there they all were. The wonderful Sandi Toksvig, who is now a Virago author, raised our spirits (I had asked her to speak because I knew it was going to be important to laugh) and then she and Margaret Atwood lit the candle on the cake. I looked out into the audience of old and new Viragos and breathed a great sigh of relief.

Margaret took the mic, and with one of her sly grins recited her poem for us:

> Back then, to Soho's seedier nooks,
> Came a band of lasses keen on books.
> They stormed the land of spangles and garters,
> One room on Wardour Street, they hired for starters.
> Up dimly lit stairways they bravely groped
> While men in mackintoshes leered and hoped.
> They had leather satchels and sensible shoesies,
> Though some mistook them for upmarket floozies.
> And though there *was* the odd bit of fighting
> They took on the task of—women's writing!
> (A notion THEN some set great store on
> Was that women's writing was an oxymoron)
> But though doubters pointed and quipped and jeered,
> They rolled up their sleeves and persevered.
> Their revenues were often less than slender,
> But on writers they lavished care so tender.
> And readers too were deeply grateful
> For Virago's high-heaped female plateful.

Though their first author tours were do-it-yourself trips,
Soon they were into dumpbins and shelf strips.
They stopped re-boiling the coffee grounds,
And they grew by leaps and they grew by bounds.
Tonight we've put on our shirts and dresses
To toast Virago's many successes
So raise a glass to the half-gnawed fruit
Of knowledge and clap and stamp and hoot.
And cheer an appropriately rowdy cheer
Hooray for Virago's thirtieth year!

### PART FOUR

# The Power to Publish is a Wonderful Thing

## CHAPTER ELEVEN

# The Intimacy of Editing

The first adult book I edited was Michèle Roberts's novel *Daughters of the House*. I took advice from my fellow editors, 'followed my gut' and trusted this already most accomplished author. The novel got outstanding reviews and was shortlisted for the 1992 Booker Prize. I was nearing the end of my sixteen-week maternity leave (which is what we got in those days) for my second child, Zak, when I heard the news that Michèle had made the shortlist. I stood in a call box, as we were in Suffolk with no land line, and whooped with delight.

A few weeks later, now back at work, I struggled to find something glamorous to dress my post-baby body in. On the evening of the Booker dinner I rushed home from the office to breast-feed my son, stuffed breast pads into my already too-tight gown and dashed to the ceremony. Halfway through, I could feel I was leaking everywhere. Sadly we didn't win—that year, for the first time in history, the prize was split between two authors, Michael Ondaatje and Barry Unsworth. But we were there, and *Daughters of the House* went on to win the prestigious WH Smith Literary Award, which had previously gone to the likes of Laurie Lee, Jean Rhys, Philip Larkin, Seamus Heaney, and Doris Lessing. Sir Simon Hornby, the chairman of WH Smith Group, wrote in their brochure, 'It's a particular pleasure to honour this author . . . I am delighted that by selecting Michèle Roberts they [judges Philip Ziegler, Hermione Lee, and John Carey] have, at the same time, enabled us to give due recognition to Virago Press, which has contributed so much to British publishing over the past two decades.'

Oh, I thought, through leaky breasts and the tussles of returning to work as the mother of two small children, this editing lark is not so hard. Ha! I quickly learned it was not at all that simple.

To be honest, *Daughters of the House* didn't need much editing: some clarity, signposting, and, in places, a bit more 'air' around Michèle's exquisite sentences to let them breathe. Her creation was beautifully mysterious, and purposely opaque in places. I listened to her as much as she did to me: I was a rookie, while she had already published several novels. And I was hooked.

To be a midwife—as I like to think of editors—to be at the birth of a creation, can be amazing. Writing—and therefore editing— is tough, close work, exhausting and sometimes bloody, but helping an author as she forges words, ideas, and characters into a shape and then watching as it alchemizes into life: for me, that is a hard-won, deep pleasure.

There are two aspects of my career that I feel strongly about. The first is the privilege and challenge of being part of a group of women who have created Virago and kept it a vigorous and vibrant imprint; the second is trying to provide authors with an editing and publishing experience of good calibre. Of course, if only that would always happen! I know I fall short at times.

What is editing? It's sitting up at the table to read, paying close attention to every line and word, pencil in hand to mark the places where one is bored or confused or excited and engaged. It's being preternaturally alert to one's responses to the text.

A publisher recently reminded me that when she was a young editor I said, to reassure her, 'Editing is just reading with your eyes wide open.' I laughed. After more than two decades of editing, I still think that. It's being alive to the author's intentions and trusting one's instinct. It's imaginative and emotional immersion in the text, and it's being present for the long haul, ready and willing to read a manuscript many, many times.

Editing is an intimate experience. Writing—of fiction or non-fiction—is exposing. Writing tells the reader what the author thinks about, what the author feels, what the author sees, what the author hears, and what the author imagines. Writing also shows the author's talent, facility, and dexterity with words. Writing well, with clarity, is a technical challenge; writing with an originality that surprises and delights the reader, writing that shows something new, that makes words paint a picture— that is a great art. Even the attempt to reach those heights is revealing of the author's self.

Publishing rests on the shoulders of people who sit alone, hunched over their keyboards, faced with a blank page, often cursed by a gloomy and dismissive voice in their ear. To be honest, I don't think most people even in the trade really, truly comprehend that. When at Virago we invite authors in to the office to celebrate a prize or a bestseller, I am always amused to see the visible representation of publishing, of how many people it takes to publish a book: the editor, the literary agent, the copy-editor, the proof-reader, the jacket designer, the production controller, the print-run manager, the rights manager, the contracts manager, the royalties manager, the publicist, the marketer, the sales team (home, export, wholesalers), the warehouse people, the van drivers—not to forget the Managing

Director and the Finance Director—and then, once the book leaves us, the librarians and the booksellers.

But the book is drawn from the mind of one. However much discussion goes on between author and editor, the idea, the manifestation, the final book is the author's. One person to create the book and a crowd of us to publish it: all our jobs depend on the author's. An odd balance. Of course, the author needs us, the publisher, but we can always be replaced with another set of publishing people. The author is unique.

To be one of the first to read what another human being writes from their private self is a privilege and a job that I take seriously. It is an intense relationship, which is why I use the word intimacy in the chapter title; and it's one that requires trust. There are many editors in the world and I cannot speak for them, but for me the editor's first job is to understand the author's vision—to get inside their head—as only then will the author trust and believe the editor is on their side and meaningful collaboration can take place. I remember, with great pleasure, editing the psychotherapist Susie Orbach's essays. She said what she liked about our work together was that I was able 'to get into the writers' mind'. At times, the link between therapy and editing is similar: the job of the editor, like the therapist, is to get the author to fully imagine and then get to their goal—and at intense times editor and author do probably see or speak to each other once a week.

Toni Morrison said of editing that 'within the relationship if there is some trust, some willingness to listen, remarkable things can happen'.

The ego belongs with the writer—I believe that and have been wary of the editor with the ego. The job as editor is to shepherd, to cajole, to inspire even—but it is a backroom job. And yet ... and yet I have also come to believe that an editor can be the catalyst for the alchemy in a writer's mind. The editor has to have the talent, the capacity, the optimism to read through the flaws, the confusions, the wrong turnings, to make that leap of imagination, particularly in fiction: to believe that these thousands of words of made-up people and this story created out of nothing will make a great book. Like the author, you too have to have hope.

Says Linda Grant: 'There's a point where the novel, unwritten, exists inside you, whole, a kind of shimmering tangible thing which only requires you to transcribe it.' The editor has to treasure that shimmering idea with respect; it would be easy to destroy it before it solidifies on the page. The editor has to reach as high as the author, possibly higher!

In editing both fiction and non-fiction I first want to praise the great things and to be able to find the words that can take the author further—as most everyone improves with rewrites and drafts and edits. Rare is the person who writes without that. Many authors are experienced and robust, and expect careful, thoughtful editing, but in my experience the best creativity comes from a feeling of confidence. It's an editor's job to keep that confidence uppermost, even while rigorously editing, even while doubts are haunting the project—*especially* while doubts are haunting it.

An author said recently to me, 'I can't write with uncertainty.' I respect that. The editor needs to keep faith for them both. The editor needs to hold the author, to let them know they have their back—but also to let them know that they will be pushed to their limit to create their best. Like a sports coach, I suppose.

Margaret Atwood takes the sport analogy seriously. She has a team. Though she has hundreds of publishers around the world, her close-knit group of English language editors, in her native Canada, in America, and in Britain, are 'her people'. She had often called on them all to comment on the near-final drafts of her novels, and in January 2008 she called upon them all again. As her UK paperback publisher, I went along. Margaret wanted our opinion—as a group—on *Maddadam*, the third and final instalment in her dystopian trilogy that began with *Oryx and Crake*.

The early part of her manuscript was sent to us in the days leading up to the meeting and then those of us not in Canada flew to Toronto to meet the Canadians, particularly Ellen Seligman, who had been Margaret's editor at McClelland & Stewart for two decades. Vivienne Schuster, her then agent, and I feverishly read the section we'd been sent just before our flight. Once in Toronto we taxied through the freezing streets to the Park Plaza Hotel and found the others. We would see Margaret herself the next day. We were six—editors and agents—and though we all knew each other, were all experienced editors, and had long worked with her, the feeling of needing to step up, to be good enough, made us all laugh nervously. Of course it was Margaret and her manuscript that were under (willing) scrutiny. But even so . . . we editors had that sense of taking an exam. Never mind being perceptive and articulate—could we read fast enough? 'I'm a slow reader,' came from many of us. 'I'm jet-lagged,' from both Viv and me.

Margaret's then US agent, the wonderfully named Phoebe Larmore, dressed in her usual swathes of mauve, gathered us around a table and with Vivienne gave us each a package containing the entire and now completed manuscript in a box, tied with a ribbon. Each was a different colour: mine was a limey green edged in cream. We were also given a very Atwood-humoured endurance goody bag: aspirins, throat lozenges, chocolate, bottled water, and energy bars. We planned when we were to meet again, and then, as if a starting gun had been fired, we rose and dashed to our rooms, and fell into the pages of a dark and witty world. I was immediately reminded of my cover copy for the first of the trilogy: 'Pigs might not fly but they are strangely altered . . . Welcome to the outrageous imagination of Margaret Atwood', and I was there again. Bliss.

We met later—most of us having read it all—and talked about our feelings and suggestions over supper. Such an impressive, exciting talent has Margaret—I think of that enormous brain—that, as usual, she had pushed out the boundaries with tremendous originality and with terror too. We found ourselves, to our relief, in agreement on suggested edits. We passed our sense of fellow-editor test, or maybe that was comradeship fostered by the wine and jet-lag. It felt good.

The next day we gathered in a suite and rearranged the furniture. The American hardback editor, Nan Talese, could not make the meeting so she was dialled up on speakerphone and placed on a footstool in the centre of the group. Margaret arrived, pink-cheeked from her walk, with a large smile for us all, and sat down. Phoebe felt it would be good to acknowledge the auspiciousness of the event with the lighting of a candle. We nodded and the activity was explained to Nan on the footstool. The candle was lit: immediately the smoke detectors screamed and the fire alarm was set off, and a few minutes later we watched from the windows as fire engines pulled up outside the hotel. Who else could write a book that would bring the fire department running?

Then we focused. We had our notes, and we spoke and Margaret listened, sagely asked questions, nodded, asked more questions, took notes, and pushed for answers. We discussed the title.

After, through snowy streets, for which only Margaret was properly dressed, we went to her house for the supper her partner Graeme had prepared for us all. Ellen Seligman loaned me a scarf as she could see I was cold. 'I always bring extra clothes when I visit here,' she said, nodding at the energy-conscious Margaret. 'They never keep their heat very high.' Because it had all gone well, or maybe just because it was an extraordinary collection of women (and Graeme), we had a splendid time. I think Margaret got what she wanted. I admire her for asking for that openness and level of scrutiny: she asked for honesty and we gave it. Never before or since have I been in anything of its like. A seminar, perhaps—but with the author of the book in question leading the discussion. (Extraordinary!)

An editor is only any good to an author if they are honest, but an editor can find positive ways of pushing, positive ways of showing what *is* working, positive ways of indicating when a writer is heading in a direction that makes the writing lift off the page. Honesty, absolutely, always; but framed in a way that suggests a solution. As Maya Angelou said, 'When someone feels they must tell you the brutal truth usually all you remember is the brutality.' Though a challenge can be productive, as proved by the way Maya Angelou's editor got her to agree to write her memoir.

Sarah Dunant and I have had a long, productive relationship, one that I think both of us would cheerfully characterize as being creatively challenging: we have always really enjoyed an intense and sparky, even abrasive, time together. We'd worked together for years when she began her first Italian Renaissance novel. She decided that she would narrate the story in the voice of a fifteen-year-old girl, but I worried the girl was just too young, too well born, and too secluded to give the novel the scope it needed. Sarah insisted it could be done. Fittingly, we were in an Italian restaurant; we'd finished eating and were still discussing this point long and hard. There was nothing left on the white tablecloth and the restaurant had almost emptied out when I finally said 'Okay then, prove it!' Chin up, smiling, she said, 'I will.'

The outstanding, moving—and bestselling—*The Birth of Venus* was the glorious result and the beginning of Sarah's new career as a historical novelist.

How tough one can be with a writer of course depends on the author, but also on the relationship. If the author thinks an editor doesn't understand their vison then the discussions get mired in defensiveness. Certainly, the editor is not always right about why a book is not working, and frank observations produce results only if there is trust between author and editor. Even then it's a risk.

Sarah reminds me that after she'd more than won me over with her protagonist I had a final question: 'What did they eat during the Italian Renaissance?' She gave me a long, colourful reply about food. I pointed out that the book covers six years and no one has a meal. There was a dreadful pause and then we laughed, and what great banquets she wrote as a result.

Sarah has taught me how to tease out what is in the author's mind but not yet on the page and, crucially, how to balance ownership of the text with an author. It must be respectful but it must also be a partnership because publishing only works if the editor is as committed to the book as the author.

Though not every author wants an editor's views. One of our Virago editors once asked an author into the office to discuss her manuscript, which she had printed out and carefully annotated with pencilled suggestions and edits. The author looked at it, then took the entire pile of paper, walked to the open window, tossed it all out into the street, and left.

I once suggested to Nina Bawden, who wrote splendid, taut novels about what goes on behind the façade of happy families, some small edits that she agreed with, and then that I thought one strand of her story could be expanded just a bit. She listened quietly and then said the finished novel was like a wall; if she took out one brick the whole thing would fall down.

So, no. Sometimes the dialogue is drawn to a close.

Sarah Waters, like Margaret Atwood and Sarah Dunant, has more than one reader and editor. She listens carefully and notes when things need fixing. But when I suggest something that doesn't quite chime with her, she says, 'Mmm, maybe,' and I know that's a polite no.

An editor must draw observations and comments from the text. The editing suggestions and conundrum-solving ideas only ring true to an author when they can feel they are organic to the book. When that happens it's almost like hitting 'tilt' at the machines: you can see the author light up and the penny dropping all the way. So rewarding.

What I have found takes the most courage is to send an author back 'just one more time'. Many will have written maybe four, five, or six drafts and often taken several years. When an author is at that point they are understandably very tired and even blind to the text. But sometimes there are just a few final tweaks, nuances, shades of meaning that could put the final gloss on the book. I hold my breath and send that email.

Linda Grant and I had been editing a novel together very happily over several months, and when we were nearly finished—in fact Linda thought we were—I suggested just one more thing and immediately got an email in return: 'ENOUGH!'

The book goes out into the world with only the author's name. And if they want to include something I don't agree with, I will tell them but I will respect their decision. It's their book. And no editor forgets that the history of publishing is littered with editors who got it wrong. Think how many editors turned down *Harry Potter*.

So when Linda said 'ENOUGH!' I backed down. She was right. Though I think—or choose to believe—it was a compliment to be thanked in her acknowledgments for being 'relentless' . . .

Joan Bakewell, the redoubtable journalist and now life peer, decided in her late seventies that she wanted to write a novel, and put her very capable mind to that pursuit. When she came into the office to talk through the suggested edits, she revealed herself to be a swot. She would thank us and then happily depart with the marked-up manuscript, which she laughingly referred to as her 'homework'.

Writing novels is like solving a puzzle you've set yourself—then knowing what to withhold from the reader to build drama, working out what to do with your characters, how to describe the scenes that convince the reader. One of the most pleasurable aspects of working with great fiction writers is watching their characters come alive, becoming tangible, human; what

Toni Morrison calls moving 'from the curl all of the way to a full-fledged person'. I know they haunt writers as they create them, but while we are working together I find they inhabit me too. Sarah Waters and I once sat in a café for hours discussing Duncan in *The Night Watch*, who was in prison. If anyone had listened in they would have heard us talking about why he would behave that way, what was in his background that would make him think the way he does, why couldn't he see what others could, that he was being naive, not watching his back, and was going to get into trouble. They would have thought we were talking about a real man. And by this time in the writing and the editing we were.

And that is why readers believe that too. Readers also find that the characters inhabit them—sometimes for life—because we are in their very lives and minds and secrets. I have always loved the writer James Baldwin's quote about *I Know Why the Caged Bird Sings* because in praising his friend's memoir he shows us how he understands the power of well-drawn characters: 'I know that not since the days of my childhood, when people in books were more real than people one saw every day, have I found myself so moved.'

To help an author write their life story is another thing again—or actually, maybe not. Writers who create remarkable memoirs are in some ways not far from being a novelist: just like fiction, it has to have main characters, a narrative arc, drama and tension, and resolution. In so many ways, if they are good, memoirs are really not at all truly like life. That is not to say they are not truthful and authentic and real. That, of course, is at the core of autobiography: they must be genuine. But they are, of necessity, an edited life, and editing means leaving people and things out, possibly truncating episodes, and not telling *every* truth. I am with Oscar Wilde on this: life imitates art more than art imitates life. It's not the job of a memoir, or indeed art, to record each and every fact, but instead, like fiction, to make a shape of a life. But even if making a shape has a certain unreality compared to an exact record of what happened, it doesn't follow, as he says, that lying 'is the proper aim of art'.

To me, what *must* be at the heart of memoir is emotional truth. The facts can be changed, names can be disguised, people written out, and timelines altered: sometimes all of these things must happen to protect the innocent, but the heart must be honest.

But there is honesty—and then there is ruthlessness. Nina Bawden wrote, only slightly tongue-in-cheek, about writers, 'They make use of their own tragedies to make a better story. They batten on their relations. They are terrible people. They "put people in books"...Writers are not to be trusted.'

Novelists, like memoirists, plunder their own experiences as well as those of their friends and family, but at least in fiction the truth is veiled, however thinly. I have had a few memoirists who have written unnecessary, casually cruel things about their family, until phrases are pointed out to them and changes have been made. Where it is more interesting, though, is when an author tells things that reveal more about themselves than they are aware of, and in some cases are far from flattering. My job as editor is to highlight this, to tell them how they are coming across to the reader. When I edited Rosie Thomas's spirited and exciting *Border Crossing*, the story of a vintage car rally from Beijing to Paris, I felt obliged to say that at certain points she was showing herself to be a bit disagreeable. I had no problem with that, but I wanted to make sure she was happy with her own portrayal. Oh yes, she knew exactly what she was doing, and so we went to print as it was. I admired that.

Lyndall Gordon's approach to biography taught me something important about editing autobiography and memoir. When she embarks on a subject she works hard first to find out what that person thought about the narrative of their own life, and only once she has surmised what that was can she write their story. For example, Mary Wollstonecraft, she believed, saw herself as a woman who could reinvent herself: from being victim of a brutal father to finding the brief relief of being a governess, to working with a benevolent editor and writing *A Vindication of the Rights of Woman*, to being a revolutionary in France. Even when her despair after the infidelity of the man she loved caused her to try to drown herself in the Thames, even then, once she recovered, she reinvented herself as campaigner, speaking up for the rights of women. Says Lyndall, 'I wanted to counter the image of her as veering and wanton. I learned that she saw herself as entirely devoted and serious.' And it is that Mary Wollstonecraft who is revealed in Lyndall's biography.

I found this idea that there was a narrative thread running through most people's lives, and, importantly, one they were conscious of, most helpful in helping a memoirist draw together the strands that made up their own life. The journalist Katharine Whitehorn was struggling with her autobiography, *Selective Memory*, and so I asked her to think about how she viewed her life; what was the aspect that joined it all up? Together we worked out that she felt that good luck was the keynote of her life: luck had always come her way. And even though this view doesn't account for her obvious talent, that sense of the wonder and pleasure of always being in the right place at the right time was a great revelation. It gave us the organizing principle of the book and the backbone of the story.

I feel it is the job of the editor to protect the writer, to be their harshest reader, and to speak honestly to them. Once they have that information it is up to them what they do with it.

Lyndall Gordon decided to write a book about the original-ity and poetic spirit that her mother managed to keep alive in a small-minded, provincial place in South Africa of the 1940s and 50s—a spirit that influenced her daughter to become a most exciting and intuitive biographer. It became obvious to us both that Lyndall, who had previously understood her role in her mother's life as a willing helper and 'sister', was uncovering a pain-ful divide as their lives and dreams diverged. It was a moment of intense collaboration as then bravely, honestly, Lyndall changed tack and pursued this new realization. We're both very proud of her *Divided Lives*.

It's not entirely unusual to find that there is something unwrit-ten, unspoken, something about the story that doesn't make sense, doesn't add up. Until we both have found that piece of the puzzle, there is something hollow, something ringing falsely in the book. I would hope to have built up enough trust with the author that they can tell me the thing—usually about a fam-ily member or friend—that they don't want to share with their readers. One debut author was giving an ex-boyfriend quite a bit of space in her memoir. I thought he was standing in for things she didn't want to talk openly about, but I also felt that because their break-up was still fresh her perspective wasn't as clear as it would be even a few months later when we published the book and she might be sorry he was given so much air time. She laughed and agreed.

It's only once we have the truth that together we can work out how to show it.

Sometimes distance and time mean that an author is very ready to distil a difficult relationship, to see beyond its immediacy and portray the complications in a more rounded way. Sally Phipps has a very clear-eyed view of her novelist mother, Molly Keane, and of her mother's view of her and her sister too. On her deathbed Molly had suggested that Sally write a biography of her: a gift and a burden that Sally had taken to heart. She had been writing her mother's life for well over ten years when it came to me in its near-to-finished state. Sally was by this time in her late sixties and not a typist, not a computer user, and without email. I decided after one short meeting in London and several phone calls that the only way to finish the edit was to go to her in County Cork in Ireland. She suggested we edit at the extraordinary Ballymaloe House Hotel, and we drove there from the airport. From the boot of the car Sally retrieved a deep wicker basket in which sat her manuscript. 'Doesn't everyone carry things like this?' In we went and sat together for two straight days, reading, often out loud, every line of the more than 100,000-word book alongside my suggested edits and with references to a small notebook in which Sally had made notes on her original manuscript. The staff—who loved Sally and had known Molly—gave us the conservatory to work in, and as we studied the book together a storm blew up around us; first snow covered the grass and the windows and then torrential rain pounded down, creating a tumultuous roiling in the river running past the hotel, which overflowed its banks. The helpful staff brought out many little heaters, which they banked in a circle around us, and on we went into the evening and through the storm, finally stopping for the famous Ballymaloe supper. A quick sleep and we resumed, after which Sally took me back through the now deeply flooded roads to her stone cottage, where I sat in my coat as she made me soup; we warmed ourselves in front of an open peat fire. I love Sally and am a big fan of her mother, but I hadn't quite expected to experience so literally the temperature of the houses in which Molly had grown up. I went back to my warm London house, with the full manuscript of the splendid *Molly Keane* ready for the typesetters, though not in a basket!

When, to my great surprise, I won Editor of the Year at the 2010 British Book Awards, Susie Boyt gave me a celebratory supper at her house and surrounded me with a tableful of my authors. It was so marvellous, and embarrassing, but actually a little discombobulating too. When I am editing or publishing a writer it's intense and as if they are my only author. And now there they all were together!

Susie Boyt's courageous and wildly original memoir, *My Judy Garland Life*, taught me how an author can give of herself whole-heartedly and yet also keep her soul intact. Bold and beautiful, it tells of the hero worship of a woman who, for Susie, 'seemed to miraculously transform the harsher truths of life into something wonderful, where all feelings however dark are good and true because they're *yours*'. This the young Susie took as encouragement to 'bypass all the indignity of the strong feelings I was grappling with'. Brilliant memoir like this is a tricky, fascinating, brave balance of total honesty but not honesty in total—that is, not telling absolutely everything. Susie wisely kept much back.

It's important to know how to protect and take care of yourself as an author. I watch authors carefully for that tipping point.

I learned this in the early 1980s, when we published the iconic American writer Tillie Olsen, author of the fiction *Tell Me a Riddle* and *Yonnondio*, and the non-fiction *Silences*, an original work about women and writing. Tillie came to London. Startlingly, she wanted to read out loud to an audience the entire text of *Tell Me a Riddle*, which though short was still a test of some hours' endurance. I arranged it in the upstairs room of a pub in Hampstead, and with our hearts in our mouths we waited—and then watched as the room filled to overflowing with adoring fans. It was a moving evening and a great success, and at the end Tillie gave more and more of herself, listening, talking, crying with her readers. It was the same as we went around other events in London; people asked and she gave and gave. I saw that it was what sustained her but it looked like giving away yourself, dissipating your courage even. Though lucky people who received it . . .

The editor is sometimes regarded as the gatekeeper, the means to publication: the one who can say yes, let's acquire this book, and then later, after editing, let's go to print, so it sometimes seems that they have the upper hand in the relationship. But that is not true. An author–editor relationship is a balancing act: the question of where the power lies changes all the time. Though a good relationship is held together with mutual respect and admiration, neither side will forget that the relationship is underpinned by a contract. It's certainly not all about money, but it *is* about money. And either side of that contractual relationship can decide that it is no longer working; perhaps the author wants a new publishing house and that will be a good career move for them; perhaps the editor senses the sort of book the author is writing is no longer popular with readers.

Either side can sever the ties. And that is usually painful—for both sides.

I publish many of Emma Donoghue's books, including *Slammerkin*, which I loved. For various complicated but entirely valid reasons understood and agreed by Emma and me and her agent, when the manuscript of *Room* was finished it was sent to many editors and I had to compete for it with other publishers. I knew immediately it was an astonishing novel, about a young woman and her child held hostage for years in a small room by a brutal man. But what made this book so touching, brave, and special was that Emma chose to tell it as a love story between a mother and her son. I felt it would be a breakout book for her. I didn't predict a Booker shortlist and a movie, but I knew it would succeed and I desperately wanted to publish it. I offered a large advance but Picador offered more and I lost it. Emma's agent rang me on my mobile to tell me the bad news just as I was walking up to my front door. I felt the blow of disappointment so keenly that I actually shed tears. I stood in my front garden sniffing, saying to myself, 'It's only a book, it's only a book, it's only a book.' But it didn't feel like that. When you invest your whole life in the written word it's never *only* a book. I felt sadness at the loss of a future relationship with Emma but glad that we thankfully still have her on our backlist.

So editing is about a relationship that is intense and intimate, based on a financial transaction. Another curious balance.

I learned this deep respect for authors from Carmen and from Ursula. Even though their loyalty lay with Virago, both had a tremendous affinity with their authors. Both were willing to take chances on new writers, and I don't recall a time when contracts got cancelled because the writer failed to deliver their manuscript on time—which does happen in publishing houses. In fact when Angela Carter was struggling to write *The Sadeian Woman*, Carmen continually encouraged her but was also highly aware that her £1,000 advance meant that Angela couldn't afford to devote her life to the project. It was published in 1979, many years after the initial contract.

And it was Carmen's sensitivity to her authors that led her to rage at Chatto when she couldn't get the same money for an Angela Carter novel as Salman Rushdie, Graham Swift, and Fay Weldon were commanding.

Here, of course, is the uncomfortable rub: money and the value of creativity. A publishing house takes a gamble on a writer and a project, paying money up front on the promise of either a proposal or a finished manuscript, that the book will be good, will find a market, and will earn that advance and more. But it is so very far from a pure numbers calculation: everything is in the mix—competition, loyalty, fashion, balance of power—as well as the written word. It's at this stage of publishing that commerce and the need for profit butt up hard against creativity and the author's worth. And then 'the deal' becomes the focus. Who gets the best out of it? The author or the publisher? Obviously, the perfect deal is one where both parties finish happily, feeling they both got their fair dues. This *is* where the ideal does meet business squarely, but it is not quite as frequent as one would like.

Once on the other side of the agreement, the editor–author conversations begin. Partly because of the sense of intimacy, partly because the author and editor—along with the agent—now feel like a team up against the world, a relationship begins. It has all the intensity of any deep relationship, plus the fact that the editor is now the advocate of the book—doing battle, as it were, on behalf of the author. It is like falling in love.

I adored the late Irish novelist and poetry evangelist Josephine Hart. What I witnessed in Josephine was the courage to respond to the written word emotionally and honestly. Even though I met her well on in my career, I learned much from her: she reminded me of the danger of cynicism and irony, of protecting yourself from truth and beauty. In her book *Catching Life by the Throat: How to Read Poetry and Why* she wrote, 'Poetry has never let me down . . . I was a word child in a country of word children where life was language before it was anything else. Poets were not only heroes, they were indeed the gods of language.' She had a passionate, elemental relationship with art and her novels show that she was not afraid of big, unruly, raw—ferocious even—feelings. She knew that is what literature is for.

She thrilled to our proposed Virago Modern Classics cover for *Damage*, which showed a beautiful thorny scarlet rose, and sent me two dozen long-stemmed red roses with a line from the poet Marianne Moore, 'Your thorns are the best part of you.'

We editors are here to serve the writers, first and foremost—and I firmly believe that—but I also know that there is creativity and even savageness and sharp edges in the act of editing and publishing. A few thorns are a good thing.

# Does Any Other Successful Publisher Get Asked Constantly if They are Still Necessary?

In 2017 I stepped back to become Chair and happily made Sarah Savitt, a brilliant woman who I knew was going to bring new ideas, strategies, and fun, Virago Publisher. I said, laughing somewhat ruefully, 'I promise I am going to allow myself to say this just once, but speaking as someone who slogged through the post-feminist era, it has to be said this is a great time to be Publisher at Virago!' She had the grace to laugh too.

And we both know it *is* a great time. At last publishers are reaching out to find and publish books by marginalized voices; publishing houses are taking real steps to try to change their almost all white, middle-class staff; there is proper gender pay gap analysis; conversations around gender norms and definitions are being opened up even further, with transgender and non-binary experiences being explored and celebrated; the necessity of intersectionality is acknowledged. One result is that feminism—in the media and in books—is suddenly saleable.

I am not especially sanguine about regarding feminism as a trend rather than a political movement but I recognize the way fashions influence book-buying, and of course Virago benefits hugely. What does make me anxious about trending is not only that much released in the name of feminism is really very thin bandwagon publishing, but, more importantly, seeing feminism this way implies that it is merely the current fashion—until the next thing comes along.

It looks like the feminism of the current generation—trendy or otherwise—is not going to go away and the strides we are making now will not be negated. I think that's true and maybe we are really at the tipping point. But didn't we also think that was true in the 1970s and 80s? And then we hit the 90s and found out that political movements can retreat and reform as well as advance.

Virago had ridden the crest of the Women's Liberation Movement of the 1970s and enjoyed fame as one of the leading feminist publishers of the 1980s. The changes in feminism towards the end of the 1980s and in the early 90s showed increasing diversity or, if one looked at it another way, fragmentation.

In the 1980s feminist concerns were wide-ranging: Andrea Dworkin's important argument about pornography; Gloria Steinem's *Outrageous Acts and Everyday Rebellions*; Judith Butler's discussion of socially constructed gender and essentialism; lesbian poetry and politics; a close study of sexism and language; and particularly from women of colour, the insistence of intersectionality, as defined by Kimberlé Crenshaw in 1989.

As usual at Virago, we were doing many things in the 1980s: reclaiming female literary history with the Virago Modern Classics; launching new fiction writers; recording the lives of women—famous, infamous, and unknown; and reflecting some of the feminist concerns of the time. It was the decade in which we kept the faith with American feminists Kate Millett and Adrienne Rich, and British feminists Lynne Segal and Beatrix Campbell.

When I look at our catalogue for just six months of 1987 I am amazed by our ambition: we launched the Virago Upstarts; published *The Handmaid's Tale* and a women's travel guide; re-launched the famous Swiss psychoanalyst Alice Miller with a revised version of *The Drama of Being a Child*; continued our Virago Pioneers; and published more Virago poetry, more Virago Travellers, and Virago Non-fiction Classics—and twenty-four Virago Modern Classic novels. We had seventeen members of staff, but all the same . . .

And we completed our management buy-out in July of that year.

We also began exploring and reimagining the crime genre with writers such as Amanda Cross (pseudonym of the feminist writer Carolyn Heilbrun). The Women's Press was making a real success of feminist science fiction. Feminist novelists were pushing the boundaries.

Meanwhile, feminist polemic continued to roar from the United States. Britain has often looked to America to the feminist writers who write in commandingly confident prose: proffering new theses in popular ways and unabashedly wearing the line that first was emblazoned on Marilyn French's novel *The Women's Room*: 'This book will change your life.'

In 1990, in my new job as Publisher, an extraordinary manuscript landed on my desk—it was by a young American woman who I remembered had been an intern at Virago a few years before. Over the years we had many extremely good interns, and at one point we'd had an arrangement with Oxford University

to offer some of their Rhodes scholars a few months with
Virago. One clever young student stood out: she was quick and
so very helpful in editorial, and especially good at blurb-writing.
She had a broad smile and tremendously willing nature, and
whenever there was a pause in the work she wanted to talk
about feminism and beauty. She was determined, blessed with
confidence and good looks; she was talented and there was no
doubt she would go far.

That manuscript was *The Beauty Myth: How Images of Beauty
are Used Against Women* and the debut author was Naomi Wolf.
I bid for it immediately—only to be outbid by one Carmen
Callil at Chatto! Of course Carmen herself would see the
importance of a book like this, but what it showed was that her
company also saw it: feminism was bankable. Over at Hamish
Hamilton, Alexandra Pringle published Marilyn French's *The
War Against Women* and Katie Roiphe's controversial *The Morning
After: Sex, Fear, and Feminism*, and in 1993 Carmen published
*Backlash: The Undeclared War Against Women* by Susan Faludi.
Feminist books, particularly the big, bold American ones,
equalled good money for publishers. (Though as a result Virago,
with smaller resources, was often unable to compete for the
books.)

In fact, both *The Beauty Myth* and *Backlash* were dire warn-
ings against the idea that women's empowerment was an
easy win and nearly achieved; that feminism was now mainstream. Both demonstrated—in different ways—that society's fear of women's gains meant that the battle had become
more subtle, more nuanced, and therefore harder to identify
and struggle against, not least because at times 'the enemy'
was within.

Naomi Wolf, reflecting many years later on the time of writing her book, says: 'I realised that in every generation in which there was a great push forward by women, some ideal arose to colonise their energies and thus make sure that they did not get too far. And then, I saw, in every generation that had seen such an awakening, the next generation was told to go home—it was "post-feminism" time—the battles had all been won.' She describes how in the 1990s the media were saying that young women did not want feminism.

Susan Faludi's *Backlash*, a bold and impressive book, revealed the deep fear of powerful, successful women and what some parts of society would do to put women back in their place. She wrote, for example, about how the media embraced belittling scare stories such as the infertility epidemic and the man shortage. Based on specious surveys, these articles were the harbingers of what we now know as fake news.

However, even though both these books were very successful in their day, the commercial tide was beginning to ebb on this moment of feminist polemic. Eve Ensler's eye-opening *The Vagina Monologues* play (later a Virago publication) opened in 1996, but it was the same year that *Bridget Jones's Diary* by Helen Fielding became the single girl's bestseller. Career, self-image, friends, lovers, and downfalls—they were all brilliantly revealed. Many independent working women in their twenties and thirties lapped up *Bridget Jones*, saying, 'This is my life.'

Was this the new female empowerment? It was freed of what feminist Natasha Walter called 'excessive attachment to a politically correct idealism'. Her view was that there was a new spirit propelling young women who had come of age in a time when it looked like women could achieve what they wanted.

Natasha believed that feminism was thriving—it just didn't call itself feminism and it belonged to men as well as women; and she, along with others, felt that women should turn their attention to political and economic inequities, and stop policing behaviour. She called her book *The New Feminism* and it was acquired by Philippa Harrison at Little, Brown the year before Virago arrived in the fold. Little, Brown published the hardback and I published the paperback at Virago in 1999.

The cover copy was bright and breezy:

A major polemic on British feminism which sets the agenda for the 21st century. *The New Feminism* is a breath of fresh air. Where has British feminism gone? Has it retreated into the academy, did it burn out at Greenham Common, has it emigrated to the United States? . . . In defining this new feminism, Natasha Walter celebrates women's growing power, casts aside the dogma of previous generations, and argues that the old adage 'The Personal is Political' does more harm than good. Because above all, this new feminism is frankly materialist. Who cares about how women dress, how they talk, how they make love? First, feminism must deliver political power and economic equality. With tremendous wit, verve and intelligence, *The New Feminism* marks out fresh ground in feminist debate.

The British response to the book spoke volumes about the messy, frustrated, fragmented state of feminism on the eve of the twenty-first century. Older feminists, on the whole, were not kind, unhappy as they were to see—as they thought—their style of feminism disparaged. Recognized as being a figurehead of the third wave of feminism along with Naomi Wolf and

Rebecca Walker (author and daughter of Alice Walker), Natasha Walter did get a few of the older feminists on side: 'At her spirited best, she is a symbol ... of power and confidence, and a hopeful sign of new feminist stories in a more egalitarian future,' said Elaine Showalter in the *Guardian*, but the reviewers who really liked it had already decided that old-style feminism has had its day: 'Better than a dose of Paglia any day.'

The press, and many young women too, said feminism was passé. To older feminists, porn culture was looking frighteningly mainstream, but for some of the young, empowerment was defined as girls enjoying sexy behaviour and pole-dancing classes.

The upshot was—in so many quarters—that feminism was out of date. The mainstream said women 'had it all' and it was time to stop moaning. Within radical politics, the conversation fragmented into identity politics: lesbian, black, ecological, disability; the umbrella term 'feminism' could not easily encompass them.

So how do you publish politically? When you know all is not right, as Susan Faludi pointed out, when feminism seemed to have lost its broader goals of social change, responsible citizenship, the advancement of human creativity, the building of a mature and vital public world.

But though there *were* feminists who felt this way, we were up against the tide of opinion that naysayed feminism, and that belief lasted until the mid to late 2000s. In 2006, Susan Faludi bewailed this:

> We live in a time when the very fundaments of feminism have been recast in commercial terms—and rolled at our feet like

three golden apples. The feminist ethic of economic independence has become the golden apple of buying power . . . The
feminist ethic of self-determination has turned into the golden
apple of 'self-improvement'—an improvement dedicated
mostly to one's physical appearance, self-esteem, and the
fool's errand of reclaiming one's youth. And the feminist
ethic of public agency has shape-shifted into the golden apple
of publicity—the pursuit of a popularity that hinges not on
how much one changes the world, but on how marvelously
one fits into its harness.

I can chart this period of feminist polemic publishing with
Natasha Walter's books: the time between *The New Feminism*
of 1998 to 2006, when Natasha, though still bruised from her
early publication, came to see me with the idea for a new book,
*Living Dolls*.

Philippa Harrison had left and Ursula Mackenzie was now
Little, Brown Publisher, with David Young as CEO. One of
Ursula's first innovations was to change the acquisition process;
she opened it up to sales, publicity, rights, marketing, and finance
people, to whom editors presented their proposed books. When
I presented Natasha's new proposal I talked to a large room full
of slightly sceptical people. They knew—as I did—that straightforward feminist polemic was no longer a big seller, but nonetheless everyone agreed Virago should be doing this, and of
course Natasha was our author and we are loyal to writers. Our
sales projection was not overly optimistic. I costed on modest
figures, made my offer, and Natasha began writing.

But there was one striking feature of that acquisition meeting.
I clearly remember the young women at the table vehemently

saying, 'At last ... someone is talking about this!' And 'this' was sexism. What Natasha Walter wanted to talk about was the invidiousness of sexism; how irony and put-downs of political correctness were making invisible the fact that sexism was alive and well, and particularly how the sexualized culture encouraged the body ideal—as with the days of *Fat is a Feminist Issue* and *The Beauty Myth*—and meant that girls and women were internalizing sexism. The young women in that room knew that the need for feminist analysis had not gone away, because sexism had certainly not disappeared.

*Living Dolls* took a while to write. Feminist investigation takes time. Defining the slipperiness of sexism takes great care. Finding ways to explain to readers that yes, they *seem* to have what they want—education, equal pay rights, a right to demand safety and a life of non-violence—and it looks like they have choice too, but do they? I remember the hours she spent trying to pin it down exactly. It wasn't like Betty Friedan's 'the problem that has no name'—this problem did have a clear name, sexism, but the task was the same: making that problem visible. Showing women they weren't 'mad'. Showing women—and men—the work to be done. And showing the new seeds of change. It felt as if we were back in the early days of feminism once again.

In her introduction to *Living Dolls*, Natasha bravely wrote how she—like so many others—had got it wrong:

> I once believed that we only had to put in place the conditions for equality for the remnants of old-fashioned sexism in our culture to wither away. I am ready to admit that I was wrong ... Empowerment, liberation, choice. Once the watchwords of feminism, these terms have now been co-opted

by a society that sells women an airbrushed, highly sexual-
ised and increasingly narrow vision of femininity.

Having had such a rough ride with *The New Feminism*, Natasha
and I were braced for the media onslaught. We had a launch
party for the book—with many people who knew exactly what
she was revealing and believed she was right—but those were
friends. I remember taking Natasha's hand and saying, 'Okay,
here we go, and I am with you.' We smiled grimly and were
ready. But as we came up over the parapet in 2010 we saw a
new world. We were no longer alone. People were ready for
this message, for the truth of where we had—and hadn't—got
to. *Living Dolls* was an immediate hit; readers were hungry for
Natasha's analysis. They were angry and desperate for facts,
stats, and ammunition. We reprinted and reprinted; it became
an instant feminist classic.

Sarah Savitt started her career in the post-feminist lull, in 2002,
but began acquiring books on this cusp of change at Faber. The
first book she acquired was Kat Banyard's *The Equality Illusion:
The Truth about Men and Women Today*. It is significant and pleasing
to us both that Sarah published *The Equality Illusion* in the same
month in 2010 as I published *Living Dolls*, to the same ready and
waiting readership.

In 2012 we published *Vagina: A New Biography* by Naomi Wolf,
and followed soon after with the anthologies *Fifty Shades of
Feminism* and *I Call Myself a Feminist*. These publications were
certainly not without controversy; *Vagina*, in particular, created
much heated feminist discussion in the press—but, importantly, these books won eager audiences and success. Around us
the publishing world was warming up, speaking out, waking

up. Caitlin Moran's massive hit, *How to Be a Woman*, told retailers and publishers that readers wanted feminist books, and that led to multi-variations on books that champion women, almost a new genre even—variations on rebel stories for rebel girls. We seemed to be in a brave new world where women were not afraid to be demanding, outrageous, and even funny about feminism. And where gender politics could expand to encompass transgender and non-binary authors, such as our *Trans Like Me: A Journey for All of Us* by CN Lester and *Darling Days* by iO Tillett Wright.

Sarah Savitt is very much part of this new feminism: 'I see a renewed energy around publishing not just more and a greater variety of books by women but also more and a greater variety of books by other writers whose voices have been historically marginalized, whether that's writers of colour, writers with disabilities, LGBTQ+ writers and so on. It's exciting.'

But she is wise: 'It is a great time to be Publisher of Virago for these reasons and if we achieve gender equality in the future, perhaps we will no longer be necessary—though I think it would be safer to keep going, just in case things go backwards! Knowing the history of Virago is a good reminder that change is not a straight line.'

As Margaret Busby, editor of *Daughters of Africa* and *The New Daughters of Africa: An International Anthology of Writing by Women of African Descent*, cautions, 'The aspirational mantra of inclusivity and diversity is increasingly routine, fashionable even, in today's publishing industry, but lasting change has yet to be achieved.'

Looking at our own industry tells Sarah how far we have come: 'There are energetic—and sometimes justifiably angry— discussions happening about all kinds of inequality in terms of publishing staff and working conditions.' The gender pay gap reporting in 2018 revealed significantly larger gaps than the national average at several major publishing houses, provoking many questions for her. 'Why in 2019 are almost all the CEOs of major British publishing companies men when publishing is an overwhelmingly female industry? Why is publishing so unrepresentative at all levels in terms of race and class?'

It spurred Sarah to acquire *Equal* by the journalist Carrie Gracie, who resigned as BBC China Editor over equal pay. It's right that Virago prizes an equal pay campaigner and addresses these stubbornly deep inequalities.

I love that Sarah knows books about feminism can be deliciously ironic as well as hard-hitting, that today's feminists are not afraid to laugh at themselves. She ushered in *The Guilty Feminist: From Our Noble Goals to Our Worst Hypocrisies* by Deborah Frances-White who writes,

> Proper, dedicated, lived and breathed fuck-the-patriarchy feminism is a wonderful thing for the empowerment and elevation of women everywhere but what if we're not there yet? What if we fear we will die at ninety-five, still wanting desperately to have smooth legs and a flawless forehead and without having read *The Bell Jar*? ...What if we are at base camp, and the summit looks like it's crowded with better feminists than us? ...This book is about starting today...We don't have to be perfect to dare ourselves better ...Laughing at the gap between where we want to be (Maya Angelou) and where we are (My God, I Can't Believe I Just Said That) can be cathartic, joyful, bonding...Learning to live with our contradictions and love ourselves anyway is a noble goal in itself.

Younger feminists argue, correctly, that what has been traditionally white feminism must instead centre, include, support, and understand those who have been on the margins. Virago Editorial Director Ailah Ahmed says, 'I like the adaptation of Flavia Dzodan's quote, "if your feminism isn't intersectional, it isn't feminism at all". That about sums it up for me.' She and Sarah commissioned June Eric-Udorie to edit a book about intersectionality, *Can We All Be Feminists?*, in which June writes, 'I agree wholeheartedly that building an (albeit imperfect) united sisterhood that focuses on the liberation of all women is a necessary step. But we won't get there by abandoning our own concerns and shutting off parts of ourselves. We will only get there when privileged feminists start listening — really listening, no matter how uncomfortable it might be, to women like me who exist on the margins, and amplifying our voices.'

June Eric-Udorie, who has been called a young Audre Lorde, sends me right back to 1984 when white feminists got so much right with the First International Book Fair, and so much wrong. I am thankful for this honesty and I warm to her sense that despite its shortcomings, she is grateful for feminism because it gave her a voice and a campaigning purpose: 'Feminism also gave me permission to reject the notions of being a "good" girl. I like being a rebel girl.'

I feel more optimistic than I ever have before and I am heartened and fascinated by this generation of feminists and I have seen the power we have when we support each other. But I am haunted by the fact that we name each new influx of change a 'wave'. Waves are like tides that ebb and flow, advance and retreat, and even this period, which feels more likely to succeed because it speaks to so many women, men and non-binary people and people from all races, from the grassroots up, even this, we are calling a wave. And frankly, when one looks up and sees the way world politics is moving to the right, maybe we are just waving.

I don't want to believe that, but I know what to answer when we are asked, 'Is Virago still necessary?'

I go back to books, to the words on a page that will not be erased, so we don't forget and so we can build on the energy and successes of this time. I return to Adrienne Rich:

'In a world where language and naming are power ... We need concrete artifacts, the work of hands, written words to read, images to look at, a dialogue with brave and imaginative women who came before us.'

## CHAPTER THIRTEEN

# Why Can't a Man Read Like a Woman?

When asked about feminism in the 1980s, Marguerite Yourcenar, the acclaimed author of *Memoirs of Hadrian*, said, 'I have a horror of such movements, because I think that an intelligent woman is worth an intelligent man—if you can find any—and that a stupid woman is every bit as boring as her male counterpart . . .

'I did not want to be published by [Virago]—what a *name*!— because they publish *only* women. It reminds me of ladies' compartments in nineteenth-century trains, or of a ghetto.'

I bet she was rolling in her grave when I published two volumes of her autobiography as Virago Non-fiction Classics in the late 1990s.

Though there have always been many extraordinary women writers delighted to be on the Virago list, not everyone wants to be a Virago author. Some see it as a club of which they don't wish to be a member.

I think it is often because they are anxious that they then won't be read by men—and in that, the meta-message I hear is: I won't be taken as seriously.

The Women's Prize for Fiction (originally the Orange Prize for Fiction) has also always had its naysayers, and not only men.

A. S. Byatt and Jenny Diski, for example, did not want their books entered.

Who publishes you, what prizes you win do matter—up to a point. But only up to a point.

With fiction, what seems to matter more is the gender of the writer; because even in this new world of outspoken writers and readers it appears that not all words are equal. Something seems to happen to a novel when it has a woman's name on the spine.

What Virago and the Women's Prize continue to highlight, even after more than forty years in Virago's case, is not that women struggle more than men to get published—though some non-fiction subjects are spotted and encouraged only by women's presses—no, getting published isn't the problem. What has long been the big hurdle is how women's writing is regarded.

Novels by women are most often seen as books for women only, and this is just not true of novels by men.

I do see that there is an argument which says that 'ghettoizing' women's writing, such as in Virago or the Women's Prize, does not work against this problem but actually reinforces it, but to that I would say, what we actually do is expose the otherwise invisible problem of women's talent not being seen as equal to men's. We do not subscribe to a sort of 'gender-blind', anonymous creed; we alert readers to the fact that these books are by women; that these *great* books are by women and are worth reading by all. If instead we are not honest about how there is a difference in the way a book is perceived if it has a man's or a woman's name on the spine; if we ignore the truth that authors' names carry a gendered message; if we pretend that choosing books to read, to review, to win prizes is a perfectly neutral, even-handed game, we mask the issue.

Grace Paley, referring to women in the past who used initials or male pseudonyms, and to her own first poetry submissions as G. C. Paley, brilliantly sums up the paradox: 'Women hid in order to be seen.'

You can hide, or you can 'come out' as female.

And you might as well come out as female and name yourself because the fact is, as Joyce Carol Oates ruefully noted, 'The woman who writes is a writer by her own definition, but a "woman writer" by others' definitions.'

We've got rid of 'poetess' and 'authoress', but we still have 'woman writer'. You will never hear the term 'man writer'. He's a writer: genderless apparently, but certainly neutral and therefore universal and of universal appeal.

Women readers do see universality of meaning and relevance in men's novels, as on the whole women read across genres and genders. Of course, everyone has favourite writers and individual tastes, but women readers show again and again that even if they favour women, they will almost certainly also read many books by men. They may not even notice their choices.

This is particularly true of literary fiction, and I want to look at literary fiction because even though it might attract fewer readers than, say, crime or romantic fiction or 'beach novels', what it does command is headlines, prizes, reviews, features, author appearances at festivals: in other words, high visibility and respect. A headline in the *Observer* to mark the Booker Prize at fifty says it all: 'Flawed—but still the best way to judge our literature'.

And I think literature is still a good way to judge our society. Literary fiction animates readers, makes us think—even changes how we think—and survives after we die. These are the books that become set texts, are translated into other languages, and are incorporated into the literary canon. These are the books that society—or rather, those who have the platform to make such judgements—deem great.

The Virago Modern Classics began in 1978 with the idea of blasting this canon wide open: to challenge the narrow notion of 'great' and also to challenge the idea of who gets to decide what is great.

Because who decides what is noteworthy needs to be illuminated. For years women have highlighted the fact that book review pages and literary prizes have been dominated by men. Back in 1990 Margaret Atwood said reviewing was 'where you are likely to see gender bias, bias of all kinds', but it only seems to have changed marginally since then.

VIDA, a 'non-profit feminist organization committed to creating transparency around the lack of gender parity in the literary landscape', has been doing heroic work measuring male and female review coverage—and who writes the reviews—in the American press and some of the British papers, and finding parity woefully slow. In Britain, the Emilia Report into the Gender Gap for Authors by Danuta Keane, published in spring 2019, showed that though there has been an increase in the number of women reviewers, male writers are still more reviewed than women, even when writing comparable fiction.

The report quotes the writer Kate Mosse, co-founder of the Women's Prize for Fiction: 'Literature with a capital L is still not seen as a neutral literary voice if it is women writing from their own point of view.'

Which brings me to the prizes.

After February 1992, when the writer many of us would call the great Angela Carter died, a group of us—publishers, agents, and writers—gathered in the Kentish Town, north London, flat of the then Curtis Brown agent Anne McDermid. We were outraged that none of Angela's novels had ever troubled the shortlist of the Booker, but nor had other women fared well. In the Booker's first thirty years the shortlists tallied 63 per cent male, and in the five years preceding our meeting only five women had been short-listed, compared to twenty four men. In those first thirty years, eleven women won. (Over the subsequent years, the prize has gone to nine female writers—boosted by two women, Margaret Atwood and Bernadine Evaristo, sharing the prize in 2019—which means that in fifty years of the prize only twenty novels by women have won, and of those women Hilary Mantel, writing about Thomas Cromwell, won twice.) A look at the judges shows that even with an almost equal number of men and women on the panel more men than women made the shortlists. Did women, too, subscribe to the idea that the prize was for big, important novels by men? What was the prevailing notion of 'great'?

We planned a new and bold prize for fiction by women that would challenge the Booker Prize. We wanted to demonstrate to the judges, the writers, and the world that they were looking at authors either through a clouded lens or they had their eyes shut. We would counter their predominantly male prize with a women-only award and, most importantly, we'd raise the purse. The Booker at the time awarded £25,000; we would make ours £30,000. We wanted to indicate from the start that we were not an insignificant extra, a small protesting voice. This group eventually whittled itself down to a small committee of women (of which I was not a member) including Kate Mosse, who took the prize to extraordinary glory and success; one that is still a combative challenge to the Booker. In provoking discussions about visibility for women novelists, just like Virago does, the Women's Prize—like the new Jhakal Prize—does not let drop the conversations about what is great literature and who decides. I see us as so much more than mere conscience-pricking—not least as many of the winning books have far outsold the Booker winners—but that certainly is one of our jobs.

But it's not only women who have noted the Booker blindness. Robert McCrum, looking back over the half-century of the Booker, notes,

> Having been right about the English literature of India, Australia and the rest, the prize misjudged the other big story of these decades, the emergence of a brilliant new generation of female novelists. In hindsight, this was predictable. A book prize cooked up [in 1968] by middle-aged men in the smoke-filled rooms of London's clubland was likely to have a tin ear when it came to the innovations of contemporary female writers at the cutting edge. While a feminist literary revolution led by Virago transformed the reading lives of a new generation, Booker was struggling...It did not recognise Elizabeth Taylor in 1971 (*Mrs Palfrey at the Claremont*); passed over Beryl Bainbridge five times; missed Muriel Spark in 1981 (*Loitering with Intent*), and never even shortlisted Angela Carter's *Nights at the Circus*.

Even though it is gratifying to be proved right and to see Virago recognized, what is striking to me is his acknowledgment that middle-aged men were likely to have tin ears when it came to women writers.

Why *are* the men tone deaf?

It seems to me that there are two reasons. First, there is a perception of what readers *think* the book is going to be about—before they even pick it up. Secondly, and this is in some ways more shocking, I think a novel written by a woman is read differently from one written by a man. What we have here is not gendered writing, but gendered *reading*. It's a term I first learned from Lisa Appignanesi, and it makes everything very clear.

I love the Booker winner Anne Enright's slightly outrageous observation:

> It is tempting to [...conclude] that men and women are read differently, even when they write the same thing. If a man writes 'The cat sat on the mat' we admire the economy of his prose; if a woman does we find it banal. If a man writes 'The cat sat on the mat' we are taken by the simplicity of his sentence structure, its toughness and precision. We understand the connection between 'cat' and 'mat', sense the grace of the animal, admire the way the percussive monosyllables sharpen the geometrics of the mat beneath [...] If, on the other hand, a woman writes 'The cat sat on the mat,' her concerns are clearly domestic, and sort of limiting. Time to go below the comments line and make jokes about pussy...I am kidding, of course. These are anxieties, projections, phantasmagoria—things to which women are particularly prone.

She finishes this 'projection' with a deprecating note about women's anxieties, and I am not surprised. The number of times I have sat beside some of the most famous novelists in the English language as they sign books for long queues and have to listen as every age of man hastens to say, 'It's not for me. My wife loves your books,' are legion. And insulting, boring, and belittling.

Does reading novels about women demean men? Are they anxious about being associated with femaleness? What do they think femaleness is about?

Most women writers know they are up against this prejudice—from individuals, the review pages, and the literary festivals. It's confirmed by those men who are not tin-eared.

The novelist John Boyne wrote: 'I've been publishing novels for almost 20 years [and] I've become increasingly aware of double standards in the industry. A man is treated like a literary writer from the start, but a woman usually has to earn that commendation.' At a literary festival in 2017, he noticed that 'a trio of established male writers were referred to . . . as "giants of world literature", while a panel of female writers of equal stature were . . . "wonderful storytellers" . . . [But] I think women are better novelists than men. There, I've said it. While it's obviously an enormous generalisation, it's no more ludicrous than some half-wit proudly claiming never to read books by women.'

I wonder if the words 'domestic novel' hover over most books with a woman's name on the cover, and if 'domestic' is standing in for 'emotion', 'family', 'love'. Yet we know that if you are a man and write about the intimate, about feelings, that term does not apply; instead, impressive writers such as Ian McEwan, Richard Ford, Michael Ondaatje, Colm Tóibín, Julian Barnes *et al.* are applauded for writing about intimacy and the important things.

I remember standing in my kitchen and cheering out loud when the writer Helen Simpson responded to what sounded like a criticism about writing domestic short stories on Radio 4's *Woman's Hour*. Her answer cut through to the truth: 'Calling a work of fiction domestic is a political not a literary judgement.'

Gendered reading is making a judgement: assuming this novel is going to be about things of interest to women only.

I am making a speech about Virago at the British Institute in Florence. At the end a man—friendly, interested— stands up and waves a piece of paper, and says, 'If this was a story with no name attached, could you tell if it was written by a man or woman?'

I want to sigh. This is an old question that has besieged Virago and the other feminist presses from the start. Do men write differently from women? And— definitely the subconscious question- -which is better? The answer is no, the greatest likelihood is that I could not tell. But what I realize I should have said—and, of course, the best response always comes to one later, in bed that night— is what differences do you *think* you would find, even before reading, once you knew the gender of the writer?

We should have moved on from the time when Anthony Burgess said approvingly of Olivia Manning that she was never, like so many women novelists, limited to experiences of her own sex, but I really am not sure we have.

I think in challenging the perception, significance, and reception of novels by women— in prizes and reviews among others— we are showing up the underlying assumptions. We are saying there is no such thing as a limiting female experience and nor is there a male universal one. We are also putting paid to the idea of domestic as pejorative and inferior when it is in the hands of the female novelist.

In 2013, outraged by the way that *Fifty Shades of Grey* was ushering in a 'wave of essentialism once more sweeping the woman's world', authors and friends Lisa Appignanesi, Rachel Holmes, and Susie Orbach edited a volume of essays we called *Fifty Shades of Feminism* and published to great success. In her piece, Siri Hustvedt, renowned novelist married to another renowned novelist, so able to witness different responses to his and her work, wrote, 'We, all of us, women and men, encode masculinity and femininity in implicit metaphorical schemas that divide the world in half. Science and mathematics are hard, rational, real, serious and masculine. Literature and art are soft, irrational, unreal, frivolous and feminine . . . Anything that becomes associated with girls and women loses status, whether it is a profession, a book, a movie or a disease.' In a later interview she goes on to explain why she thinks male writers have an equal number of men and women readers whereas female writers are read primarily by women: 'A male novelist hardens and dignifies the form, while a female novelist is doubly penalised as a woman working in an unserious form.'

Are women authors also afraid of what happens to their readership when they 'come out' as female? Interestingly, the novelist Rachel Cusk wrote that 'the woman writer still risks' taking female and female experiences as her subject and she certainly has taken much flak over the years for writing honestly about them.

What is sad about listening yet again to an author or agent on her behalf ask me, 'Will men read the book?' is that the frank answer is, if current circumstances are anything to go on, and men continue to read little literary fiction and even less by women, then probably not.

That is both enraging and depressing; and also fascinating that we women still seem to think we have to measure success by how much we capture a male readership. That is partly because we all see that the cultural upper hand is still held by white men, but it's also because from time immemorial we women have read and discussed novels by men—and it's only natural to want the favour returned.

Sarah Churchwell, who wrote *Careless People: Murder, Mayhem and the Invention of the Great Gatsby* for us, concurs: 'Male readers . . . rarely use the compliment "universal" to describe a book written by a woman: in fact, it's difficult to recall a single instance.

'Patriarchy works unseen to valorise men's perspective, and invalidate women's. When we don't recognise the way it shapes the world, then we do not understand that world properly: our perspective becomes unreliable. In other words, patriarchy continues to gaslight us all'

*Gas Light* was a clever 1938 play by Patrick Hamilton. Gaslighting has come to mean the deliberate undermining of another's sanity, and about women fighting to get men to see their experience.

I remember the first time I read a contemporary novel set in Toronto, on streets I recognized, in a country that was mine. I felt a thrill of recognition, of validation; that the background to my life was worthy of being in a book—it was that important. I'd had no understanding until then about how I, the reader, was identifying with characters and places that had nothing to do with me. I was in the Midwest, a young girl in a covered wagon; I was Pip, in a graveyard frightened by Magwitch; I was Tom, painting the fence; I was frightened by the black spot in

*Treasure Island*; I was Oliver, running from the law with Fagin; I was flying with Peter Pan; and I was Anne, with an 'e', with hated red hair and freckles on a small island in eastern Canada: all places, people, and time periods I had never experienced. Of course this is exactly what fiction should do for a reader: transport them to another time and place, make them live and breathe the hero or heroine's life. But suddenly to have a book that really was about me, in my neck of the woods, was eye-opening. It meant I too was important. When I think of that now, I begin to understand why women so effortlessly continue to cross into men's worlds: we've done it all our reading lives. I also note that all these books are by white authors and with white protagonists; readers of colour, male and female, and trans readers must make another leap too.

I live in hope that for the younger generation of readers, publishers, and authors coming up behind me that these observations and this conversation will soon be out of date.

I return to Anne Enright: 'There is a difference between a culture that tilts male and a culture that does not see what it is doing.'

Since we began, Virago and feminists have been showing the culture what it is doing. Maybe people can now see.

What does it take to be a successful writer? Beyond writing a brilliant book, you have to be visible, strategic—you have to be immodest. Until very recently, and even now I would say, that is still not the norm. The woman who calls attention to herself and her talent is running a risk. It's still considered better if she waits for the accolades than acts as if it is her due.

Elaine Showalter, a critic who has long been important to Virago, has observed this: 'Women have been too dignified and self-effacing to make their own claims to artistic immortality. Women novelists do not observe the rituals of male literary artistry that sustain historical memory; they have rarely produced manifestoes, aligned themselves in a notable school, named their generation (whether Lost or Beat) and their genre, or feuded heroically and publicly with a critic-double, or a female rival.'

When John Updike died, there were pieces on the radio and in the papers bemoaning the death of the Great American novel (Saul Bellow, Norman Mailer, and Updike being the pantheon). Poor America was left with only Philip Roth, and now that he too has gone we got a reprise of this lament. But what about Marilynne Robinson, Donna Tartt, Toni Morrison, Annie Proulx, Anne Tyler, Ann Patchett, Siri Husvedt, to name just a few ...?

Not long ago I was in a well-known high street bookshop and gravitated to a table labelled Great American Novelists. When I pointed out that there was not a single woman among the twenty-five or so novels to the young man who'd made the selection, he was utterly surprised—and, to give him his due, though embarrassed, he admitted he just hadn't noticed.

The critic Bryan Appleyard thinks that men don't see beyond themselves. He wrote in the *Sunday Times* in 2007: 'Great-novel writing is regarded as a pursuit as male as heading out into the woods and shooting stuff ... having bought into this view, I fell into a kind of literary-critical slumber. I have, over the past couple of years, been violently shaken awake. As a result, I can now announce with total confidence that the two greatest living novelists are women: Marilynne Robinson and Shirley Hazzard ... Both Robinson and Hazzard have had their awards and successes, but both are quiet, unhyped and deadly serious. And they're not men.'

Unhyped. Do we need to do more hyping for ourselves?

The indisputable thing that Virago does is claim space, immodestly, for writing by women. We are not defensive about that, nor should we be, as I have not noticed any other area of the art world, the reviewing world, or the reading world being defensive about shortlists of mainly men. When you get a lot of women on lists people do comment. I have yet to see a headline saying: 'Five Men Shortlisted!' or 'Men Dominate Shortlist' or 'Men win all the Prizes this year!' But I have certainly seen the reverse.

Publishers are often as bad as toy manufacturers—pink for girls and blue for boys. Naomi Alderman wrote, long before she won the Women's Prize for Fiction, 'I want to work hard and know that my work has some chance of being considered important. That no one's going to stick a flower on the front of it just because I have a vagina.'

I noted her novel *The Power* has a great cover. Maybe it's because she weighed in; maybe it's because publishers are changing.

When I published Linda Grant's novel *Upstairs at the Party*, the first-draft cover image from the designer was a picture of young people at a party—very nice, but exactly what you'd expect for a female novelist: one showing people.

I said, 'Let's imagine this book was by, say, Jonathan Franzen or George Saunders.'

Back came a strong, graphic cover with bold colours and strokes: big and important. By a woman: looking universal.

## CHAPTER FOURTEEN

# Giving and Taking Courage

There are, apparently, monstrous authors who can write humane and wonderful books, but I think the integrity of a writer's soul cannot be hidden for long. Their writing reveals the truth about them.

All fiction writers show exasperation when readers imply that their novels are autobiographical, but in my experience an author's true nature is visible—even in fictional writing, their personality seeps through their prose. Personality, that is, not actual experiences. When we published Sarah Dunant's novel *Transgressions*, which had some graphic sex scenes, I idly asked if her mother had read the novel and she was horrified. No! Sarah wouldn't let her! Her mother, like many readers, believed if Sarah could write it—she must have lived it.

What I admired about Carmen Callil's book *Bad Faith* is that in this factual account of a Nazi collaborator and 'Commissioner for Jewish Affairs' who managed the Vichy government's dirty work one keenly feels her sense of injustice. As you read, between the lines you feel the absolute rage on behalf of innocent people who died, and this tells you something about the author.

As readers read a novel they know they are falling in love with certain characters and stories. But something subliminal is also going on, as the reader gives themselves over to an author.

I think that by the end of the book a reader not only judges the novel, they judge the author too. We think the author must be as kind, or humane, or funny, or clever—or the opposite—as their creation.

In her book *Outrages: Sex, Censorship and the Criminalisation of Love*, Naomi Wolf talks about Walt Whitman: 'It wasn't just the language of *Leaves of Grass* that sparked . . . a response. Many readers also fell in love with the poet himself. Whitman was certainly complicit in this seduction. He made choices throughout his career that would continue to lead people not just to love his writing but to wish to touch, confess to, and even make love to the poet himself.'

Marilynne Robinson's novels are a perfect example of personality shining through the work. I have seen her wave her hand, dismissing the very idea of writing about characters she doesn't care about, love even. And her novels bear this out: even Jack, the weak-willed, destructive son in her Gilead novels is obviously someone she cares about deeply. There are no out-and-out bad guys in a Marilynne Robinson novel. The result of this compassion is that readers fall equally for the novels and their creator.

The late Shirley Hazzard, author of most exquisite novels including *Transit of Venus* and *The Great Fire*, understood that when we read deeply we give ourselves over to a novel. She called it 'in part an act of submission, akin to generosity or love'. Shirley was with us in June 2004 when *The Great Fire* was shortlisted for the Orange Prize. While she was in London she received the marvellous news that she'd won the prestigious Miles Franklin Award in Australia. She couldn't be there, but she wrote an acceptance speech to be read out, which I typed and sent by email. I remember the care with which she pored over the speech, rewriting and carefully choosing her words to capture the exactness of her feelings:

'Our world that seems charged with war is also the world in which the frail filament of expression miraculously persists, and the phenomenon of the accurate word...Thanks to this mystery of art and diverse beauty, we can meet in affinity across oceans and continents and centuries, and celebrate books.'

'A frail filament of expression miraculously persisting' is a beautiful mirroring of Shirley and her writing. Carefully dressed in high-necked blouses, a pretty brooch at her throat, hair pinned in a loose, elegant bun, and with lovely, long expressive hands; I see her now as she rode with me in the back of taxis marvelling at London, quoting strands of poetry, both of us delighting in our friendship. Her novels and her book about Graham Greene are robust beauties, deceptively delicate. Like her.

An agent, Jonny Geller, once said to me that a successful novel must have an aura, a sort of 'charge' about it. I agree. Readers pick up a feeling about a book—from reviews, from how it looks, how it's talked about—and respond accordingly. It's almost another way of saying word of mouth, but I think it's more inchoate, more subtle than that: it's a feeling. (And the book that generates no aura is silent—and silenced too.) It's that same feeling about the author. Readers can pick up a sense of the author from interviews and features, but even when a reader has little or no access to an author they generate their own feeling about them—just from their prose. We feel we know—almost intimately—the writers we admire, who write books we love. We transfer our feelings about their writing to them. I say 'we' because I do it too, even though I have met authors I admire and discovered some are not quite as lovely as their prose.

I think about these things because as a publisher I want to give an author the very best chance in the marketplace. I think about why readers absolutely adore certain authors and how we can encourage that, about how we can create an aura for authors and their books. The simple conclusion is that, just like any kind of love, you can't force it. We can market intelligently and demonstrate the thrill and pleasures of a particular novel, and indeed do well by it and the author, but the truth cannot be manufactured. It's in the very prose. The honesty is there, and the reader feels it. I think of J. M. Coetzee, for example, and feel in his work, his watchful, guarded prose, that he is a private, distant person—which I understand to be true of him.

And it's not always all about adoration; some writers such as Rachel Cusk and the late Jenny Diski—bracing writers—reveal an unlikeable side of themselves that readers enthusiastically respond to. That too is about honesty.

Margaret Atwood has a party trick: she can read palms. I was once with her and Beryl Bainbridge in a pub after they had both done their turns at a literary festival. Margaret took Beryl's hand (to Beryl's mild consternation) and after studying it for a while she looked her fellow writer in the eye and laughed: 'You're not as scatty as you make out.' Here is a storyteller not afraid to go beneath the obvious—even in real life! And to tell the truth.

The power of good and truthful writing is important to Margaret Atwood. She says: 'I happen to believe that at its best writing is considerably more and other than mere self-expression . . . Good writing is not "expressing yourself". It is opening yourself, discarding yourself, so that the language and the world may be evoked through you. Evocation is quite different from expression . . . Evocation, calling up, is what writing does for the reader. Writing is also a kind of sooth-saying, a truth telling. It is naming of the world, a reverse incarnation: the flesh becoming word. It is also a witnessing. Come with me, the writer is saying to the reader. There is a story I have to tell you, there is something you need to know. The writer is both an eye-witness and an I-witness . . . The writer bears witness. Bearing witness is not the same as self-expression.'

This is obviously particular in some ways to Margaret Atwood and her own version of sooth-saying, but I think her point is larger and applicable to other writers. She tells us that writing is a truth-telling and my view is that the truth it tells is also about the writer.

In a packed hall in north London a white, middle-aged man stands up; be-suited, he stands out in the casually dressed group. He waits for a microphone to be handed to him, then turns to Marilynne Robinson: 'Your books changed my life.'

In Ledbury, at a library event, part of a literary festival, Donna Coonan and I give a talk about Virago and then afterwards, while we are packing up our books, a small, dark-haired, late-middle-aged woman quietly comes up to me. 'The Virago Modern Classics saved my life.'

'Your novels give me steely courage.' People have often written like this to Sarah Waters, to tell them how deeply she has affected them.

Reading takes you outward. Reading gives us entertainment, education, information, escapism, fun, wisdom; its nourishment gives us strength, from humour or from recognition, or fellow feeling, and it gives us knowledge, but so often it's also much more than that: it gives us the bravery to allow ourselves to be inspired.

Is it surprising to hear how people have gained strength, companionship, or a deeper knowledge of themselves through reading? I don't think so: I think part of the courage a reader draws is from a perception that the writers themselves had the bravery to write openly and honestly—even in fiction. As Sarah Waters says, 'We write best when we write about what is closest to our hearts.' Readers feel that.

Sonali Deraniyagala wrote one of the most devastating books I have ever published, or indeed read, after she lost her entire family in Sri Lanka—two sons, husband, mother, and father— to the 2004 tsunami. She was the sole survivor, and found that the only way she could remotely recover was to hold her family in her heart by writing her memories of their lives together in her beautiful book *Wave*. It was devastatingly hard, but she says it would have been harder to turn away from them. Her courage in writing she gives to us.

Sometimes it's a matter of books reaching into lonely lives, and sometimes, aside from giving great pleasure, books are also a validation. Marilynne Robinson has talked many times of the wonder of each of us—'To be human is a very high and complicated privilege'—which implies not only that we are to be valued individually but also, importantly, that we have obligations: that we're part of a community.

I ask Marilynne what response she gives when readers tell her she changed their lives. She said she wishes she had a worthy answer, something she supposes she might have if she knew more of what the readers mean; however, she feels that their reaction is a deeply private one, not to be pried at, opened, examined. She lets people know of her grateful appreciation, though. Indeed, I have seen at signings how she takes her time, looks readers in the eye, and listens carefully. She feels it is a blessing, not to be taken for granted, to be able to reach such an audience.

Sometimes courage is unwitting. When I was editing the politician Shirley Williams's autobiography *Climbing the Bookshelves* I often remarked on her bravery and she laughed at that, saying no, she wasn't brave at all, but she knew herself to have a fearlessness, claiming it came from a desire to throw herself into things without the impediment or worry of consequence. She said it was quite another thing from courage, but I am not sure I see the distinction. To me she is brave and I do know that she gets it honestly too: in her mother, Vera Brittain, she had a role model, a woman not afraid to stand up against the popular military spirit of her time and speak the truth, as she saw it, about pacifism.

I saw another kind of courage in Rachel Seiffert. I had wanted desperately to publish her first book, *The Dark Room*, which was an astonishing novel in three parts; remarkable in both its form and its story about the Nazis' rise to power, told from differing points of view. I didn't win the chance to publish that novel, which went on to be shortlisted for the Booker Prize, but I kept myself on the agent's radar and when I met Rachel at events made sure she knew how keen I was. In the end, her original editor changed jobs and I became the lucky publisher of two novels, *The Long Walk Home* and *A Boy in Winter*. The latter told the story of Nazi devastation in a small town in the Ukraine and Rachel wrote a *Guardian* piece to explain something about her German family—that her grandparents were active in the Nazi Party. It's brave to stand up and be counted with others, in street demonstrations or marches, but to stand alone, to reveal something of pain, hurt, and shame in one's own family, to be on the wrong side of history and to tell that truth: that takes remarkable courage.

And even when you are on the right side of history, to tell your story, to decide to reveal your heartache and pain in the name of a larger cause, is heroic. Nadia Murad's peaceful village existence was ripped apart in August 2014 when the so-called Islamic State (ISIS) attacked Kocho, her village, beginning its savage campaign—its genocide—against the Yazidis. Nadia lost six of her nine brothers, along with hundreds of other men from her village in the Kocho massacre. Her mother was killed after being deemed 'too old' to be enslaved, while Nadia and her two sisters were taken by ISIS to be sexual slaves.

After enduring unimaginable violence and brutality, Nadia escaped.

She told her story with Jenna Krajeski in *The Last Girl: My Story of Captivity and My Fight against the Islamic State* because she wanted to be the last girl to whom this happened. Nadia's testimony is not just one of violence, but of love and family life, and a story of her innate determination and strength. I think of Atwood, who wrote that the writer retains three attributes that power-mad regimes cannot tolerate: a human imagination, the power to communicate, and hope.

Nadia shared the 2018 Nobel Peace Prize with Denis Mukwege for their efforts to end the use of sexual violence as a weapon of war.

But there is another kind of courage a writer needs: that of self-belief, the courage to claim the importance, the space, and the time for writing. This is getting better for women who write, but I think it is still not easy for many women, particularly mothers, to combine life and writing. Tillie Olsen's *Silences*, which we published in 1980, revealed a list of women writers without children, and sometimes without a husband or partner, who wrote and published books. Her list of some such women from the twentieth century alone is eye-opening: Willa Cather, Gertrude Stein, Edith Wharton, Virginia Woolf, Elizabeth Bowen, Katharine Mansfield, Isak Dinesen, Katherine Anne Porter, Dorothy Richardson, Henry Handel Richardson, Dorothy Parker, Lillian Hellman, Eudora Welty, Djuna Barnes, Anaïs Nin, Zora Neale Hurston, Christina Stead, Carson McCullers, Flannery O'Connor, Jean Stafford, Janet Frame, Iris Murdoch, Lorraine Hansberry.

And it is certainly true that many women, again especially those with children, do not start writing until they are in their thirties.

Tillie Olsen wrote about the conviction one needs to wrte: 'Conviction as to the importance of what one has to say, one's right to say it. And the will, the measureless store of belief in oneself to be able to come to, cleave to, find the form for one's own life comprehensions.'

The strength to write bolder, bigger, better often comes from other writers. Hilary Mantel said: 'The question is not who influences you, but which people give you courage. When I began, the female writer who gave me courage . . . was Beryl Bainbridge . . . her books were so off the wall, they were so screamingly funny in a black way, and so oblique, that I thought, If she can get away with this, so can I.'

In recent years I have been interviewing writers at literary festivals and I have adopted Hilary Mantel's question. I ask which writers gave them courage. It takes authors a few moments to think—it's a momentous question—but they always have an answer; they know their writing is emboldened, liberated, inspired even, by others.

In 2006 I published a book of Patti Smith's poetry. Every author cares about their cover images, and one would expect a poet to mind how their poems are placed on the page, but Patti Smith cared not just about all of that, but also about the quality of the paper. She wanted to know what weight of paper we were using. As a self-confessed neurotic about book production details, I just loved it. *Auguries of Innocence* was inspired by William Blake, and when she came over from America as part of a music tour she gave us a few days of her time, which culminated in her giving the Blake Society Annual Lecture at the impressive St James's Church in Piccadilly. Patti Smith, of course, does not 'give a lecture': she read, she sang, she played the guitar, she made mistakes and laughingly confessed that she could play only in A minor, and was backed on the acoustic guitar by a friend she had bumped into in a second-hand bookshop on Charing Cross Road earlier that day. It was a life-enhancing evening. I had seen her the year before, when her agent, Betsy Lerner, also a Virago author, invited me to a performance at the Meltdown festival in London. Seeing Patti Smith sing and speak passionately, laugh out loud, strum her guitar, and jump wildly across the stage at the age of nearly sixty was utterly surprising and inspirational.

I felt the same uplift and watched another audience swell to pride and tears with the great comic and humanist Sandi Toksvig when she, as part of her extensive tour for her novel *Valentine Grey*, stood small on the vast stage of Richmond Theatre and asked us to rise and join her in conducting Beethoven's Fifth. It's a long story . . . but all one needs to know is that by this time in the show we would have done anything she asked. And we did.

I looked at dear Sandi on the stage and thought, here is an outspoken political critic, a gay woman, a mother of three, a feminist: a 'type', we are lead to believe, thanks to the tabloids, that gives middle England some anxieties. But instead they know and love her. She has opened herself to them and they have responded. Sandi has written one of the most genuinely creative and rewarding memoirs Virago has ever published, *Between the Stops: The View of My Life from the Top of the Number 12 Bus*.

'I think we're genetically programmed to tell stories; it's how we make sense of the world. In order to successfully negotiate the world you have to able to put yourself in imaginary scenarios, in other people's stories. Empathy is a great driver of fiction—and of reading: that's a very basic need we have . . .' I think Sarah Waters is right: a good novel can tell us something that we cannot experience or know ourselves; it transports us. I rail against the idea of a novel only being appealing if the characters are 'relatable' or likeable; of course it's deeply pleasurable to find aspects of your story, your background, your country in a novel, but what I want is to have even those feelings enlarged in a way that will take me further than myself. Surely the only criterion is are they credible? Going well outside oneself, exploring the other, is what good books are about.

Knowing our readers and wanting to reach out, to open ourselves to those who don't know us—or don't care about us—has been at the heart of Virago from the start. Crudely, it might be called 'marketing feminism', and indeed people have said that about Virago. But we have always planned to balance our books, in every sense of that phrase. I know and I understand the queasiness that 'marketing' evokes. But empathy and understanding, curiosity, and listening closely to the other: might that be another definition of reaching out to people? Might that even be a way to change people's minds? My view is that we change things by knowing where one must stand, unbending, but also by knowing where to meet part way; where to make things easier and more inviting for people. And indeed for us, the gatekeepers, to understand that we don't know it all; we have to listen to learn.

We're trying our best, is what I will say and what I surmise the current Viragos would too. But maybe they'll do it differently. That's for the next generation of Viragos to work out. What is so heartening is to see in them the same fervour, intelligence, style, taste, drive—and even bloody-mindedness—that from the beginning has characterized the women who have made the choices about Virago books.

This is my bite of the Virago apple. The apple logo, which came to Virago via Carmen's amusing green apple on one leg she had designed for her publicity company, symbolizes the myth about the first woman who took a bite of knowledge—and suffered the consequences. I like instead to think she relished that juicy bite, and that she'd enjoy knowing her apple became the symbol for a publishing house that mirrors the marvellous march of women. That brings them words that nourish.

Who owns dear Virago? Many of the battles and the dramas and the anger and the pleasures rest on this question. We Viragos have fought over who literally owns it and who should own it, and we—and others—have gloried in owning it. Feminists have claimed it from the beginning: demanding, suggesting, and celebrating the press. Readers have identified with Virago; felt they are part of a club, thrilled to the like-minded authors and readers who have given them so much pleasure and a sense of recognition, who have introduced new voices to them. We have thousands of fans now; social media has brought us even closer to our readers. Authors have come to us with enthusiasm. Booksellers have supported us, as have our current owners. When we—the Virago shareholders—argued over to whom to sell our company, we were conscious of our readers and our authors; we referred to the Virago in the room. Whatever we did, we said, she must go on. As Publisher and now as Virago Chair, still working with my authors, I have kept that faith throughout the years we've been part of Little, Brown. I know that the women—and men—who work with Virago feel the same way. Virago will always be her own woman; heroic, just like her name.

One of Carmen's famous quotes is, 'The power to publish is a wonderful thing.' She's right. The excitement of bringing into the world something unique, a book that began as a glimmer of an idea, or writing that might give tremendous joy or even create change—that, to me, is a power of the deepest pleasure.

# Notes

PART ONE

Page no

*'The sense of limitless freedom...'*: Angela Carter, 'Notes from the  1
front line', in Michelene Wandor (ed.), *On Gender and Writing*
(London: Pandora, 1983).

CHAPTER ONE

*'In England, then, being Canadian...'*: Margaret Atwood, 'Dump  4
bins and shelf strips', *A Virago Keepsake to Celebrate Twenty Years of
Publishing* (London: Virago, 1993)

*'help in the struggle for World Peace...'*: Left Book Club brochure,  9
1936, quoted in Ruth Dudley Edwards, *Victor Gollancz: A
Biography* (London: Gollancz, 1987).

*'I was inspired by the explosive energy of underground press's...'*:  10
Quoted at https://www.cardiffwomensaid.org.uk/second-wave-
feminism/.

*'in the '70s I asked the head of BBC News...'*: Joan Bakewell, 'Dame  10
Joan Bakewell: The battle isn't over for women on TV', https://
graziadaily.co.uk/life/tv-and-film/bafta-joan-bakewell/, 1 May
2019.

*'It seems cool, vibrant, sexy...'*: Amy Annette, Martha Mosse, and  11
Alice Stride, 'Introduction', in Victoria Pepe, Rachel Holmes,
Amy Annette, Alice Stride, and Martha Mosse (eds), *I Call Myself
a Feminist* (London: Virago, 2015).

*'Well, I liked you...'*: Interview with the author.  11

*'to put women's liberation on the news stands'*: Quoted in Marsha Rowe  12
(ed.), *Spare Rib Reader* (London: Penguin, 1982).

'*There is the most urgent need ...*': Ibid.                              12

'*one day, when having a drink ...*': Carmen Callil, 'The stories of   12
our lives', *Guardian*, 26 April 2008.

'*Rosie and I sat on the floor of my flat ...*': Carmen Callil, personal   13
notes.

'*a strong, courageous, outspoken woman ...*': Callil, 'The stories of   13
our lives'.

'*It was not enough to publish for ourselves*': Carmen Callil, 'The   13
future of feminist publishing', *The Bookseller*, 1 March 1986. An
edited version of a speech at the Women in Publishing conference, 1985.

'*It was as if an explosion had gone off ...*': Val McDermid, 'Letter:   14
Val McDermid on the importance of Kate Millett, author of
*Sexual Politics*', *Observer*, 10 September 2017.

'*She bowled me over ...*': Rosie Boycott, in 'What Germaine Greer   15
and *The Female Eunuch* mean to me', *Observer*, 26 January 2014.

'*slipped to me like Samizdat ...*': Nuala O'Faolain, 'You've come a   15
long way, baby', *Guardian*, 13 September 2003.

'*in your most intimate organ—the brain*': A. L. Kennedy, 'Someone   15
to Watch Over Me', *A Point of View*, BBC Radio 4, 22 September
2013.

'*Reading is a way of becoming ...*': Ibid.                              16

'*We must survive ...*': Polly Toynbee, 'Virago Press gives women   18
writers a voice', *Guardian*, 26 January 1981.

'*rules, censorship and silence ...*': Callil, 'The stories of our lives'.   18

'*The editor and publisher Ursula Owen ...*': Simon Hattenstone,   19
'Profile: Ursula Owen', *Guardian*, 21 July 2001.

'*dismantling the grand narratives*': Virago podcast, 26 February   20
2018.

'*The sense of limitless freedom…*': Angela Carter, 'Notes from the 21 front line', in Michelene Wandor (ed.), *On Gender and Writing* (London: Pandora, 1983).

## CHAPTER TWO

'*The one thing that's really memorable…*': Sabine Durrant, 'How we 23 met: Carmen Callil and Harriet Spicer', *Independent on Sunday*, 23 May 1993.

'*Harriet was always very elegant…*': Ibid. 23

'*In our year with Quartet we had learned…*': Ursula Owen, 24 'Feminist Publishing', in Peter Owen (ed.), *Publishing: The Future* (London: Peter Owen, 1988)

'*Would you mind guaranteeing my overdraft…*': *Virago: Changing the 24 World One Page at a Time*, BBC Four, 31 October 2016.

'*We were determined to reclaim a history…*': Owen, 'Feminist 26 Publishing'.

'*searching through libraries and coming, with astonishment…*': 26 Carmen Callil, 'The future of feminist publishing', *The Bookseller*, 1 March 1986. An edited version of a speech at the Women in Publishing conference, 1985.

'*more famous than the books by men that inspired it*': Mark Bostridge, 28 'Introduction', *Testament of Youth* (London: Virago, 2018).

'*Virago was founded with two main aims…*': Callil, 'The future of 28 feminist publishing'.

'*It was in my blood and I loved the tangible object*': Interview with 28 the author.

'*I loved the atmosphere…*': Interview with the author. 28

'*dethrone the myth of [inherent] femininity*': Simone de Beauvoir, *The 28 Second Sex* (1949; London: Penguin, 1972).

'There are the people who think women...': Polly Toynbee, 'Virago   29
Press gives women writers a voice', *Guardian*, 26 January 1981.

'a way of masking power': Jo Freeman, 'The Tyranny of   32
Structurelessness' (n.p., 1970).

'She hired me and I started as her slave...': Scarlett Sabet, 'Really I   34
was a reader', *Violet Book* (October 2018).

'no moral context', 'putting ideas into children's heads': See Jane   37
Cousins Mills, '"Putting ideas into their heads": advising the
young', *Feminist Review*, 28 (spring 1988).

'another example of twentieth-century arrogance': Robert Howarth,   37
'Twentieth century arrogance', *Third Way* (February 1980).

'She is an ebullient energetic character...': Toynbee, 'Virago Press   39
gives women writers a voice'.

'there were cats galore...': Durrant, 'How we met'.   42

'"It is only when women start to organize..."': From Sheila   43
Rowbotham, *Women, Resistance and Revolution* (London: Vintage,
1974).

'As with all publishers, books are our lifeblood...': Virago Press cata-   45
logue, 1993.

## CHAPTER THREE

'a market-driven company, but...': *British Book News*, 1990.   47

'now and in the future patriarchal attitudes...': Eva Figes, *Patriarchal*   48
*Attitudes* (London: Faber & Faber, 1970).

'with a series of books and position papers...': From 'Women's lib-   49
eration meets Miller-Mailer-Manson man', in Gore Vidal,
*Homage to Daniel Shays: Collected Essays, 1952–1972* (New York:
Vintage, 1973).

'Those early days of feminism were serious days...': Carmen Callil, 'The   49
stories of our lives', *Guardian*, 26 April 2008.

*'the silent women whose voices have been denied us...'*: Acceptance    54
speech, National Book Award for Poetry, 1974.

*'the long process of making visible the experiences of women...'*:    54
'Conditions for work: the common world of women', in
Adrienne Rich, *On Lies, Secrets and Silence* (London: Virago,
1980).

*'When a woman tells the truth she is creating the possibility...'*:    54
'Women and honor: some notes on lying', in ibid.

*'felt as though the top of my head was being attacked...'*; Margaret    54
Atwood, 'Diving into the wreck', *New York Times*, 30 December
1973.

*she sent me a Christmas card*: Reprinted with the permission of the    56
Adrienne Rich Literary Estate.

*'Feminism begins but cannot end with the discovery...'*; Rich,    56
'Conditions for work'.

*'Woman as Other is such a familiar trope...'*: Katha Pollitt, 'Adrienne    57
Rich's news in verse', *New Yorker*, 30 March 2012.

*'We cannot wait to speak until we are perfectly clear...'*: 'Split at the    57
root', in Adrienne Rich, *Blood, Bread and Poetry: Selected Prose
1979–1985* (New York: W. W. Norton, 1986).

*'somewhat combative pacifist and co-operative anarchist'*: Quoted in    57
Alexandra Schwarz, 'The art and activism of Grace Paley', *New
Yorker*, 1 May 2017.

*'When you write, you illuminate what's hidden...'*: Interview on    58
*Fresh Air*, NPR, 1985. Quoted in ibid.

*'I wanted to write about women and children...'*: Quoted in Jonathan    58
Dee, Barbara Jones, and Larissa MacFarquhar, 'Grace Paley,
The art of fiction No. 131', *Paris Review*, 124 (fall 1992).

*'It doesn't preach...'*: Schwartz, 'The art and activism of Grace    59
Paley'.

*'While we owe a great deal…'*: Mishal Husain, *The Skills: From First* 62
*Job to Dream Job — What Every Woman Needs to Know* (London: 4th
Estate, 2018).

*'the ultimate effect upon the woman's mental and emotional health…'*: 62
Susan Brownmiller, *Against Our Will: Men, Women and Rape* (New
York: Simon & Schuster, 1975).

*'People in the movement were starting to say…'*: Rachel Cooke, 'US 62
feminist Susan Brownmiller on why her groundbreaking book on
rape is still relevant', *Observer*, 18 February 2018.

*'We didn't do book signings…'*: Lynn Alderson, 'Sisterwrite book- 64
shop', Lesbian History Group website, 8 December 2016,
https://lesbianhistorygroup.wordpress.com/2016/12/08
/sisterwrite-bookshop-lynn-alderson/.

## CHAPTER FOUR

*'I wanted to celebrate women's lives…'*: Virago Modern Classics 70
40th: Tessa Hadley, Elizabeth Day, Donna Coonan, and Carmen
Callil in Conversation, Foyles, 3 May 2018.

*'It's not too much…'*: Margaret Drabble, Virago leaflet. 71

*'Virago changed English reading habits for ever'*: Philip Hensher, 71
'Dead white male seeks publisher', *Independent*, 21 July 2006.

*'Antonia White, a novelist wonderful to know…'*: Virago Modern 71
Classics 40th.

*'If one novel could tell the story of my life…'*: Carmen Callil, 'The 71
stories of our lives', *Guardian*, 26 April 2008.

*'would unseat some of my deepest assumptions as a reader'*: 72
Jonathan Coe, 'My literary love affair', *Guardian*, 6 October
2007.

*'It reminds you that we connect…'*: Virago Modern Classics 40th. 72

*'like looking through someone's LPs to see if they were okay'*: Ibid. 73

*'It was the '80s, the heyday of dreadful literary theory…'*: Ibid. 73

*'I realised that many of the titles I loved…'*: 'Thirty Years of Virago 73
Modern Classics', Virago brochure, 2008.

*'I was reading for female experience'*: Virago Modern Classics 40th. 73

*'To find the jacket was* enthralling': *Virago: Changing the World One* 74
*Page at a Time*, BBC Four, 31 October 2016.

*'The biggest contribution came from writers'*: Callil, 'The stories of 76
our lives'.

*'Carmen Callil persuaded Alfred Knopf…'*: A. S. Byatt, 'Willa 77
Cather', *A Virago Keepsake to Celebrate Twenty Years of Publishing*
(London: Virago, 1993).

*'I have a note from her thanking…'*: Rosamond Lehmann. reprinted 77
with permission of her Literary Executor.

*'Anita Brookner and I would go for dinner with her…'*; Virago 78
Modern Classics 40th.

*'Afflicted as I was with three years' study…'*: Carmen Callil, 'Virago 78
reprints: redressing the balance', *Times Literary Supplement*, 12
September 1980.

*'A considerable body of women novelists…'*: Callil, 'The stories of 79
our lives'.

*'She also had a genius with language…'*: Talk at Edinburgh Book 81
Festival. Reprinted *Harper's Bazaar* (April 2018).

*'stiletto sharpness and infinite kindness'*: Sally Phipps, *Molly Keane:* 82
*A Life* (London: Virago, 2017).

*'a tiny bombshell'*: Ibid.   82

*'Thinking about you a lot…'*: Molly Keane, reprinted with 82
permission of her Estate.

*'Have married an Englishman…'*: Reprinted in Elaine Dundy, *Life* 85
*Itself!* (London: Virago, 2001).

*'people forget how many of the writers…'*: Email to the author.   86

*'Lovers of literature of either sex…'*: Anthony Burgess, 'Pilgrimage', 86
*Guardian*, 9 December 1979.

*'I take the view that a small canvas…'*: 'Thirty Years of Virago   87
Modern Classics', Virago brochure, 2008.

CHAPTER FIVE

*In 1975 in the UK*: Women's Research and Resources Centre, 1981.   92
*'Women's studies comes out of research inspired…'*: Bristol Women's   93
Study Group, *Half the Sky: An Introduction to Women's Studies* (London:
Virago, 1979).
*'By feminism we mean'* Lynn Alderson, 'Sisterwrite bookshop',   93
Lesbian History Group website, 8 December 2016, https://
lesbianhistorygroup.wordpress.com/2016/12/08/sisterwrite-
bookshop-lynn-alderson/. *feminist we mean both an awareness…'*: Ibid.
*'host of feminist predecessors—feminist radicals…'*: Barbara Taylor,   94
'Making History: The Virago Reprint Library', *A Virago Keepsake
to Celebrate Twenty Years of Publishing* (London: Virago, 1993).
*'"People should know," she said…'*: Amrit Wilson, *Finding a Voice:*   95
*Asian Women in Britain* (Virago, 1978; Montreal: Daraja Press,
2018).
*'many white figures of authority…'*: Ibid.   95
*'For the first time, here was a book…'*: Quoted in ibid.   95
*'shameless immorality'*: Quoted in 'Afterword by the German'   96
Editor, *A Woman in Berlin* (London: Virago, 2005).
*'We often feel that we are unfitted by our education…'*: Dorothy   98
Thompson (ed.), *Over Our Dead Bodies: Women Against the Bomb*
(London: Virago, 1983).
*'I think one of the reasons why I was never properly domesticated…'*: In   99
Jackie Bennett and Rosemary Forgan (ed.), *There's Something About
a Convent Girl* (London: Virago, 1991).
*'Young feminists—whether you call yourself one…'* Amy Annette,   103
Martha Mosse, and Alice Stride, 'Introduction', in Victoria Pepe,

Rachel Holmes, Amy Annette, Alice Stride, and Martha Mosse (eds), *I Call Myself a Feminist* (London: Virago, 2015).

## CHAPTER SIX

*'A country needs to hear its own voice'*: Margaret Atwood, *Suvival: A Thematic Guide to Canadian Literature* (Toronto: House of Anansi, 1972).  105

*In the early 1970s*: John Bowman, 'Fill in the blank: As Canadian as _____', CBC News YourCommunity Blog, 7 June 2013, https://www.cbc.ca/newsblogs/yourcommunity/2013/06/as-canadian-as.html.  106

*'someone with a logical reason to think he may be one'*: Mavis Gallant, *Home Truths* (Toronto: Macmillan of Canada, 1981).  106

*'Virago felt like home to me...'*: Margaret Atwood, 'Dump Bins and Shelf Strips', *A Virago Keepsake to Celebrate Twenty Years of Publishing* (London: Virago, 1993).  106

*'When times are tough...'*: Margaret Atwood, 'Witches', in *Second Words: Selected Critical Prose* (Toronto: House of Anansi, 1982).  109

*'Why do men feel threatened by women?...'*: Margaret Atwood, 'Writing the male character', in *Second Words*.  109

*'Murderess. It rustles, like a taffeta skirt across the floor'*: Margaret Atwood, *Alias Grace* (1996; London: Virago, 1997).  110

*'The writer retains three attributes...'*: Atwood, 'Writing the male character'.  112

*'The research into courtesans, convents, women...'*: Sarah Dunant, 'Sarah Dunant: "The answers history gives us depend on the questions we ask it"', *Guardian*, 29 July 2017.  113

*'One of feminism's great achievements...'*: Ibid.  114

*'art is the nearest thing to life...'*: George Eliot, 'The natural history of German life', *Westminster Review*, XIX (July 1856).  114

'*imagining—generously—life that is not your life*': From interview    115
with Neel Mukherjee, Queen Elizabeth Hall, 20 October 2018.

'*culture and education are basically ...*': Ibid.    116

'*we have learned what looks like learning*': Ibid.    116

'*She stimulates the mind and satisfies the heart*': Sue Wilson, *Scotland*    116
*on Sunday*.

'*The very patchiness of lesbian history ...*': 'Afterword', *Tipping the*    118
*Velvet: 20th Anniversary Edition* (London: Virago, 2018).

'*To me, lesbian stories are the norm, not the aberration*': Sarah Waters,    118
email response to reader via Virago inbox.

'*Storytelling makes us human*': Virago podcast, 26 February    118
2018.

'*Such a brilliant writer ...*': A. N. Wilson, *Daily Mail*.    118

### PART THREE

'*Tell all the truth but tell it slant*': Emily Dickinson, 'Tell all the    119
truth but tell it slant', from Ralph W. Franklin (ed.), *The Poems*
*of Emily Dickinson: Reading Edition* (Cambridge, MA: The Belknap
Press of Harvard University Press, 1998).

### CHAPTER SEVEN

'*You have to realize we were like family*': *Virago: Changing the World*    122
*One Page at a Time*, BBC Four, 31 October 2016.

'*Whatever happened, no one ever wishes they hadn't worked there*':    122
Conversation with the author.

'*By the end of 1986 the group situation was grave ...*': Ursula Owen,    126
'Feminist Publishing', in Peter Owen (ed.), *Publishing: The Future*
(London: Peter Owen, 1988).

'*The author Graham Greene ...*': Edwin McDowell, 'Random    127
House to buy British group', *New York Times*, 8 May 1997.

*'The book is never just about the text...'*: Conversation with the    130
author.

CHAPTER EIGHT

*'Tell all the truth but tell it slant'*: Emily Dickinson, 'Tell all the    133
truth but tell it slant', from Ralph W. Franklin (ed.), *The Poems
of Emily Dickinson: Reading Edition* (Cambridge, MA: The Belknap
Press of Harvard University Press, 1998).

*'In the mid-80s, I was once invited...'*: Zoe Fairbairns, 'Feminist    134
publishing—then, now and in the future', talk at Nottingham
Mechanics, 22 April 2017.

*'It is indicative of the power of the movement...'*: Feminist Book Fair    135
press release.

*'I will never forget the sheer ebullience...'*: 'Writing women', in Ritu    137
Menon (ed.), *Making a Difference: Memoirs of the Women's Movement
in India* (New Delhi: Women Unlimited, 2011).

*'it was about the people who read books...'*: Fairbairns, 'Feminist    137
publishing'.

*'I remember the booksellers who became...'*: Email to the author.    138

*'If you went looking for the Women's Liberation Movement...'*: Lynn    139
Alderson, 'Sisterwrite bookshop', Lesbian History Group website, 8 December 2016, https://lesbianhistorygroup.wordpress.
com/2016/12/08/sisterwrite-bookshop-lynn-alderson/.

*'a monstrosity of racism'*: Pratibha Parman and Jackie Kay,    140
'Frontiers', in Joan Wylie Hall (ed.), *Conversations with Audre
Lorde* (Jackson: University Press of Mississippi, 2004).

*'In those early days of the black feminist movement...'*: Jackie Kay,    141
'Feminist, lesbian, warrior, poet: rediscovering the work of
Audre Lorde', *New Statesman*, 30 September 2017.

*'There was a fervour that greeted Audre...'*: Ibid.    141

*'My mission in life is not merely to survive...'*: Maya Angelou, 142
*Rainbow in the Cloud: The Wit and Wisdom of Maya Angelou* (London:
Virago, 2014).

*'the rhythms and imagery of the good...'*: Maya Angelou, *I Know Why* 143
*the Caged Bird Sings* (1969; London: Virago, 1984).

*'I speak to the black experience...'*: Virago poster.                        143

*'Sister, Mama loves to see you read...'*: Angelou, *I Know Why the Caged* 143
*Bird Sings*.

*'She opened the first page...'*: Ibid.                                        143

*'You may not control all the events...'*: Angelou, *Rainbow in the* 146
*Cloud*.

*'History, despite its wrenching pain...'*: Ibid.                             146

*a sweet letter from August 1987*: Reproduced with the permission 149
of the Estate of Maya Angelou.

*'I envision Maya as a kind of General of Compassion...'*: Alice Walker, 150
'Maya Angelou was more beautiful than she realised', *Guardian*,
29 May 2014.

*'clever and sassy'*: Quoted in Lauren Gambino, 'Obama: Maya 150
Angelou's words "carried a little black girl to the White House"',
*Guardian*, 7 June 2014.

*'describes Black women's celebration of their culture...'*: Beverley 152
Bryan, Stella Dadzie, and Suzanne Scafe, *The Heart of the Race:
Black Women's Lives in Britain* (London: Virago, 1985).

*'You know you can only ask that question...'*: Elissa Schappell with 152
Claudia Brodsky Lacour, 'Toni Morrison, The art of fiction No.
134', *Paris Review*, 128 (fall 1993).

*'I remember the day Salman Rushdie was described...'*: Yasmin Alibhai- 152
Brown, *Who Do We Think We Are? Imagining the New Britain*
(London: Allen Lane, 2000).

*'It's not patronage, not affirmative action...'*: Schappell and Lacour, 154
'Toni Morrison'.

'the desire for a multi-cultural list does not...': Margaret Busby and 154
Lennie Goodings, *The Bookseller*, 23 September 1988.

'publishers want to make money...': Marsha Hunt, 'Saga that led to 155
a miracle', *Herald*, 8 August 1995.

'the distance between the self...': Patricia J Williams, *Seeing A Color-* 156
*Blind Future: The Paradox of Race. The Reith Lectures* (London:
Virago, 1997)

'We don't want to be saved by Western feminists...': Masih Alinjed, 156
BBC News, 22 September 2018.

'things don't have to be the way things are...': Joanna Bourke, 157
Feminist Book Fair 2018.

'The feminist pundit class is not attuned to race and class': Lola 157
Olufemi, ibid.

CHAPTER NINE

'I set out in a very tepid, tentative sort of way...': Rob Nixon, 'An 164
interview with Pat Barker', *Contemporary Literature*, 45:1 (spring
2004).

'Regional, working-class voices are very, very marginalized...': Ibid. 165

'All those bloody dons sitting around...': Ibid. 166

'I felt I had got myself into a box...': Ibid. 166

'I am just finishing this for the girls': Quoted in publisher's preface 167
to Angela Carter (ed.), *The Second Virago Book of Fairy Tales*
(London: Virago, 1992).

'She gave of herself—her ideas...': Marina Warner, 'Introduction', 167
ibid.

'seems to show grand narratives being prised open...': 'Afterword', 169
*Tipping the Velvet: 20th Anniversary Edition* (London: Virago, 2018).

'There's an idea that there's this great mainstream...': Jonathan Dee, 170
Barbara Jones, and Larissa MacFarquhar, 'Grace Paley, The art
of fiction No. 131', *Paris Review*, 124 (fall 1992).

*'I have always believed in a way ...'*: Rachel Cooke, 'Maggie Nelson:    171
"There is no catharsis ... the stories we tell ourselves don't heal
us"', *Observer*, 21 May 2017.

*'Acceptance of the "given-ness" of the marketplace ...'*: 'For a heroic    171
writers movement', in Toni Morrison, *What Moves at the Margin:
Selected Nonfiction* (Jackson: University Press of Mississippi, 2008).

## CHAPTER TEN

*'Promotional paraphernalia from balloons to bookmarks ...'*: Catherine    173
Lockerbie, 'Taming of the shrewd behind a write-on success',
*The Scotsman*, 18 June 1993.

*'Today women reign over Random House ...'*: Catherine Bennett,    174
*Guardian*, June 1993.

*'Virago has become a victim of its own success ...'*: E. Jane Dickson,    174
'A woman's place is on the shelf', *Daily Telegraph*, 15 June 1993.

*'Virago is the feminist movement in microcosm ...'*: Natasha Walter,    174
'Still maligned, still loved, still needed', *Independent*, 19 June
1993.

*'Call me old-fashioned but ...'*: Lennie Goodings, 'Call me old-    175
fashioned, but that advertisement's sexist', *Independent*, 20 June
1993.

*'things had changed a great deal over that time ...'*: Lynn Alderson,    178
'Sisterwrite bookshop', Lesbian History Group website, 8
December 2016, https://lesbianhistorygroup.wordpress.com/
2016/12/08/sisterwrite-bookshop-lynn-alderson/.

*'They decided to take on the supermarkets and Smith's ...'*: Quoted in    179
Stuart Jeffries, 'How Waterstone's killed bookselling', *Guardian*,
10 November 2009.

*'You cut Waterstones out, and ...'*: Quoted in Stephen Hyman, 'Big-    180
box stores don't have to die', *Slate*, 15 December 2015.

'In my experience, the smaller the cheese...': Virago: Changing the 181
World One Page at a Time, BBC Four, 31 October 2016.

'The setback raises questions about the future health...': Stephen Ward, 181
'Virago's book list is trimmed as sales drop', Independent on
Sunday, 5 June 1994.

We are a literary and political publishing house...: Quoted in ibid. 182

'In challenging times you have to focus...': Bookseller, 17 February 183
1995.

'I wanted Lennie to have Virago': Virago: Changing the World One Page 184
at a Time.

'Reports of the death of feminism...': Jan Dalley, 'Was Virago too 184
successful?', Independent on Sunday, 29 October 1995.

'The Virago list is close to my heart...'. Little, Brown press release, 186
2 November 1995.

'Talk to any of her authors...': Mark Bostridge, 'The apple bites 193
back', Independent on Sunday, 18 May 2003.

'Back to Soho's seedier...': with kind permission of Margaret 194
Atwood.

## CHAPTER ELEVEN

'It's a particular pleasure to honour...': WH Smith Literary Award 199
brochure.

'within the relationship if there is some trust...': Elissa Schappell 202
with Claudia Brodsky Lacour, 'Toni Morrison, The art of fiction
No. 134', Paris Review, 128 (fall 1993).

'There's a point where the novel...': Email to the author. 203

'When someone feels they must tell you...': Maya Angelou, Rainbow in 206
the Cloud: The Wit and Wisdom of Maya Angelou (London: Virago,
2014).

*'from the curl all of the way to a full-fledged person'*: Schappell and   210
Lacour, 'Toni Morrison'.

*'I know that not since the days of my childhood ...'*: James Baldwin,   210
quoted in Don Nardo, *Maya Angelou: Poet, Performer, Activist*
(Minneapolis: Compass Point Books, 2009).

*'is the proper aim of art'*: 'The decay of lying—an observation', in   211
Oscar Wilde, *Intentions* (1891).

*'They make use of their ...'*: Nina Bawden, 'Coded Autobiography',   211
*A Virago Keepsake to Celebrate Twenty Years of Publishing* (London:
Virago, 1993).

*'I wanted to counter the image of her as veering ...'*: Email to the author.   212

*'seemed to miraculously transform the harsher truths ...'*: Susie Boyt,   215
*My Judy Garland Life* (London: Virago, 2008).

*she couldn't get the same money*: Edmund Gordon, *The Invention of*   218
*Angela Carter: A Biography* (London: Chatto & Windus, 2016).

*'Poetry has never let me down ...'*: Josephine Hart, *Catching Life by*   219
*the Throat: How to Read Poetry and Why* (London: Virago, 2006).

*'Your thorns are the best part of you'*: Marianne Moore, 'Roses Only'.   219

## CHAPTER TWELVE

*'I realised that in every generation ...'*: Naomi Wolf, *The Beauty Myth*   225
(1991; London: Penguin, 2015).

*'excessive attachment to a politically correct idealism'*: Natasha   225
Walter, *The New Feminism* (London: Virago, 1999).

*'At her spirited best, she is a symbol ...'*: Elaine Showalter, *Guardian*.   227
'Better than a dose of Paglia any day': *Marie Claire* (February   227
1999).

*We live in a time when the very fundaments ...*: Susan Faludi, *Backlash:*   227
*The Undeclared War Against American Women* (1991; New York:
Broadway Books, 2006).

*I once believed that we only had to put in place…*: Natasha Walter, 229
*Living Dolls* (London: Virago, 2010).

*'I see a renewed energy around publishing…'*: Interview with the author. 231

*'The aspirational mantra of inclusivity and diversity…'*: Margaret 231
Busby, 'From Ayòbámi Adébáyò to Zadie Smith: meet the New
Daughters of Africa', *Guardian*, 9 March 2019.

*Proper, dedicated, lived and breathed fuck-the-patriarchy feminism…*: 232
Deborah Frances-White, *The Guilty Feminist: From Our Noble Goals
to Our Worst Hypocrises* (London: Virago, 2018).

*'I like the adaptation of Flavia Dzodan's quote…'*: Conversation 233
with the author.

*'I agree wholeheartedly…'*: 'Introduction', June Eric-Udorie 233
(ed.), *Can We All Be Feminists?* (London: Virago, 2018).

*'Feminism also gave me permission…'*: Ibid. 233

*'In a world where language and naming are power…'*: 'Conditions 234
for work: the common world of women', in Adrienne Rich, *On
Lies, Secrets and Silence* (London: Virago, 1980).

## CHAPTER THIRTEEN

*'I did not want to be published by [Virago]…'*: Susha Guppy, 235
'Marguerite Yourcenar, The art of fiction No. 103', *Paris Review*,
106 (spring 1988).

*'Women hid in order to be seen'*: Jonathan Dee, Barbara Jones, and 237
Larissa MacFarquhar, 'Grace Paley, The art of fiction No. 131',
*Paris Review*, 124 (fall 1992).

*'The woman who writes is a writer…'*: Joyce Carol Oates, *(Woman)* 237
*Writer: Occasions and Opportunities* (New York: Dutton, 1988).

*'where you are likely to see gender bias, bias of all kinds'*: Mary 238
Morris, 'Margaret Atwood, The art of fiction No. 121', *Paris
Review*, 117 (winter 1990).

'*a non-profit feminist organization committed…*': https://www    238
.vidaweb.org/about-vida/.

'*Literature with a capital L…*': Quoted in Danuta Kean, 'Are you    238
serious? The Emilia report into the gender gap for authors',
March 2019.

*Having been right about the English literature of…*: Robert    240
McCrum, 'The Man Booker at 50: flawed—but still the best
way to judge our literature', *Observer*, 1 July 2018.

*It is tempting […to conclude] that men and women…*: Anne Enright,    241
'Diary', *London Review of Books*, 39:18 (21 September 2017).

'*I've been publishing novels for almost 20 years…*': John Boyne,    242
'"Women are better writers than men": novelist John Boyne
sets the record straight', *Guardian*, 12 December 2017.

'*Calling a work of fiction domestic…*': *Woman's Hour*, BBC Radio 4,    243
23 November 2015.

'*wave of essentialism once more sweeping the women's world*': 'From    244
the Editors', in Lisa Appignanesi, Rachel Holmes, and Susie
Orbach (eds), *Fifty Shades of Feminism* (London: Virago, 2013).

'*We, all of us, women and men…*': Siri Hustvedt, 'Underground    244
sexism: what was that you just said?', in ibid.

'*A male novelist hardens and dignifies the form…*': Aaron Hickling, 'Siri    244
Hustvedt: I'm writing for my life', *Observer*, 3 March 2019.

'*the woman writer still risks*': Rachel Cusk, 'Shakespeare's daugh-    244
ters', *Guardian*, 12 December 2009.

'*Male readers…rarely use the compliment…*': Sarah Churchwell,    245
'Pushing back: why it's time for women to rewrite the story',
*Guardian*, 17 February 2018.

'*There is a difference between a culture…*': Enright, 'Diary'.    246

'*Women have been too dignified and self-effacing…*': Elaine    246
Showalter, 'The female frontier', *Guardian*, 9 May 2009.

'Great-novel writing is regarded as a pursuit...': Bryan Appleyard,    247
'Twilight of the greats?', *Sunday Times*, 30 December 2007.

'I want to work hard and know that my work...': Naomi Alderman,    248
'Wild West Video', in Appignanesi, Holmes, and Orbach (eds),
*Fifty Shades of Feminism*.


CHAPTER FOURTEEN

'It wasn't just the language of Leaves of Grass...': Naomi Wolf,    250
*Outrages: Sex, Censorship and the Criminalisation of Love* (London:
Virago, 2019).

'in part an act of submission, akin to generosity or love': Quoted in    250
Brigitta Olubas, 'Remembering Shirley Hazzard: "art is the only
afterlife of which we have evidence"', http://theconversation.
com/remembering-shirley-hazzard-art-is-the-only-afterlife-
of-which-we-have-evidence-70519, 16 December 2016.

'Our world that seems charged with war...': Acceptance speech,    251
Miles Franklin Award, 2004.

'I happen to believe that at its best writing...': Margaret Atwood,    252
'An end to an audience?', public lecture, Dalhousie University,
part of the Dorothy J. Killam Lecture Series, 8 October 1980.
Reprinted in *Second Words: Selected Critical Prose* (Toronto: House
of Anansi, 1982).

'We write best when we write about...': Sarah Waters, email response    254
to reader via Virago inbox.

'To be human is a very high and complicated privilege': 'Marilynne    254
Robinson webchat – your questions answered on *Gilead*,
Trump and the joys of quiet', *Guardian* Books blog, 26 January
2018.

'Conviction as to the importance of what one...': Tillie Olsen, *Silences*    257
(London: Virago, 1980).

'*The question is not who influences you…*': Mona Simpson, 'Hilary   257
Mantel, The art of fiction No. 226', *Paris Review*, 212 (spring
2015).

'*I think we're genetically programmed to tell stories…*': Virago pod-   259
cast, 26 February 2018.

# Index

5 Wardour Street ix, 6, 25, 33, 123
41 William IV Street 123

Aaron, Hank 148
Abacus 155, 188
Abbey, Sally 117, 189, 190, 191
Adams, Ruth
  *I'm Not Complaining* 79
Adebayo, Diran 157
  *Some Kind of Black* 155
Adichie, Chimamanda Ngozie 153
*After Noon Plus* (Thames
  Television) 145
Ahmed, Ailah 112–13, 189, 233
Aiken, Joan 89
Akira Press 154
Alderman, Naomi 248
  *The Power* 248
Alderson, Lynn, Sisterwrite 64,
  74, 76, 78, 139, 178
Alexander, Sally 27, 43
  *Becoming a Woman: And Other Essays
    in 19th and 20th Century
    Feminist History* 94
  *Her Infinite Variety* 173
Ali, Monica 153
Alibhai-Brown, Yasmin 152
Alinejad, Masih
  *The Wind in My Hair: My Fight for
    Freedom in Modern Iran* 156
Allen & Unwin 136
Allfrey, Ellah Wakatama 155
Allison and Busby 154
Alther, Lisa 136
*Amazones d'Hier* 11

Amis, Kingsley 48
Anansi, House of, Toronto 25, 106
Anarchist Feminists 136
André Deutsch 12, 81
Angelou, Maya 52, 65, 102, 126,
  139, 142–51, 188, 189, 206
  'And Still I Rise' 102
  *I Know Why the Caged Bird Sings*
    14, 142, 143, 144, 151, 210
Annette, Amy 103, 149, 162
Annette, John 58, 78
Annette, Zak 148, 199
Annis, Francesca 173
Anonymous
  *A Woman in Berlin* 96
Appignanesi, Lisa 30, 32, 241
  *Fifty Shades of Feminism* (ed.) 244
  *Mad, Bad and Sad: Women and the
    Mind Doctors* 100
Appignanesi, Richard 30
Appleyard, Bryan 247
Arawadi 154
Arcadia 32
Arsenal Women's Group 20
Arvon Foundation 164
Athill, Diana 81
Attallah, Naim 64
Atwood, Margaret 65, 72, 83,
  105–12, 126, 153, 181, 188,
  189, 191, 208, 225, 238,
  252–3, 256
  on Adrienne Rich 54–5
  *Alias Grace* 110, 111, 189
  *The Blind Assassin* 110, 189
  *Bluebeard's Egg* 111

Atwood, Margaret (*cont.*)
  and Canada 4, 105, 107
  *Cat's Eye* 109, 111
  *The Circle Game* 105
  *The Edible Woman* 14, 106, 107
  *The Handmaid's Tale* 109, 111,
    170, 223
  *The Testaments* 109, 111
  *Lady Oracle* 107
  *Maddadam* 204–6
  'On Virago's 30th Birthday'
    194–5
  *Oryx and Crake* 110, 113, 204
  *The Robber Bride* 109–10
  *Surfacing* 75, 107
  *Survival* 105
  'The Whirlpool Rapids' 111
Austen, Jane 71
Australian Classics 83

Badran, Margot and Miriam
  Cooke (eds)
  *Opening the Gates: A Century of
    Arab Women's Writing* 101
Bailey, Paul 76
Bainbridge, Beryl 240, 252, 257
Baker, Dorothy
  *Cassandra at the Wedding* 77
Bakewell, Joan 10, 209
Baldwin, James 145, 151, 210
Bambara, Toni Cade 137
Bamford, David 189
Banyard, Kat
  *The Equality Illusion: The Truth
    about Men and Women
    Today* 230
Barker, Pat 134, 136, 161,
    164–6
  *The Ghost Road* 166
  *Union Street* 164, 166

Barnes, Djuna 84, 257
Barnes, Julian 242
Battle Axe 136
Bawden, Nina 86, 89, 112, 191,
    208, 211
Baxter, Sarah 148
BBC TV
  Virago documentary 122
Beauman, Nicola
  *A Very Great Profession: The Women's
    Novel 1914–39* 79
Beauman, Sally 76
Bedford, Sybille 76
Beevor, Antony 96
Beginners' Guides 30
Behn, Aphra 94
Bell, Florence
  *At the Works* 26–7
Belle, Jennifer
  *Going Down* 191
Belott, Elena
  *Little Girls* 31
Benjamin, Jessica 100
Bennett, Catherine 174
Bennett, Jackie (ed)
  *There's Something About
    a Convent Girl* 99
Berger, John 33
  *Pig Earth* 31
  *Ways of Seeing* 31
Berryman, Tamsyn 187
Best of British 153
Best of Young British
  Novelists 134
Best of Young British Writers 153
Beswick, Richard 188
Bevan, Aneurin 165
Black Ink 154
Black Lesbian Group
  (BLG) 141

Black Womantalk  154
Black Women Talk  136
Blackwell's  136, 138
Blake, William  258
Bloodaxe Books  136
Bloomsbury  107, 110, 130, 184–6
Bogle-L'Ouverture  154
Book Action for Nuclear
    Disarmament  138
Book Marketing Council  81, 134
Book Trust  155
Booker Prize  110, 153, 166, 199,
    225, 237, 239–40, 255
Bookmarks  136
Bookplus  136
Boothe, John  12, 41–2
Borogrove Bookshop, Victoria,
    British Columbia  16
Bostridge, Mark  28, 193–4
Bourke, Joanna
    Rape: A History from 1860 to the
    Present  156–7
Bowen, Elizabeth  83, 257
Boycott, Rosie  12, 13, 15, 17
Boyne, John  242
Boyt, Susie  215
    My Judy Garland Life  215
Braddon, Mary E.  84
Brandenberg, Gert  137
Breeze, Jean Binta  151
Brettenham House, Lancaster
    Place  187
Brighton Women and Science
    Group (ed.)
    Alice through the Microscope  92
Brilliance  136
Bristol Women's Studies Group  92
British Book Awards  215
Brittain, Vera  93, 255
    Testament of Youth  27, 43

Brontë sisters  160
Brookner, Anita  76, 78
Broughton, Rhoda  84
Bryan, Beverley; Dadzie, Stella;
    Scafe, Suzanne
    The Heart of the Race: Black
    Women's Lives in Britain  152
Brownmiller, Susan
    Against our Will: Men, Women and
    Rape  14, 62
Buford, Bill  134
Burgess, Anthony  86, 243
Busby, Margaret  154, 155
    Daughters of Africa (ed.)  231
    The New Daughters of Africa: An
    International Anthology of
    Writing by Women of African
    Descent (ed.)  231
Butalia, Urvashi  136, 137
Butler, Judith  222
Butterworth, Sue  139
Byatt, A. S.  76, 77, 236

Calder, Liz  43, 107, 110, 130,
    184–5
Callil, Carmen  193, 260, 261
    Bad Faith  249
    Chair  124, 126, 180, 182–3
    and Chatto & Windus  80, 121,
    123, 184, 224
    at CVBC  123, 124, 126, 142,
    164, 180
    Managing Director  ix, 6, 7, 9,
    10, 11, 17–19, 24–5, 27–9,
    33–6, 38–9, 40, 41–2, 43–4,
    49, 87–8, 217–18
    and publicity  130
    and Quartet  12–13, 24
    resignation  183–4, 186
    and Rothschilds  127, 128

Callil, Carmen (*cont.*)
  Virago Modern Classics 70,
    74–6, 77, 78–9, 87, 107
  *see also* Carmen Callil
    Publicity Ltd
*Cambridge Women's Liberation*
  *Newsletter* 11
Cambridge Women's Studies
  Group 92
Campbell, Beatrix 43, 53–4, 223
  *Wigan Pier Revisited* 59–60
Campbell, Cheryl 27
Canada x, 11, 16, 25, 105–6, 107
  Human Rights Act (1977) 29
Carcanet 183
Carey, John 200
Carmen Callil Publicity Ltd 12,
  17, 23
Carpentier, Alejo 31
Carswell, Catherine 83
Carter, Angela 1, 21, 25, 43, 73,
    98, 161–5, 166–8, 239
  *Angela Carter's Book of Fairy*
    *Tales* 167
  *The First Virago Book of Fairy*
    *Tales* 167
  *The Magic Toyshop* 72, 161
  *Nights at the Circus* 240
  *Nothing Sacred* 162
  *Perrault's Fairy Tales* 167
  *The Sadeian Woman* 161, 218
  *The Second Virago Book of Fairy*
    *Tales* 167
Cather, Willa 73, 76, 77, 84, 85, 257
Centerprise Bookshop, Hackney,
  London 30, 136
Central Books 136
Chamberlain, Mary
  *Fenwomen* 23
Change 136

Chatto, Bodley Head and Jonathan
  Cape Ltd. (CBC) 121, 123
Chatto, Virago, Bodley Head and
  Cape (CVBC) 123–5, 126,
    127, 128, 129, 142, 218
Chatto & Windus 121, 123
Chester, Gail 135
Cheyne Place, Chelsea 23–4
Cholmeley, Jane 139
Cholmondeley, Mary 84
Chopin, Kate 80
Christie, Julie 98
Churchwell, Sarah
  *Careless People: Murder, Mayhem*
    *and the Invention of the Great*
    *Gatsby* 245
*City Limits (magazine)* 34
Clapp, Susannah 76
Clarke, Desmond 134
Cliff, Michelle 55
Clinton, Bill 144
Co-operative Women's Guild
  26, 27
Coach House, Toronto 25, 106
Coates, Tim 179
Coe, Jonathan 72
Coetzee, J. M. 252
Colette 75
Collector's Cards 74
Collins, Merle 151
Compendium 139
Compton-Burnett, Ivy 71
Comyns, Barbara 74
  *The Vet's Daughter* 80
Cooke, Miriam *see* Badran, Margot
  and Miriam Cooke (eds)
Cooke, Rachel 72–3
  *Her Brilliant Career: Ten*
    *Extraordinary Women of*
    *the Fifties* 70

Coonan, Donna 70, 85, 87, 88–9, 189, 191, 192, 253
Cooper, Karen 129
Cottam, Hilary
  Radical Help: How We Can Remake The Relationships Between Us and Revolutionise the Welfare State 97
Cousins, Jane
  Make it Happy: What Sex is all About 7, 36
Craigie, Jill 33, 98
Crenshaw, Kimberlé 222
Cross, Amanda 112, 223
Curtis Brown 239
Cusk, Rachel 244, 252

Dadzie, Stella see Bryan, Beverley
Dalley, Jan 184
Dane, Clemence 88
Daraja Press 94–5
Darling, Grace 147
DasGupta, Sayantani 156
Daunt, James 179, 180
Davies, Margaret Llewelyn (ed.)
  Life as we Have Known It 26
  Maternity: Letters from Working Class Women 26
Davies, Robertson 106
Davin, Anna 27, 44
Davis, Angela
  If They Come in the Morning 14
Dawson, Jeremy 128
Day, Elizabeth 70, 73
de Beauvoir, Simone 28–9
  The Second Sex 14
de Lanerolle, Ros 154
de Soissons, Susan 148
Delafield, E. M. 86
Delmar, Rosalind 27, 43

Deraniyagala, Sonali
  Wave 254
Desai, Kiran 153
Desert Flower Foundation 96–7
Deutsch, André 107
Devlin, Polly 76, 82, 83
Dialogue 155
Dickinson, Emily 102, 119, 133
Dickson, E. Jane 174
Dillons 178, 179
Dillsworth, Elise 155
Dinesen, Isak 257
Dirie, Waris 156
  Desert Flower 96–7
Diski, Jenny 236, 252
Diversity in Publishing Network (DIPNet) 155
Dizzy Heights 136
Donoghue, Emma 217
  Room 217
  Slammerkin 217
Dorling Kindersley 136
Dover Street, Mayfair 69, 123
Doyle, Ursula 112, 189
Drabble, Margaret 71, 76
  The Millstone 14
Drake, Barbara
  Women and Trade Unions 27
Du Maurier, Daphne 86
  Rebecca 89
Duffy, Maureen 88
Dunant, Sarah 112, 113–14, 191, 206–8
  The Birth of Venus 113, 207
  Transgressions 113, 249
  War of the Words (ed.) 99
Dundy, Elaine
  The Dud Avocado 84
  Life Itself! 84
Dunn, Nell 76, 86

Dworkin, Andrea  222
Dzodan, Flavia  233

Eddo-Lodge, Renni
    *Why I am No Longer Talking to
        White People About Race*  157
Edmund Gordon  168
Eichborn  96
*Einstein for Beginners*  31
el Sadaawi, Nawal  136
Eliot, George  114
    *The Lifted Veil*  83
Elliott Advisors  179
Ellmann, Lucy
    *Sweet Desserts*  112
Eltahawy, Mona
    *Headscarves and Hymens: Why the
        Middle East Needs a Sexual
        Revolution*  91
Emecheta, Buchi  153
Emilia Report into the Gender Gap
    for Authors  238
Enright, Anne  241, 246
Ensler, Eve
    *The Vagina Monologues*  225
Ephron, Nora  84
Eric-Udorie, June 91, 103
    *Can We All Be Feminists?*  103, 233
Evaristo, Bernardine  153, 225
*Everywoman*  11

Fabian Women's Group  27
Fairbairns, Zoe  134, 136, 137
    *Stand We at Last*  112
Falling Wall Press  136
Faludi, Susan  227–8
    *Backlash: The Undeclared War
        Against Women*  224, 225
Fanon, Frantz  31
Farrell, M. J.  81–2

Fawcett Society  61, 166
Feiffer, Judy  151
Feiffer, Jules  151
*Feminism for Beginners*  31
Feminist Book Fairs  134, 156–7
    *see also* First International
        Feminist Book Fair
Feminist Book Week  135, 138
*Feminist Review, The*  11, 136
Ferrier, Susan  83
Fielding, Helen
    *Bridget Jones's Diary*  225
*Fifty Shades of Feminism*  156, 230, 244
Figes, Eva  136
    *Patriarchal Attitudes*  14, 48
Figes, Kate  100
First International Feminist Book
    Fair  135–41, 233
Fitzgerald, Penelope  76
Florence, Peter  147–8
Fontana  136
Foot, Michael  33
Foot, Paul  76
Ford, Richard  242
Forgan, Rosemary (ed)
    *There's Something About a Convent
        Girl*  99
Forward, Toby  160–1
Foulston, Jill  189
Foyles  ix, 70, 178, 179
Frame, Janet  89, 257
Frances-White, Deborah  65
    *The Guilty Feminist*  101, 232
Frank Cass publishers  19
Franklin, Miles  83
Fraser, Sylvia
    *My Father's House*  101
Freeman, Jo
    'The Tyranny of
        Structurelessness'  32

Freire, Paulo 31
French, Marilyn
   *The War Against Women* 224
   *The Women's Room* 14, 223
*Freud for Beginners* 31
Friday, Nancy
   *My Secret Garden: Women's Sexual*
      *Fantasies* 23–4
Friedan, Betty 229
   *The Feminine Mystique* 14

Gallant, Mavis 106
GAP (Greater Access to
   Publishing) 154, 155
Gavron, Bob 24, 125, 127, 180,
   182, 183, 185
Gavron, Kate 183, 185
Gay Men's Press 80
Geller, Jonny 251
Gibbons, Stella 86
Gibson, Graeme 111–12, 206
Gilman, Charlotte Perkins 84
Gilot, Françoise
   *Life with Picasso* 100
Glendinning, Victoria 76
Godden, Rumer 89
Gollancz, Victor 9, 136
Gordon, Lyndall 212
   *Divided Lives* 213
   *Lives Like Loaded Guns* 102
Gracie, Carrie
   *Equal* 232
Graham, Lauren
   *Gilmore Girls* (TV series) 101
   *Talking as Fast As I Can* 101
Granada 12, 136
Grant, Linda 116–17, 191, 203, 209
   *Still Here* 116
   *Upstairs at the Party* 248
*Granta* 134, 153

Greene, Graham 80, 127, 251
Greene, Graham C. 127
Greenham Common Women 98
Greer, Germaine 18, 43, 76,
   99–100
   *The Female Eunuch* 12, 15
Gregory, Jane 43
Griffin, Kate 17, 36, 121, 123,
   138, 184, 193
Grunfeld, Ernst 24
Guardian Fiction Prize 112, 166
Guy, Rosa 140–1

Hachette 122, 189, 190
Hadley, Tessa 70, 73
Hale, Hilary 187–8
*Half the Sky: An Introduction to*
   *Women's Studies* 92
Hall, Radclyffe
   *The Well of Loneliness* 86
Hamilton, Patrick
   *Gas Light* (play) 245
Hamish Hamilton 131, 175,
   183, 224
Hamlyn, Paul 24
Han Suyin 88
Hancock, Sheila 173
Hanff, Helene 84
   *Charing Cross Road* ix
Hansberry, Lorraine 257
Hanson, Michele
   *Treasure: The Trials of a Teenage*
      *Terror* 102
Harlem Writers Group 146
Harman, Harriet 98
Harper & Row 136
*Harper's Bazaar* 81
Harrison, Philippa 121,
   184–5, 186–7, 188–90, 193,
   226, 228

Hart, Josephine 219
    Catching Life by the Throat: How to
        Read Poetry and Why 219
    Damage 219
Harvester Press 136
Hatchards 179
Hauptmann, Gaby
    In Search of an Impotent Man 191
Hay on Wye Literary Festival 147
Hazzard, Shirley 83, 191, 247
    The Great Fire 113, 250
    Greene on Capri 251
    Miles Franklin Award 250–1
    Transit of Venus 250
Head, Bessie 85
Hebert, Anne 106
Heffers 138
Heilbrun, Carolyn (as Amanda
    Cross) 112, 223
Heinemann Education 136
Hellman, Lillian 257
Hensher, Philip 71
Her Infinite Variety 173
Herizons 11
Highsmith, Patricia 84, 89
Hillers, Marta 96
History Workshop Journal 25–6
Hitchens, Christopher 147
HMV Group 179
Hobsbawm, Julia 129, 148
Hodgson, Antonia 102
Hogarth Press 80, 124
Holmes, Rachel
    Fifty Shades of Feminism (ed.) 244
    I Call Myself a Feminist 103
Holroyd, Michael 71
Holtby, Winifred 86
Hornby, Sir Simon 199
Hossain, Attia 85
Housemans 139

Hughes, Dorothy Pitman 12
Hunt, Marsha
    Joy 155
Hurston, Zora Neale 72, 84, 257
    Their Eyes Were Watching God 85
Husain, Mishal 62
Husain, Shahrukh 167
Hustvedt, Siri 244, 247
Hutchinson Education 136

I Call Myself a Feminist 11, 230
ICA (Institute of Contemporary
    Arts) 55, 78, 162–3
Ink (newspaper) 18
Inky Fingers 154
International Marxist Group
    newspaper 31
International PEN 65
Ishiguro, Kazuo 134, 166

Jameson, Storm 74, 80
    Company Parade 80
    Journey from the North 80
    Women Against Men 80
Jenkins, Elizabeth 76, 86
    The Tortoise and the Hare 77
Jenkins, Emily
    Tongue First: Adventures in Physical
        Culture 191
Jessica Kingsley 189
Jhalak Prize 157, 240
John, Errol
    Moon on a Rainbow Shawl 147
Johnson, Amryl 151
Jonathan Cape 86, 107
Jones, Gayl
    Corregidora 85
Jones, Tayari 153
Jordan, Neil
    Night in Tunisia 31

Journeyman 136
Joyce, James 87

Kali, India 137
Karia Press 154
Karnak House 154
Kay, Jackie 141
Kaysen, Susanna
  Girl, Interrupted 100
Keane, Danuta 238
Keane, Molly 74, 76, 81–3,
    214, 215
  Conversation Piece 82
  Good Behaviour 81, 83
  Loving and Giving 81, 82
  as M. J. Farrell 81–2
  Time After Time 81
Kennedy, A. L. 15
Kennedy, Helena 147
Kennedy, Margaret 76
Kent, David 188
Keppel, Alice 75
Khan, Rahila 159–60
King, Charlie 190
King, Martin Luther
    146, 151
Kingsolver, Barbara 112
Kishwar, Madhu 137
Klein, Melanie 100
Knight, Lynn 17, 36, 86, 121, 124,
    181, 193
Knopf 24, 77, 171
Kollontai, Alexandra 33, 40
Korneliussen, Niviaq
  Crimson 113
Krajeski, Jenna 256
Kuzwayo, Ellen 137

Lacey, Robert 37
  Majesty 4

Lang, Andrew 167
Larmore, Phoebe 204–5
Laurence, Margaret 83, 106
  The Diviners 16, 83
  The Stone Angel 83
Laverty, Maura 83
Lawrence & Wishart 136
Leary, Timothy 29
Leavis, F. R.
  The Great Tradition 78–9
Lee, Hermione 76, 85, 200
Lee, Jennie 165
Lee, Jessica J. 65
Lehmann, Rosamond 74, 76,
    77–8, 134
  Invitation to the Waltz 70
  The Weather in the Streets 70
Lerner, Betsy 258
Lesbian Landmarks 88
Lesbiennes d'Aujourd'hui 11
Lessing, Doris 41, 199
  The Golden Notebook 14
Lester, C. N.
  Trans Like Me: A Journey for
    All of Us 231
Letterbox Library 136
Leverson, Ada
  The Little Ottleys 77
Levine, Ellen 115
Levy, Andrea 153
  Small Island 113
Levy, Ariel 190
Liddington, Jill and Jill Norris
  One Hand Tied Behind Us 94
Little, Brown 52, 121, 155, 184–5,
    186–8, 226, 228, 261
Lockerbie, Catherine 173–4
Loomis, Bob 151
Lorde, Audre 54, 140, 141, 233
Lovegrove, Sharmaine 155

Macaulay, Rose  76, 86
McCarthy, Mary  84, 89
McClelland & Stewart  106, 204
McCrindle, Jean
    Her Infinite Variety  173
McCrum, Robert  115, 240
McCullers, Carson  257
McCullough, Colleen
    The Thorn Birds  4
McDermid, Anne  239
McDermid, Val  14
McEwan, Ian  134, 166, 242
McIntosh, Mary see Segal, Lynne
    and Mary McIntosh (eds)
Mackay, Shena  86
Mackenzie, Ursula  190, 193, 228
McLain, Paula
    The Paris Wife  112
MacLeod, Sheila
    The Art of Starvation: A Story of
        Anorexia and Survival  96
Macmillan  136
McMorrough, Fiona  148, 186
McNeil, Gill  186
Maitland, Sara  136
Malcolm X  151
Mamut, Alexander  179
Manchester University Press  136
Mandela Street, Camden
        Town  128–9, 183
Manning, Olivia  243
Mansfield, Katharine  257
Mantel, Hilary  239, 257
Mao for Beginners  31
Maraini, Dacia  136
Marshall, Paule  85
Martin Luther King Award  94
Marx for Beginners  30–1
Maschler, Tom  127
Master, Simon  127–8

Mayor, F. M.  76
Media Diversified  157
Mehta, Sonny  24, 28
Mekhennet, Souad
    I was Told to Come Alone: Behind the
        Lines of Jihad  95
Menon, Ritu  137
Mernissi, Fatima
    Islam and Democracy  101
Messud, Claire
    The Woman Upstairs  112
Methuen  136
Mew, Charlotte  75
Middlebrook, Diane Wood
    Suits Me  102
Miles Franklin Award  250–1
Miller, Alice  100
    The Drama of Being a Child  223
Miller, Ellen
    Like Being Killed  191
Miller, William  41
Millett, Kate  223
    Sexual Politics  14
Milner, Marion  100
Miner, Valerie  136
Mitchell, Juliet  100
Mitchison, Naomi  83
Mitford, Jessica  144, 147
Mitford, Nancy  75
Molloy, Frances  36
Montefiore, Lucinda  112, 129
Moore, Marianne  219
Moran, Caitlin
    How to Be a Woman  231
Morrison, Toni  142, 152, 154,
        170, 171, 202, 210, 247
    The Bluest Eye  14
Mosse, Kate  65, 238, 239–40
    Becoming a Mother  100
Mosse, Martha  103

*Ms.* (magazine) 10–11, 111
Mukwege, Denis 256
Munro, Alice 106
Murad, Nadia 256
    *The Last Girl: My Story of Captivity
    and My Fight against the Islamic
    State* 256
Murdoch, Iris 257

Namjoshi, Suniti 137
National Book Critics Circle
    Award 115
National Union of Journalists 129
Nelson, Maggie
    *The Argonauts* 171
Nesbit, E. 89
Net Book Agreement 176, 177
New Beacon Books 154
New York Review Books 80
Newton, Nigel 111
Nicholas Treadwell Gallery 136
Nichols, Grace 151
    *The Fat Black Woman's Poems*
        151–2
Nicholson, Mavis 145–6
Nin, Anaïs 257
Nobel Peace Prize 256
Norman, Jessye 150
Norris, Jill *see* Liddington, Jill and
    Jill Norris
Norton 136
Nourry, Arnaud 190

Oates, Joyce Carol 237
Obama, Barack 116, 144, 151
Obama, Michelle 150, 151
O'Brien, Kate 83
O'Connor, Flannery 257
O'Faolain, Julia 83
O'Faolain, Nuala 15

Oliphant, Mrs 76, 83
Olivia
    *Olivia* 77
Olsen, Tillie 216, 257
    *Silences* 216, 257
    *Tell Me a Riddle* 216
    *Yonnondio* 216
Olufemi, Lola 157
    *Feminism Interrupted: Disrupting
        Power* 157
Ondaatje, Michael 106, 199, 242
Onlywomen 47, 63, 136
Ono, Yoko
    *Acorn* 102
Orange Prize 65, 113, 115, 153,
        250 *see also* The Women's
    Prize for Fiction
Orbach, Susie 65, 100, 136, 202
    *Fat is a Feminist Issue* 14, 229
    *Fifty Shades of Feminism*
        (ed.) 244
Organization of Women of African
    and Asian Descent
    (OWAAD) 141
Orwell, George
    *The Road to Wigan Pier* 59
Osborne, Frances
    *The Bolter* 102
Ottakars 178, 179
*Outwrite* 11
Owen, Ursula 193
    and Chatto & Windus 121, 122
    Editorial Director 7, 9, 17,
        19–20, 24, 25–6, 34, 35,
        39, 41, 42, 43, 44, 59, 88,
        94, 100
    *Her Infinite Variety* 173
    and the Labour Party 131, 175
    Managing Director 124, 126,
        130, 185–6, 217–18

Owen, Ursula (*cont.*)
  and Maya Angelou  144, 147
  Virago Modern Classics  76

Paladin  28
Paley, Grace  53–4, 57–9, 84,
   163–4, 170, 237
  *Enormous Changes at the Last
    Minute*  57
  *Later the Same Day*  57
  *Little Disturbances of Man*  57, 79
Pan  24
Pandora  136
Pankhurst, Emmeline
  *My Own Story*  27
Pankhurst, Sylvia  94
Paretsky, Sara  112
Parker, Dorothy  257
Parker, Rozsika
  *Torn in Two*  100
Parkin, Jane  129
Parmar, Pratibha  97
Partnoy, Alicia
  *The Little School*  101
Patchett, Ann  247
Patel, Smita  129
Peace Book Week  138
Pearce, Mark  162
Penguin  48, 74, 136, 181
Pepe, Victoria  189
  *et al.* (eds) *I Call Myself a Feminist:
    The View from Twenty-Five Women
    under Thirty*  103
Pergamon  136
Persephone  79
Petrie, Ruthie  17, 100, 101, 112,
   121, 130, 147, 152, 159–60,
   181, 193
Petry, Ann
  *The Street*  85

Phipps, Sally
  *Molly Keane: A Life*  82, 214–15
Picador  28, 217
Piercy, Marge  136
Pines, Dinora  100
Pipeline books  138
Pluto  48, 136
Pollitt, Katha  57
Pope, Steve  155
Porter, Cathy  40, 69, 94
Porter, Katherine Anne  257
Poultney, Michael  138
Pringle, Alexandra  17, 20, 34–6,
   74, 75, 76, 78, 100, 112, 122,
   193
  at Bloomsbury  107, 110–11
  Editorial Director  124, 126,
    162, 185
  at Hamish Hamilton  131, 175,
    183, 224
  at Toby Eady's  183
Proulx, Annie  247
Pulitzer Prize  115
Pulsifer, Gary  31
Pym, Barbara  71, 86, 89

Quartet  12, 14, 23, 24, 64, 136
*Quest*  11
Quick, Diana  98

Radical Book Fair  135
Random House  127, 128,
   144, 151, 174, 180, 183,
   184, 186
Rebuck, Gail  183, 184, 185–6
*Red Rag*  11
Reeves, Maud Pember  94
  *Round About a Pound a Week*  26
Reith Lectures  156
Renault, Mary  86

*Revolutionary and Radical Feminist
    Newsletter*  11
Rice, Margery Spring
    *Working-Class Wives*  26
Rich, Adrienne  53–4, 91, 140,
    223, 234
    *Diving into the Wreck*  54
    *On Lies, Secrets and Silence*  55
    *Of Woman Born: Motherhood as
    Experience and Institution*
    14, 55
Richardson, Dorothy  257
    *Pilgrimage*  86
Richardson, Henry Handel  76,
    83, 257
Rifat, Alifa  137
Roberts, Michèle  166, 191
    *Daughters of the House*  199–200
Robinson, Marilynne  114–16,
    191, 247, 250, 253, 254–5
    *Gilead*  115
    *Home*  115
    *Housekeeping*  115
    *Lila*  115
Robinson-Patman Act (1936)  177
Roche, Christine
    *I'm Not a Feminist But…*  102
Roiphe, Katie
    *The Morning After: Sex, Fear, and
    Feminism*  224
Rose, Jacqueline
    *The Haunting of Sylvia Plath*  102
Rothschild Ventures  46, 127, 128,
    180–1
Routledge  136
Rowbotham, Sheila  43, 94, 98
    *Hidden from History*  14, 26
Rowe, Marsha  12, 13, 17
Rowling, J. K.  65
    *Harry Potter*  209

Rowntree Trust  24
Roy, Arundhati  153
Rushdie, Salman  83, 85, 134, 147,
    152–3, 166, 218
    *Midnight's Children*  153
Russell, Bertrand  40
Russell, Dora
    *The Tamarisk Tree: My School and
    the Years of War*  40

Sackville-West, Vita  75, 76
*Saga* (magazine)  155
Sandon, Susan  148, 173
Sangam Books  136
Sargood, Corinna  167
Saunders, George  248
Savitt, Sarah  101, 189, 221, 230,
    231–2
Scafe, Suzanne *see* Bryan, Beverley
Schreiner, Olive  76
    *Women and Labour*  27
Schuster, Vivienne  110–11, 204
Scopottone, Sandra  112
Scottish & Northern Book
    Distribution Cooperative
    136, 138
Scottish Classics  83
Searle, Chris  33
Segal, Lynne  100, 223
Segal, Lynne and Mary McIntosh
    (eds)
    *Sex Exposed*  99
Seierstad, Åsne  65
    *The Bookseller of Kabul*  101
Seiffert, Rachel  191, 255–6
    *A Boy in Winter*  255
    *The Dark Room*  255
    *The Long Walk Home*  255
Seligman, Ellen  204, 206
Serge, Victor  31

Settle & Bendall  136

Sex Discrimination Act (1975)  29

Shamsie, Kamila  85, 153

Shaw, Fiona  173

Shaw, George Bernard  80

Sheba  48, 63, 135, 136, 142

Shelley, David  190

Shirazi, Manny  136

Showalter, Elaine  43, 227, 246–7
    *A Literature of Their Own: Brontë to*
        *Lessing*  71, 102

*Shrew*  11

Shukla, Nikesh  157

Silgardo, Melanie  129, 186

Silver Moon Bookshop  136, 139

Simpson, Helen  242–3

Sinclair, May  76

Singh, Sunny  157

*Sinister Wisdom*  11

Sisterbite  139

Sisterwrite  64, 136, 139, 178

Slovo, Gillian  112, 191
    *The Ice Road*  113

Smith, Ali  168
    *Free Love*  112
    *Like*  112

Smith, Barbara  137

Smith, Patti  258
    *Auguries of Innocence*  258
    *Babel*  7

Smith, Stevie  73
    *The Holiday*  75
    *Me Again: The Uncollected*
        *Writings*  102

Smith, Zadie  153, 170

Snow, Jon  147, 149

Sontag, Susan  162–3, 164, 165–6

Spain, Nancy  88

*Spare Rib*  8, 12, 17, 21, 65, 121

Spare Rib Collective  43

Spare Tyre Theatre Company  98

Spark, Muriel  83, 89
    *Loitering with Intent*  240

Spedding, Carole  135

Spencer-Thomas, Fiona  4

Sphere  136

Spicer, Harriet  193
    and Chatto & Windus  121,
        122–3
    Managing Director  45, 124,
        131, 147, 175, 180, 183,
        185–6
    Production Director  7, 9, 17, 20,
        23, 24, 28, 33, 35, 41, 47, 51
    Virago Modern Classics  76

St Aubin de Teran, Lisa  112

St Ives printers  24

Stafford, Jean  257

Stead, Christina  83, 257
    *Letty Fox: Her Luck*  75
    *For Love Alone*  75

Steedman, Carolyn  100

Stein, Gertrude  83, 88, 257

Steinem, Gloria  12
    *Outrageous Acts and Everyday*
        *Rebellions*  222

Stevenson, Juliet  173

Strachey, Ray  94
    *The Cause*  27

Streatfeild, Noel  89

Stride, Alice  103

Stuckey, Lydia  150

Swift, Becky  129, 193

Swift, Graham  218

Syal, Meera  95, 173

Tahsin, Arzu  129

Talese, Nan  205

Tannen, Deborah  100

Tartt, Donna  247

Taylor, Barbara
  *Eve and the New Jerusalem:*
    *Socialism and Feminism in the*
    *Nineteenth Century* 93–4
Taylor, Elizabeth 72, 76, 86
  *Mrs Palfrey at the Claremont* 240
Taylor, Imogen 189
Thatcher, Margaret 5, 82
Thaw, Abigail 173
Third World Publications 136
Thirkell, Angela 83
Thomas, Rosie
  *Border Crossing* 211–12
Thompson, Dorothy (ed.)
  *Over Our Dead Bodies: Women*
    *Against the Bomb* 98
Thompson, E. P.
  *The Making of the English Working*
    *Class* 25
Thompson, Glenn 30, 31
Time Warner 185, 190
Tipton, Billy 102
Todd, Janet
  *The Sign of Angelica* 79
Tóibín, Colm 242
Toksvig, Sandi 65, 194
  *Between the Stops: The View of My*
    *Life from the Top of the Number*
    *12 Bus* 259
  *Valentine Grey* 258–9
Tolstoya, Tatyana 112
Toynbee, Polly 39
Tracy, Jo 129
Travers, P. L. 89
Trefusis, Violet 75
Tremain, Rose 134
Trevor Brown Associates 136
Trevor, William 83
Triangle Translations 136
*Trotsky for Beginners* 31

*Trouble & Strife* 11
Tyler, Anne 247
Tynan, Kenneth 84–5

Uglow, Jenny 76
Unsworth, Barry 199

Vauxhall Bridge Road 183
Victorian Classics 10, 84
VIDA 238
Vidal, Gore 49, 166–7
Viney, Charlie 188
Virago Advisory Group 42–3
Virago Bookshop 139
Virago Children's Classics 89
Virago Irish Classics 74, 82, 83
Virago Modern Classics 71, 89,
    124, 166, 191, 219, 222, 223,
    238, 253
Virago Non-fiction Classics
    223, 235
Virago Pioneers 100, 223
Virago Reprint Library 26, 88
Virago Travellers 88, 223
Virago Upstarts 130, 223
Virago Vs 117, 190–1

Walker, Alice 54, 97, 137, 142,
    149, 150, 227
  *The Color Purple* 14
Walker, Rebecca 227
Walkowitz, Judith
  *City of Dreadful Delight* 94
Walley, Claire
  *Changing the World One Page at a*
    *Time* (TV documentary) 24
Walter, Harriet 173
Walter, Natasha 65, 174, 225–6, 227
  *Living Dolls* 174, 228–30
  *The New Feminism* 226, 228, 230

Wandor, Michelene 136

Ward, Harriet 40

Ward, Mrs Humphrey 74

Warner, Marina 99, 1467

Warner, Sylvia Townsend 73, 86
  *Mr Fortune's Maggot* 75
  *The True Heart* 75

*Wasafiri* 11

Waterhouse, Keith
  *Billy Liar* 164

Waters, Sarah 20, 65, 82, 117–18,
      168–70, 191, 208, 253, 254,
      259
  *Affinity* 117
  *The Night Watch* 210
  *Tipping the Velvet* 117, 169, 191

Waterstone, Tim 178, 179,
      180, 183

Waterstones 178–80

Watts, Janet 76

Webb, Mary 86

Webster, Katrina 121

Weldon, Fay 98, 218

Wells, H. G. 80

Welty, Eudora 84, 257
  *Losing Battles* 85

Wesker, Arnold 31

West, Dorothy 85

West, Rebecca 74, 75, 76,
      80–1, 134
  *The Fountain Overflows* 81

WH Smith 137, 179

WH Smith Literary Award 199

Wharton, Edith 76, 84, 85, 257

Whipple, Dorothy 79

Whitbread, Helena (ed.)
  *I Know my Own Heart: The Diary of
      Anne Lister* 94

White, Antonia 74, 76
  *Frost in May* 71, 75

White, Sarah 187

Whitehorn, Katharine
  *Selective Memory* 212–13

Whitman, Walt
  *Leaves of Grass* 250

Wilde, Oscar 211

Wildwood House 41

William Collins publishers 3

Williams, Patricia J.
  *Seeing a Colour-Blind Future* 156

Williams, Raymond
  *Culture and Society* 26

Williams, Shirley
  *Climbing the Bookshelves* 255

Williams, Sian 30

*Willowherb Review, The* 65

Wilson, Amrit
  *Finding a Voice* 94

Wilson, Barbara 112

Wilson, Melba
  *Healthy and Wise: Black Women and
      Health* 152

Winfrey, Oprah 150

Winsloe, Christa 88

Winterson, Jeanette 169

*WIRES* 11

Wolf, Naomi 65, 224, 225, 226
  *The Beauty Myth: How Images of
      Beauty are Used Against
      Women* 61, 224, 229
  *Outrages: Sex, Censorship and the
      Criminalisation of Love* 250
  *Vagina: A New Biography* 230

Wollstonecraft, Mary 41, 212
  *A Vindication of the Rights of
      Woman* 212

Women and Media 51

Women for Refugee Women 65

Women in Publishing (WIP) 136,
      137, 174

*Women in Society* 92
Women's Equality Party  61, 65
Women's Press, Toronto  25
Women's Press, London  47, 64,
       79–80, 88, 136 142,
       154, 223
Women's Press Bookclub,
       The  136
Women's Prize for Fiction
       65, 153, 235, 236, 238,
       240, 248
   *see also* Orange Prize
*Women's Review of Books, The*  11
Women's Therapy Centre  65
Woolf, Leonard  40, 124
Woolf, Virginia  26, 40, 87,
       174, 257
Workers Educational
       Association  136
WOW (Women of the World)
       festival  103
Wright, iO Tillett
   *Darling Days*  231

Writers and Readers Publishing
       Co-operative  30, 31, 32,
       37–8, 41, 129, 136
Writers Guild  136

X-Press  155

Yonge, Charlotte, M.  83
York, Susannah  98
Young, David  190,
       193, 228
Young, E. H.  76
*Young Person's Guide to Saving the
       Planet, The*  131
Yourcenar, Marguerite
   *Memoirs of Hadrian*  235

Zed Books  136
Zhang, C. Pam
   *How Much of These Hills is
       Gold*  113
Ziegler, Philip  200
Zora Press  154

# Acknowledgements

I have many people to thank for helping me get this story onto the page. With huge appreciation I thank those who gave me so much: Margaret Atwood, Richard Beswick, Carmen Callil, Clair Chapwell, Donna Coonan, Susan de Soissons, Sarah Dunant, Zoe Gullen, Hilary Hale, Anne Karpf, Ruthie Petrie, Megan Phillips, Cathy Robertson, Sarah Savitt, Harriet Spicer, Dominic Wakeford, Sarah Waters, Andrew Willie.

To Jacqueline Norton of OUP, whose idea this was, I give deep thanks. I didn't know how much I wanted to write this book until you suggested it. Thanks too to Katie Bishop and Anna Silva at OUP, and to Cheryl Brant. To my Canadian team: the generous Anne McDermid and my publisher, Dan Wells of Biblioasis, a heartfelt thank-you.

I also want to thank Ailah Ahmed, Diran Adebayo, Joan Bakewell, David Bamford, Julie Barer, Joanna Bourke, Susie Boyt, Margaret Busby, Virginia Brownlow, Beatrix Campbell, Maria Campbell, Elizabeth Day, Rachel Cooke, Emma Donoghue, Zoe Fairbairns, Mary (Wuzzy) Fawdry, Lyndall Gordon, Linda Grant, Kate Griffin, Tessa Hadley, Marie Hrynczak, David Kent, Charlie King, Janey King, Lynn Knight, Wendy Kysow, Robert Manser, Souad Mekhennet, Lesley Morrison, Judith Murray, Lola Olufemi, Susie Orbach, Ursula Owen, Sally Phipps, Alexandra Pringle, Marilynne Robinson, Rachel Seiffert, David Shelley, Duncan Spilling, Sandi Toksvig, Natasha Walter, Amrit Wilson, and Naomi Wolf, for help or for quotes or for early reads.

To June and Bill Goodings, who have been inspiring parents and important readers for me, and to my brothers, Brian, Craig, and

Shawn, and my sister, Laurel, I owe tremendous gratitude. My daughter, Amy, an essential and smart early reader and my son, Zak, a loyal supporter, were in my mind throughout the writing of this book: I want them to inherit a more equal world and they themselves already give me great hope.

John Annette, my dear husband, has lived these many Virago years alongside me and has never wavered in his interest and loyalty—which has included reading and discussing this book many, many times. I know how lucky I am. Thank you. Thank you.